Buying a H...
Budget For D...

Handy Contact Informa...

Try these numbers and Web sites for help finding the right person for the job.

- ✔ **Estate agent:** The National Association of Estate Agents at www.naea.org.uk or call 01926 496800.

- ✔ **Licensed conveyancer:** The Council for Licensed Conveyancers at www.conveyancers.gov.uk or call 01245 349599.

- ✔ **Solicitor:** The Law Society at www.lawsociety.org.uk or 020 7242 1222.

  - In Northern Ireland, try the Law Society of Northern Ireland (www.lawsoc-ni.org) or call 028 90 231614.

  - In Scotland, contact the Society on 0131 226 7411 or visit www.lawscot.org.uk.

- ✔ **Surveyor:** Royal Institution of Chartered Surveyors (RICS) at www.rics.org or on 0870 333 1600. In Scotland, RICS Scotland on 0131 225 7078 or www.rics-scotland.org.uk.

Tips on Buying the Right Property

Although everyone's requirements are different when it comes to buying property, keep these few general rules in mind:

- ✔ Be clear in your mind about what you want before arranging to view any properties (see Chapter 3 for more on this).

- ✔ Research the area carefully, particularly if you aren't familiar with it.

- ✔ Don't let the agent or seller rush you into a decision: Take your time and trust your instincts (head to Chapter 8 for more details on this).

- ✔ Ask yourself whether you can see yourself living in that property. If you aren't sure, keep looking.

- ✔ Ask the seller about the neighbours and whether he has had any problems with them. If he has made a complaint about them to the police or council, he is legally obliged to tell you if you ask.

- ✔ Time the commute to work and the school run at the time of day you are likely to make these journeys.

- ✔ Visit the property after dark. If troublemakers are hanging around on street corners, you may not feel safe walking home late at night.

- ✔ Commission a survey. If you don't, you may miss serious structural problems that are expensive to rectify once you have bought the property. Head to Chapter 9 for more on surveys.

For Dummies: Bestselling Book Series for Beginners

Buying a Home on a Budget For Dummies®

Cheat Sheet

Mortgage Do's and Don'ts

Your home is likely to be your most expensive purchase – ever. So getting the finance right is vital.

- ✔ Don't accept the first mortgage offered to you by your bank. Shop around to see whether it's competitive (see Chapter 4 for more details).

- ✔ Do use an independent mortgage broker to find a home loan; this can save you time and effort searching the market for the best deal.

- ✔ Don't overstretch yourself: Work out whether you can afford to meet the repayments if interest rates rise. (Chapter 2 has more on budgeting.)

- ✔ Do put down a deposit if you can. If you've got a deposit, you'll not only get a better mortgage rate, your monthly repayments will be lower and you won't have to pay Mortgage Indemnity Guarantee (see Chapter 2 for more on this).

- ✔ Don't get a mortgage with extended redemption penalties. Paying a penalty for switching mortgages before an offer comes to an end is fair enough. But don't accept a mortgage with penalties that extend beyond this period. Check out Chapter 4 for more details on what to avoid.

- ✔ Do shop around for buildings insurance. Some lenders charge borrowers a one-off fee if they don't take out the buildings or contents insurance with them. It may be cheaper to pay this and buy your insurance else-where (head to Chapter 4 for more on insurance).

Extra Costs You Have to Pay For

On top of the property purchase price, you must remember to budget for a number of extras. These include

- ✔ Solicitor's fees, local searches, and Land Registry fee (see Chapter 10 for details in England, Wales, and Northern Ireland, or Chapter 11 if you're buying in Scotland).

- ✔ Stamp duty on properties over £60,000, or £150,000 in certain disadvantaged areas (see Chapter 2 for the low-down on rates).

- ✔ Mortgage lender's valuation and survey. It's tempting to skimp on the survey but you may regret it in the long run. (There's more on these costs in Chapter 9.)

- ✔ Mortgage application fee, booking fee, arrangement fee, and mortgage broker fee (where applicable). Head to Chapter 2 for more on lenders' fees; Chapter 4 has more on what a broker charges.

- ✔ Buildings insurance. You can't get a mortgage without it. See Chapter 4 for how to get the best deal on this necessity.

- ✔ Removal costs. One way of saving money is to do the move yourself, so persuade strong mates with vans to lend a hand.

Wiley, the Wiley Publishing logo, For Dummies, the Dummies Man logo, the For Dummies Bestselling Book Series logo and all related trade dress are trademarks or registered trademarks of John Wiley & Sons, Inc. and/or its affiliates. All other trademarks are property of their respective owners.

For Dummies: Bestselling Book Series for Beginners

About the Author

Melanie Bien is personal finance editor of the *Independent on Sunday*. She also writes and edits the paper's property section. For the past seven years, she has written about property for a variety of national newspapers, magazines, and Web sites. She has also written several books and pamphlets to accompany television programmes on property makeovers and design, buying, renovating, and selling property.

She is also author of *Buying and Selling Property For Dummies* and co-author of *Renting Out Your Property For Dummies*. She lives in East London with her boyfriend Andrew and their two cats, Wilma and Lulu.

Dedication

To Andrew, JB, and my parents, for all your support, enthusiasm, and endless encouragement.

Author's Acknowledgements

I would like to thank Jason Dunne at John Wiley & Sons for having the faith in me to write yet another book for the company! I also acknowledge a depth of gratitude to Amie Tibble, my excellent editor, for her help, direction, feedback and constructive criticism during the process. Also, many thanks to Samantha Clapp for dealing with my queries patiently and quickly, and to everyone who works behind the scenes at Wiley for their efforts in making this book possible.

I would also like to thank mortgage brokers David Hollingworth and Ray Boulger for their help, patience, and invaluable knowledge.

Thanks also to those friends I had to cancel at the last minute for being not only understanding but also encouraging: it was more to do with deadlines looming than the allure of the conveyancing process, honest.

And finally, thanks to my family for their untiring support and encouragement. To my mother for the wonderful reflexology treatments which helped me relax, my father for his knowledge and sound advice, and my brother, for getting me away from it all to the Arsenal every weekend.

And to Andrew, who understood that I had to write when he would rather go down the pub, made endless cups of tea to keep me going, and put up with my obsession with making even the tightest budget stretch to affording a property – thank you.

Publisher's Acknowledgements

We're proud of this book; please send us your comments through our Dummies online registration form located at www.dummies.com/register/.

Some of the people who helped bring this book to market include the following:

Acquisitions, Editorial, and Media Development

Executive Editor: Jason Dunne

Executive Project Editor: Caroline Walmsley

Project Editors: Amie Jackowski Tibble, Daniel Mersey

Development Editor: Kathleen Dobie

Copy Editor: Kate O'Leary

Editorial Assistant: Samantha Clapp

Technical Reviewer: Tim Bennett

Cover Photos:
© Getty Images/Digital Vision

Cartoons: Ed McLachlan

Composition

Project Coordinator: Erin Smith

Layout and Graphics: Sean Decker, Kelly Emkow, Joyce Haughey, Michael Kruzil, Jacque Roth, Heather Ryan, Brent Savage, Julie Trippetti, Mary Gillot Virgin

Proofreaders: Dwight Ramsey, Charles Spencer

Indexer:
TECHBOOKS Production Services

Publishing and Editorial for Consumer Dummies

> **Diane Graves Steele,** Vice President and Publisher, Consumer Dummies
>
> **Joyce Pepple,** Acquisitions Director, Consumer Dummies
>
> **Kristin A Cocks,** Product Development Director, Consumer Dummies
>
> **Michael Spring,** Vice President and Publisher, Travel
>
> **Brice Gosnell,** Associate Publisher, Travel
>
> **Kelly Regan,** Editorial Director, Travel

Publishing for Technology Dummies

> **Andy Cummings,** Vice President and Publisher, Dummies Technology/General User

Composition Services

> **Gerry Fahey,** Vice President of Production Services
>
> **Debbie Stailey,** Director of Composition Services

Contents at a Glance

Table of Contents

Chapter 5: Getting a Mortgage with a Guarantor 75

Chapter 6: Making the Most of Being
a First-Time Buyer 87

Introduction

● ●

*W*elcome to *Buying a Home on a Budget For Dummies*. If you're struggling to climb onto the first rung of the property ladder, you need some sensible tips and money-saving advice to help you realise your dream. This book provides all the help you need to enable you to buy your first home – even if money is too tight to mention.

About This Book

Although these pages are overflowing with useful advice and information, I present it in a light, easy-to-access format. This book helps you decide whether you are ready to become a property owner, how to figure out your budget, and provides advice on making it stretch as far as possible. I include tips on negotiating a good price so you don't pay over the odds and advice on dealing with estate agents and solicitors. Just as important, this book can help you maintain your sense of humour – as well as your sanity – as you deal with these challenges and more.

Conventions Used in This Book

To help you navigate through this book, I've set up a few conventions:

- ✔ *Italic* is used for emphasis and to highlight new words and terms that are defined.
- ✔ **Boldface** text indicates the action part of numbered steps and the key term in a bulleted list.
- ✔ Monofont is used for Web addresses, whether URLs or e-mail addresses.

Also, in an effort to be even-handed with the genders, I alternate pronouns. I use male pronouns in odd-numbered chapters and female pronouns in even-numbered chapters.

What You're Not to Read

I've written this book so that you can

1) Find information easily and

2) Easily understand what you find.

And although I believe that you want to pore over every last word between the two yellow covers, I actually make it easy for you to identify material that you can skip. This is the stuff that, although interesting and related to the topic at hand, isn't essential for you to know.

- ✔ **Text in sidebars.** The sidebars are the shaded boxes that appear here and there. You may find the personal stories and observations in these sidebars interesting, but they aren't necessary reading.

- ✔ **Anything with a Technical Stuff Icon attached.** This information is interesting but not critical to your understanding of buying on a budget.

- ✔ **The stuff on the copyright page.** No kidding. You won't find anything here of interest unless you're inexplicably enamoured by legal language and reprint information.

Foolish Assumptions

In this book, I make some general assumptions about who you are:

- ✔ You may not have bought your own home because you didn't think you could afford to but now you are wondering whether – just maybe – it might be possible, despite little (or no) deposit and a low income. Perhaps some of your friends have recently taken the plunge and you're worried about getting left behind as property prices climb ever higher.

  ✔ You hope to get information on the best mortgage for
    your circumstances and whether you can save money in
    other areas – such as on legal fees or broker costs.

  ✔ You want easy-to-understand information that explains
    what you need to know about buying a property, but
    you've got better things to do (like sleeping, participating
    in your favourite leisure activity, or even relaxing on holi-
    day) than become an expert on property law. You want to
    get buying a property right while you retain control over
    your life.

How This Book Is Organised

Buying a Home on a Budget For Dummies is organised into five
parts. The chapters within each part cover specific topic areas
in more detail. So you can easily and quickly scan a topic that
interests you, or troubleshoot the source of your latest major
headache.

Part 1: Stepping onto the Property Ladder

Buying your first home is a rite of passage. The chapters in
this part help you work out whether you can afford to become
a homeowner. This part also helps you figure out whether you
need to pool resources with family or friends to help you
realise your goal. I give you lots of information on drawing up
a budget and remembering the unavoidable extras. You can
also find advice on finding the home of your dreams. Finally,
you don't want to pay over the odds so there are pointers on
buying during a slump and avoiding a property boom.

Part 11: Show Me the Money!

The most important part of buying a home on a budget is getting hold of the cash you need. In this part, I guide you through
the mortgage maze. Here you'll find all you need to know about
using a guarantor to get a bigger mortgage, the special deals

lenders offer first-time buyers, and home loans aimed at professionals who may be on a low wage now but are likely to earn much more in the future. I also look at insurance so that you can cover your back.

Part III: Finding the Right Property and Making an Offer

This part takes you from dealing with estate agents and making sure they don't pull the wool over your eyes to making an offer on a property. You'll find information on surveys and why you'd be mad to skimp on one, along with what to look for during a viewing. The legal process is also explained in full, from England, Wales, and Northern Ireland to Scotland. And if you fancy the challenge of doing up a wreck or even building your own home from scratch (you mad fool), there're plenty of tips to get you started.

Part IV: Alternative Ways of Home Buying

Because you're on a budget, you may have to be creative when raising the cash you need to buy a home. In this part, I look at the various deals available – from family offset mortgages, to renting out your spare room or even your entire home to cover the mortgage. You'll find tips on shared ownership and buying through a housing association or the Right to Buy scheme. If you are a key worker, you'll also find more information on schemes aimed specifically at you.

Part V: The Part of Tens

Here, in a concise and lively set of condensed chapters, are tips to make the difference between success and failure. In these chapters, I address the things first-time buyers need to know, tips on dealing with estate agents, and the contacts every homebuyer will find useful.

Icons Used in This Book

Scattered throughout the book are icons to guide you along your way and highlight some of the suggestions, solutions, and cautions of buying on a budget.

Keep your sights on the target for important advice and critical insights into the best practices in buying property and saving cash.

Remember these important points of information and you'll stand a better chance of buying your property successfully.

This icon highlights the dangers that homebuyers need to avoid.

This icon covers the boring stuff that only technical buffs ever know. You can skip paragraphs marked by this icon without missing the point – or you can read it and impress your friends with what you know.

This icon highlights the real-life anecdotes of myself and friends, gleaned from years of experience and mistakes when buying property. While you should learn from your own mistakes, it's even better to learn from others' – and I share some of them with you here.

This icon highlights where you can blow your budget if you're not careful.

Where to Go from Here

This book is organised so that you can go directly to the information you need. Want to know how much stamp duty you'll have to pay? Then head to Chapter 2. If you're interested in making an offer on a property, go to Chapter 9 for advice. You can use the table of contents to find broad categories of information or the index to look up more specific details.

If you're not sure what information you need first, you may want to start with Part I. Chapters 1, 2, and 3 give you all the basic information you need to get started in buying your home on a budget and direct you to other chapters in the book where you can find more detailed information.

Part I
Stepping onto the Property Ladder

"Just think – with our own house & mortgage,
we'll be as carefree as these lambs."

In this part . . .

*W*hen it comes to making decisions, they don't come much bigger – or more expensive – than the one to buy a home. This is one of the biggest purchases you will ever make. But while you may be ready, in theory, to climb onto the property ladder, finding the cash to enable you to do so may be another matter.

In this part, I guide you through the process of figuring out whether it's the right time for you to buy and how you can do so on a limited budget. This part shows you that you don't need a huge salary or thousands of pounds to put down as a deposit. There are also tips on deciding where to buy.

If you've just started to think about purchasing a property, but you're not quite sure whether you can afford to do so, this is the part for you.

Chapter 1

Becoming a Homeowner – Even If Money Is Tight

. . . .

In This Chapter

▶ Realising the benefits of becoming a homeowner

▶ Figuring out where the money is going to come from

▶ Looking at mortgage basics

▶ Finding the right home without overstretching yourself or blowing your budget

. . . .

*C*ongratulations. You've made the decision to buy a home and get a foot on the property ladder. Property is an excellent investment. In buying a home, you not only kiss grotty rented accommodations and throwing money down the drain goodbye, you invest in something that is likely to increase in value over the years. That has to be a sound move.

But there's no escaping the fact that life is hard for first-time buyers. Would-be buyers spend their twenties trying to clear student debts and struggling on low incomes – the average age of a first-time buyer was 34 in 2003 according to the Halifax, the UK's biggest mortgage lender. And as property prices edge ever upward, you may well feel that becoming a homeowner is an impossible dream.

But homeownership is attainable – you just have to be clued in to the alternatives and possibilities. A deposit isn't essential – you can borrow 100 per cent of the property purchase price. You may be single but you don't have to buy on your own – you can club together with a sibling or a mate. You don't have to earn the salary of a Premiership footballer – if you will earn more in the future than you do now, some lenders will take this into account. There are options available, and this book shows you what they are.

It is important to work out whether it is the right *time* for you to buy. In this chapter, I start by giving you the lowdown on some of the advantages of getting on the property ladder and help you decide whether you can afford it. If buying on your own isn't possible, there may be ways around this. I help you assess what assistance you can call upon to make your property ownership dream a reality.

Why Buy? Looking at the Benefits of Buying Your Own Place

Buying a home and being the master of your own property brings several benefits:

- ✔ **You stop throwing money away.** Renting provides a temporary roof overhead – no long-term benefits.

- ✔ **You can put up leopard-skin wallpaper.** Okay, maybe not leopard skin but the point is that in your place, you get to decide what goes on the walls and everything else.

  Many landlords (perhaps wisely) don't let tenants near a paint pot. But even if your landlord lets you decorate, it's a waste of your time and money.

  If you own your home, the money you spend doing it up increases its value (unless you actually choose leopard-skin wallpaper of course).

- ✔ **You get security.** One of the biggest problems with renting is that every six months when your tenancy agreement is up for renewal you could find yourself out on your ear. Your landlord may decide to sell up or to increase the rent. Your flatmate may decide he wants to move out and you can't afford the rent on your own so you've got to leave too.

  Renting brings little security. Buying your own place gives you control and if you decide to move, it is because you want to – not because you are being forced to.

✔ **You can make money.** Over the long term, property tends to rise in value – a fact you're all-too-familiar with if you have struggled to get onto the housing ladder over the past few months (or years).

But don't buy your first home with the sole aim of making money by selling it on in a couple of years. Buy a home because you can see yourself living there happily for several years: If prices go up, it will be a bonus – not the be all and end all. And if they fall in the short term, it isn't the end of the world either.

✔ **Property is a solid investment.** Property tends to rise in value over time. So if you can find a way to buy even a small flat today – and this book is full of advice on how to get the most for your money – when you eventually sell, you should realise a handsome profit.

Pondering Money Matters

You're sold on the many benefits to buying your own place: Now all you have to do is work out how you are going to pay for it. You may be ready but your finances may not be. In the following sections, I look at the costs involved and how much cash you need.

How much does it cost?

The cost of buying a home largely depends on the purchase price, which reflects the property's location, size, and whether it's particularly old or has any attractive features. The purchase price is also partly dictated by demand: The greater the demand among prospective purchasers for a property of that type, generally-speaking, the higher the price.

The purchase price is not the only expense to consider. You must also pay for a number of extras, which bump up the final bill. These include legal fees and charges for local searches and Land Registry; surveyor fees; mortgage lender's valuation, arrangement, and booking fees; and maybe even a broker's fee. You also have to pay stamp duty if the property costs more than £60,000 (or £150,000 in certain disadvantaged areas). Chapter 2 has more on what you can expect to pay for these extra items.

Some of the extra costs, such as the lender's valuation or arrangement fee, can be added onto the mortgage and paid back over the term of the loan, so you don't have to find the cash up-front. But you need to pay cash for some costs, such as the solicitor's fees and stamp duty.

How much can you afford?

Affordability is the biggest problem for first-time buyers. Most people need a *mortgage* – a loan from a bank or building society – to buy their first home. How big a mortgage you can get depends on your income. Most lenders let you borrow three to four times your annual income, if you're buying on your own – or two and a half times joint income if you're hooking up with someone else. Some lenders also look at three times the higher salary plus one times the lower salary if that suits better. (Go to Chapter 2 for more on working out your budget and Chapter 4 for details on mortgages and income multiples.)

On a low income you'll struggle to borrow enough to buy a property of any description. Consider this statistic: The average property price in the UK in March 2004 was £151,467, according to the Halifax House Price Index – 5.2 times the average salary. Given that most lenders let you borrow a maximum of four times your salary, the figures just don't add up. If you've got savings, you can put these towards a deposit, which means you can spend more on your property. However, if you're a typical first-time buyer you won't have much in the way of savings. And taking two or three years to save up a few thousand pounds is not always a good idea. (See Chapter 2 for more on coping without a deposit and how delaying your purchase may not be a good idea.)

When you've got a rough idea of how big a mortgage you think you can get, add this amount to your savings and subtract the total from the likely purchase price, along with fees and charges. The figure you're left with is the shortfall (ideally, you won't have a shortfall but realistically, most first-time buyers have less cash than they need). Whether the shortfall is hundreds or thousands of pounds, your next step is to see if it's possible to plug this gap.

Working Out Where the Money's Going to Come From

There are various ways of raising the cash you need to buy your first home. I explore the main options available to you in the following sections.

Buying a property without a big deposit or massive salary

With more than 7,000 mortgages available from over 100 lenders, there's bound to be one out there that suits you – even if you haven't got a big deposit or earn hundreds of thousands of pounds every year.

In the past, a lender simply wouldn't take you seriously and agree to let you have a mortgage if you didn't have a deposit. This is no longer the case. Several lenders are prepared to lend you the full purchase price (also known as 100 per cent loan to value). You can even borrow up to 125 per cent loan to value from some lenders: so if the property costs £100,000, you can borrow 125 per cent of this, or £125,000. So even if you haven't got a deposit, it might not be the end of the world.

Realistically, it may take several years to save up a 5 or 10 per cent deposit, depending on how good a saver you are and other demands on your wallet. But it may make sense to borrow a greater proportion of the property purchase price now, rather than put off buying for several years. In a rising property market, delaying your purchase may mean that prices continue to rise and you're priced out of the market again.

If you don't have a deposit (or have only a very small one), you won't get the cheapest mortgage rate. The best deals are offered to borrowers with sizeable deposits because they are regarded as being lower risk. A number of lenders also charge mortgage indemnity guarantee (MIG) – a one-off insurance premium if you borrow more than 90 or 95 per cent loan to value. MIG is outdated and expensive, protecting the lender – not you – yet you pay for it. Some lenders don't charge MIG: Make sure you use one of these. See Chapter 2 for more on MIG and the likely cost.

Some lenders try to help out people on low incomes by bending their lending criteria. You may be able to borrow more than the usual three times income: four times income is increasingly common; while some lenders are prepared to lend up to five or even six times your income. Think carefully before taking on a loan of this size, though (see 'Making sure you don't over-stretch yourself' later in this chapter).

Pooling resources – when you can't afford to buy on your own

Just because you can't afford to buy on your own and you don't happen to have a partner (or one you want to buy with at any rate), doesn't mean you have to give up until this situation changes. More friends and siblings are buying property together than ever before, so consider whether there is someone who you can buy with. Choose carefully, though: Not only must your co-buyer be someone you can live with, he also needs to be someone you can rely on to pay his portion of the mortgage on time every month.

If you buy with a sibling or mate, get your solicitor to draw up a legal contract stating each owner's share in the property – acknowledging their contribution to the deposit and mortgage. Then if you do fall out, you'll both know where you stand legally. (See Chapter 2 for more on buying with someone else.)

Another option is your folks. If they can lend you a few thousand pounds to put towards your deposit, you can buy a bigger place. But even if they can't afford to lend you some cash, your parents may be able to act as your guarantor. A guarantor agrees to pay your mortgage if you can't afford to – and lenders let you borrow more than your salary justifies if you use one. (See Chapter 5 for more details on guarantors.)

Getting the government to help you realise your dream

Several government-funded schemes help first-time buyers who are struggling to get on the property ladder. If you're a council tenant of at least two years standing you may be able to purchase your home under the Right to Buy scheme. Housing associations are another good source of aid: You can buy a home through shared ownership or the homebuy scheme. And if you're a key worker, you may qualify for a loan through the key worker living scheme.

Find out what you are entitled to – and make sure you claim it. It can make the difference between getting on the property ladder – or not. (In Chapters 16 to 18, I discuss these schemes in more detail.)

Understanding Mortgages

Unless you've just won the Lottery you'll need a mortgage. Understanding how they work, how much you can borrow, and the pitfalls to avoid are crucial to finding the right deal.

Getting a grip on rates

The *mortgage rate* – the amount of interest you pay your lender to borrow money to buy your home – depends on your lender's standard variable rate (SVR), which, in turn, reflects the Bank of England base rate. The decision to lower, raise, or leave the base rate alone depends on several factors, including inflation, consumer confidence, and the state of the housing market. If inflation is rising, the Bank of England's Monetary Policy Committee (MPC) raises rates in an effort to curb spending, for example.

Lenders usually respond to the MPC's decision by adjusting their SVR accordingly. Your repayments will also change if you're on a variable rate (see Chapter 4 for more details).

Making sure you don't over-stretch yourself

You may be tempted to borrow as much as possible so you can buy a bigger place – this isn't a good idea. Even if you can afford the repayments now, consider whether this will still be the case if interest rates rise. Even a 1 per cent increase can mean a big rise in your repayments. If you can't cope, your home will be repossessed. Over-stretching yourself is a bad idea: It is better to wait until you can afford to buy than doing so before you're ready.

Finding the Right Property without Blowing the Budget

As well as getting the financing sorted, you need to ensure you actually find the right property for you. By working out what you want, before you even set foot inside a property, you not only save time and effort, you're more likely to find what you want. Do you need two bedrooms or will one suffice? Do you want a garden or garage? And consider location: How important is living near work or the shops?

What you want and what you can afford are likely to be two different things. Because you are on a budget, you'll have to compromise: The sooner you accept this, the sooner you'll find a place to buy. Chapter 3 helps you assess where you are prepared to compromise – and where you aren't.

Doing It on the Cheap: Saving Cash Where You Can

You can become a homeowner on a budget – it's just not as easy as it would be if you had cash to burn. Try to avoid cutting corners (by not paying for a survey, for example), but you can still save money (by not opting for the full structural survey and getting a homebuyer's report instead). Or you can choose a mortgage where the lender refunds your valuation fee, or pays your legal bill (see Chapter 6 for details).

Whatever you do, shop around. Use an independent mortgage broker (see Chapter 4 for more on brokers) to make sure you don't pay over the odds. Use an insurance broker to arrange your cover, and compare premiums to get the best deal (Chapter 4 also has more on insurance). Compare the conveyancing costs of two or three solicitors before you instruct one – but remember that dirt-cheap may mean the service is sub-standard (see Chapter 10 for more details).

Chapter 2

Doing Sums: Looking at Financial Aspects

*O*nce you decide to buy a home, it's easy to get carried away in all the excitement. But although you're eager to start viewing potential properties, you must first work out whether you can afford to buy and how much you can spend.

First-time buyers are a dying breed because of rising house prices: There were 32 per cent fewer first-time buyers in 2003 compared with the previous year, according to the Halifax, the UK's biggest mortgage lender. And as money is tight – or you wouldn't have bought this book! – working out what you can afford is especially important.

In this chapter, I discuss the costs you need to consider, how to work out a budget, and buying without a deposit – or a measly one. I also give you advice on the best time to buy a property – and the worst – to ensure that you get the best deal and don't pay over the odds or end up owing more than your house is worth.

Figuring Out How Much You Have

Property doesn't come cheap, so you must now work out whether buying a home is actually possible. If you aren't a Lottery winner and don't have the cash to hand, you need a mortgage. Lenders use your income to calculate the maximum you can borrow (see 'Working out how much to borrow' later in this chapter). But you also need to assess how big a mortgage you can cope with.

Drawing up a budget

The first step is to calculate what mortgage repayments you can realistically afford each month. Your repayment amount should be something less than the amount of money you have left over after subtracting all your outgoings from your monthly income. I list the most common outgoings in Table 2-1. Go through the list and answer honestly how much you spend on each item every month.

Table 2-1	Working Out What You Can Afford
Category	*Amount*
MONTHLY INCOME	
Income (after tax)	£_____.
Overtime and bonuses	£_____.
TOTAL NET INCOME	£_____.
MONTHLY OUTGOINGS	
Gas/electricity/water	£_____.
Council tax	£_____.
Telephone/mobile	£_____.
Satellite TV	£_____.
Food	£_____.

Category	Amount
Travel	£ _____.
Clothing	£ _____.
Entertainment	£ _____.
Other outgoings	£ _____.
TOTAL OUTGOINGS	£ _____.
BALANCE	
Income minus outgoings	£ _____.

As a general rule, your monthly mortgage payments should be no more than a third of your income after tax; otherwise, you risk overstretching yourself. And if interest rates rise, you may find you cannot cope with the higher repayments. If the balance of Table 2-1 is less than a third of your monthly income, consider whether you can make sacrifices, such as staying in one night a week or buying fewer clothes, to bump up the bottom line. But be realistic: You can't skimp on your council tax or eat baked beans every single night of the week.

If the figures just don't add up, all may not be lost. It may be possible to meet your mortgage repayments by other means, such as buying a property with a relative or friend (see 'Getting by with a little help from your friends' later in this chapter). Or you may be happy taking in a lodger (see Chapter 14), renting out your property to tenants (see Chapter 15), or opting for a family offset mortgage (see Chapter 13). Don't give up just yet!

Keeping the extra costs in mind

As well as the purchase price, you have to budget for lots of extras. A mortgage only covers the purchase price less the deposit. You have to pay a variety of other costs out of your own pocket. These extra expenses include:

✔ **The deposit:** Most buyers put down a deposit – a percentage of the property purchase price. A deposit isn't compulsory and there is no set amount, however, some loans require a set percentage of the purchase price as a deposit, so if you don't have enough cash you won't qualify for such a deal.

The deposit demonstrates your commitment to the purchase, as it proves you're willing to risk your own cash, and also means you get a lower mortgage rate because the lender considers you less of a risk. You transfer your deposit to your solicitor just ahead of completion and he passes it on to the seller, along with the mortgage you're taking out to cover the remainder of the purchase price.

✔ **Stamp duty:** This is an unavoidable tax payable to the government on completion of the purchase. How much you pay depends on the purchase price:

- Nothing if your property costs less than £60,000 or £150,000 (in disadvantaged areas)

- 1 per cent on properties between £60,000 and £250,000

- 3 per cent on properties between £250,000 and £500,000

- 4 per cent on properties over £500,000.

Many first-time buyers come unstuck because they forget to budget for stamp duty. Remember that you need enough cash to cover it because it doesn't come out of your mortgage.

✔ **Legal fees:** You have to pay a solicitor for handling the *conveyancing* – legally transferring the property from the seller to the buyer – unless you do it on your own (see Chapter 10 for more on this). Solicitor's fees and charges vary (see Chapter 10 for England, Wales, and Northern Ireland or Chapter 11 on Scotland). Don't forget that you also have to pay 17.5 per cent VAT on the legal fees as well.

Legal fees are payable on completion along with the cost of disbursements for searches the solicitor carries out on your behalf to check whether the property has planning permission and that the seller is in a position to sell it to you, for example.

✔ **Lender's valuation and survey:** The lender's *valuation* confirms that the property is worth the amount you want to borrow. This ensures that if you default on your repayments and the lender has to sell your property, it can cover its costs. Expect to pay between £150 and £200 for the lender's valuation.

Be aware that the valuation tells you nothing about the condition of the property. To ascertain the condition, you need to commission a detailed study of the structure of the property – a survey. The survey should reveal whether the property has damp or subsidence problems, and it's carried out by a surveyor.

Even if money is tight, paying to have a survey done is a good idea because a *survey* reveals whether there are any problems that would be expensive to put right. With a survey in hand, at least you know where you stand from the beginning and can pull out or use this information to haggle over the asking price with the seller. The *home-buyer's report* is the most common survey, costing between £250 and £400.

A full *structural survey* costs anything between £500 and £1,000, but if you're buying a very old or unusual property it's worth considering. If a problem emerges later on that didn't arise in the survey, you may have grounds for compensation. However, it's a very full report, and in most cases, a homebuyer's report is probably enough. (See Chapter 9 for more information on surveys.)

✔ **Mortgage arrangement or application fee:** Some lenders charge a fee for arranging a mortgage. The amount tends to be around £300 but can be as much as double that. Some lenders let you pay it back over the term of the mortgage, while others demand it up front. Keep an eye on such fees and opt for another mortgage if they seem excessive.

✔ **Mortgage broker fee:** If you use a broker to arrange a mortgage (and I strongly recommend you do so as it increases your chances of getting the best deal), the broker may charge a fee – usually no more than 1 per cent of the mortgage.

You don't have to pay anything if the broker is on commission as the lender who gets your business pays this. Although critics argue that such brokers tend to recommend mortgages paying the highest rates of commission, I disagree. As long as you opt for a truly independent broker who has a good reputation to uphold, it shouldn't be a problem (see Chapter 4 for more on choosing a broker).

Table 2-2 gives a general idea of the expenses you should allow for if you're buying a £100,000 property.

Table 2-2 Estimated Expenses for a £100,000 Property

Expense	Amount
Stamp duty	£1,000
Solicitor's fees (including VAT)	£545
Local searches and Land Registry	£244
Mortgage arrangement fee*	£295
Mortgage lender's valuation	£150
Mortgage indemnity guarantee*	£1,000
Mortgage broker's fee*	£950
Homebuyer's report*	£450
Buildings insurance	£180
TOTAL:	**£4,814**

Non-compulsory expenses, depending on your particular circumstances.

Buildings insurance is compulsory: Every mortgage lender insists upon it. The property should be insured from the date you exchange contracts – the point at which you're contractually obliged to buy it. If the property burns down between exchange of contracts and completion, you're nevertheless committed to proceed with the purchase of the burnt-out shell so you must be covered. Contents insurance is important as it pays for the replacement of all your belongings if you are burgled or have a fire, but it isn't compulsory. You may also decide to take out payment protection to cover your mortgage if you lose your job (see Chapter 4). I look at the other costs involved in more detail in the following sections.

Other costs to bear in mind include hiring a removal firm (or a van if you're shifting your belongings yourself), any repairs that need doing, and any new furniture you may want to dress up your new home. If you're moving from a block of flats where you never cut a single blade of grass, you may have to invest in a lawnmower and other gardening equipment.

Avoiding having to pay stamp duty

In an effort to encourage investment and stimulate regeneration in disadvantaged communities, the Government has made properties costing up to £150,000 exempt from stamp duty in 2,000 areas across the country. This will obviously save you a bit of cash if you happen to be thinking about buying in one of these areas anyway.

To find out which areas qualify for stamp duty exemption, go to the Inland Revenue's Web site (www. inlandrevenue.gov.uk).

Deciding about a deposit

Traditionally, first-time buyers saved up a deposit of around 10 per cent of the property purchase price as a matter of course before they started house hunting. But saving even 5 per cent is no longer possible for many buyers. Rising house prices mean it takes a lot longer to save up such a percentage of the purchase price. Lenders have reacted accordingly by introducing 100 per cent mortgages, which don't require any deposit, so buyers don't have to 'waste' several years saving furiously for a down payment. A growing number of lenders even offer mortgages of up to 125 per cent loan to value (LTV) – enabling you to cover the purchase price and costs such as stamp duty – so you can get a foot on the property ladder before prices rise further.

Even though you no longer need a deposit as a general rule, the bigger the deposit you have, the better. Not only does a large deposit help you qualify for a lower mortgage rate because you're considered to be a lower risk, you also can choose from a wider range of home loans.

Avoiding MIG

A healthy deposit helps you avoid paying *mortgage indemnity guarantee (MIG)* – also known as a higher lending fee. *MIG* is a one-off insurance premium charged by some, but not all, lenders if you have a small deposit or no deposit at all. MIG can cost as much as a few thousand pounds so you should try to avoid paying it. Some lenders charge MIG if you take out a loan greater than 90 or 95 per cent of the property's LTV, while some charge MIG on loans bigger than 75 per cent! It is added onto your loan, covering the lender if you default on your mortgage and it has to sell your home at a loss. There is no benefit to you. Many lenders have abolished MIG, so shop around for a MIG-free deal or try drumming up a bigger deposit to avoid paying it.

You don't need a deposit but you're in a stronger position if you have one.

If you take out a 100 per cent mortgage (or bigger) you won't qualify for the most competitive rate of interest because you're considered a greater risk than if you had a deposit.

Asking granny (or the bank) for a loan

If you haven't got a deposit, investigate ways of raising one. Ask relatives whether they can stump up the readies. If they're not in a position to give you the money, you may be able to come to an agreement to pay them back over several years. (Try not to overstretch yourself though and make promises you can't keep as you will have mortgage repayments to make too, and these are your priority.)

If enquiries made with relatives draw a blank, your bank may be sympathetic and agree to extend your overdraft or let you take out a loan. Check the rates of interest before agreeing: You may find a better deal if you shop around.

Why it doesn't always pay to wait

I put down a 25 per cent deposit when I bought my flat in 1999 – just before a big hike in property prices. A friend was trying to buy at the same time but she only had £5,000 for a deposit and didn't want to pay MIG, which restricted the size of the mortgage she could take on.

She couldn't find anything in her price range so decided to put her plans on hold, save up a bigger deposit and try again. But once she'd saved up £12,000, she couldn't afford anything. Prices had risen so much she'd been priced out of the market. She had to wait four years, save a deposit of £20,000, and move out of London before she could find something half decent to buy. If she'd opted for a 100 per cent loan and bought when she first started looking, this wouldn't have happened.

Resist the temptation to take on lots of expensive debt. A cash advance on your credit card or a loan from a dodgy lender may be the only way you can raise a deposit, but at what cost?

If you borrow money, make sure you work out how much it will cost over the term of the loan and assess whether it is worth it. You'll have enough outgoings as it is without worrying about loan sharks banging on your door.

Pooling your resources

If you can't afford to buy on your own, try teaming up with someone to get a foot on the housing ladder.

Buying with a partner

The most cost-effective way of buying a property is with a partner, whether you are married or co-habiting. You can borrow more money, are likely to have a bigger deposit – as you can draw on two lots of savings – and two of you will be paying the mortgage.

There is no guarantee that you will stay with your partner – whether you're wedded or not. And if you aren't married and split up, the law treats each of you as separate individuals with no rights or liabilities in regards to each other. If the property is in your partner's name, you have no legal claim to it – even if you paid half the mortgage for the past 20 years. To protect your legal rights, ensure you own the property as *joint tenants* or *tenants in common*.

If you are *joint tenants* and your partner dies, her interest in the property passes to you and vice versa. Married couples usually buy a property as joint tenants. If you are *tenants in common*, each of you has a distinct share in the property: either 50:50 or based on how much each of you contributed to the deposit or mortgage. If you die, your share goes to your estate – not to your partner.

Get a solicitor to draw up documents staking your claim before buying property with a partner.

Get it in writing

I know a couple who bought a flat together using her savings to pay the deposit. The mortgage was put in her name and her boyfriend paid his half in cash to her each month; she paid the full amount by direct debit from her account.

Four years later, they split up acrimoniously and he discovered he had no claims on the flat. As he'd paid his share in cash he couldn't prove he'd done so. He is now renting another flat as property prices had gone up so much he can't afford to buy.

Getting by with a little help from your friends

An increasing number of buyers are clubbing together with friends or siblings or other relatives in order to get on the property ladder. While you may worry about falling out, if you choose your friends carefully and get your solicitor to draw up a contract, you've a good chance of making this arrangement a success.

The contract should state who is contributing what to the deposit and mortgage, and stipulate what happens if one of you wants to move out or sell up. You may decide to include a clause stating that no one can change the arrangements within the first five years, for example, or a clause giving the other owners first refusal to buy them out.

Most lenders allow up to four names on the mortgage deeds but offer loans based on only two salaries. So it may not be in your interests to buy with more than one person because you won't be able to borrow significantly more than if you buy with just one friend or sibling.

Drawing on parental power

Although you may be buying property in order to get away from your parents, they may be able – and more than willing – to help you do this. Even if they can't give you money to use towards a deposit, they may be able to act as guarantors and agree to cover your mortgage repayments if you default on them. (See Chapter 5 for more details on this.)

Working Out How Much to Borrow

What the lender is prepared to lend you and what you should borrow are two different things. 'How much can I afford to borrow?' is one of the most important questions you should ask yourself before applying for a mortgage.

Mortgage providers have relaxed their lending criteria over the past couple of decades, with much bigger home loans now available. But that doesn't mean you should take on the biggest mortgage you can. You have to repay it and even if you can cope initially, you may struggle if you lose your job, have to replace your car at short notice, or have to cope with rising interest rates. If you're overstretched, even a small change in circumstances can completely upset your apple cart.

Typically, you can borrow three times your income, or two and a half times joint income if you buy with a partner. So if you earn £20,000 you can borrow £60,000 on your own or £100,000 with a partner who earns the same amount. But this won't get you very far: The average cost of a house in the UK in March 2004 was £151,467, according to the Halifax House Price Index.

In an effort to bridge the gap between what you can afford and what you can borrow, some lenders have increased their *income multiple* – the number of times your salary you can borrow – to four. This enables you to buy a more expensive property. Whether you can afford the repayments is another question, though. If you can only just about cope now, how will you manage if interest rates double? Even a small increase may spell disaster.

When you're on a low income it's tempting to borrow as much as you are offered, particularly if it enables you to buy a property that might otherwise have been out of your price range. Table 2-1 can help you calculate how much you can realistically afford to repay each month – don't fool yourself into thinking you can cope with higher repayments if you've already worked out that you can't.

A handful of lenders have been rumoured to be offering bor-rowers five, or even six, times income but think really care-fully before taking on such a big loan if you are offered it. Don't overstretch yourself. Make sure you are happy with the mortgage repayments and can cope if interest rates rise. You still have to eat!

Adjusting Mortgage Terms

The majority of homebuyers take out a mortgage for a 25-year *mortgage term,* which is the length of time the borrower has to pay back the money borrowed plus interest. Because you're so used to hearing about a 25-year timeframe, you may assume that you have to take out a mortgage for this length of time. That's not the case. A mortgage term can be as short as five years or as long as you like (as long as you pay it back by the time you retire). At the end of the term, the property is yours.

There's a growing trend towards longer mortgage terms, par-ticularly among first-time buyers. The advantage of paying your mortgage back over 30, 40, or even 45 years is that your repayments are lower – ideal for those on low incomes. But the downside is that you make more repayments over the years and pay a lot more interest. Table 2-3 illustrates how much you end up paying back if you take out a £120,000 loan at 6.25 per cent over various lengths of time: The shorter the term, the higher your monthly repayment and the lower your total cost. Conversely, the longer the mortgage term, the lower your monthly repayment – but the total cost of the mortgage is higher. The mortgage term isn't set in stone: You can lengthen (or indeed shorten) it if you remortgage later on.

Table 2-3 Cost of Borrowing £120,000 Over Time at 6.25%		
Mortgage Term	*Monthly Repayment*	*Total Cost*
25 years	£791.60	£237,480.00
30 years	£738.86	£265,989.60
40 years	£681.29	£327,019.20

Source: London & Country Mortgages

Timing Your Purchase

After you work out how much you can spend, you may be tempted to wait until house prices fall so that your money goes further. Of course, if you have to move by a certain date because your landlord is chucking you out of your rented flat, you may have no say in the matter. But if there is no real hurry to buy a property, you may try timing your purchase so that it coincides with a slump in housing prices.

Nobody knows what's going to happen to property prices. Timing the market is a mug's game: If the experts can't agree on what will happen, what chance do you have? As long as you pay a fair price and don't overstretch yourself, any time is the right time for you to buy.

In practical terms, most people buy in spring or autumn, when the property market is busiest. That's not to say you can't buy in summer or winter, but many sellers refrain from putting their property on the market until spring so they have a greater chance of finding a buyer and getting the price they want. The advantage of buying in summer or winter is that agents won't be as frantic and can spend more time with you. You may also be able to knock the price down if the seller wants a quick sale.

Buying during a property boom

If prices have been rising for months and are so crazy that you can't find anything even half decent for your money, there's a strong chance the market is experiencing a boom. The problem is that if you buy at the peak of the market there's a chance you will pay well over the value. And if a crash follows, you could end up in negative equity – the worst possible position for a homeowner to find herself.

If you are in *negative equity,* your property is worth less than you paid for it. You are effectively trapped until the value of your home recovers, which could take several years. If you are forced to sell up before then, you could lose a lot of money. To avoid negative equity, make sure you don't pay over the odds in the first place – certainly not more than you can afford – and only buy if you plan to live in that property for several years.

When property prices are rising, it may seem as if they will continue moving upwards forever. But this isn't necessarily true. Historically, property prices rise over time but not without the odd blip or two along the way. If the property market does collapse just when you need to sell your home, you can bear it more easily if you haven't paid thousands of pounds more than the property was really worth, as this will minimise your losses.

Sometimes property prices just keep on rising, as they did during the late 1990s. It may be tempting to wait until prices fall before making a purchase but this could mean being on hold for years if the market is particularly buoyant. If you buy when prices are rising, you get less return on your investment but if prices continue to move upwards, it's worth getting a foot on the ladder rather than miss the boat.

Buying during a slump

The best time to buy is during a property slump. If properties are languishing on the market for months, and sellers are forced to reduce their asking price just as you're looking to buy, you're in luck. You should even be able to negotiate prices lower still, so be sure to haggle a bit. If you buy during a slump, it's a fairly safe bet that you'll get a good price for a property.

It may be tempting to hang on until prices fall even further but keep in mind that they won't continue to drop forever. Property is fairly resilient and prices eventually rise again after a fall. If you're worried that property prices may fall further once you make an offer, don't despair. Even if the market does go down further, it will recover eventually and, as long as you stay put for several years, you'll make your money back. And you can reassure yourself with the knowledge that you are getting a better deal than you would have done if you'd bought during a property boom.

Chapter 3

Finding Budget-Friendly Dwellings and Neighbourhoods

. . . .

In This Chapter

▶ Working out what sort of property you're looking for

▶ Researching the area – before arranging any viewings

▶ Finding affordable property in established areas

▶ Spotting up-and-coming areas

. . . .

*A*fter you decide that you can afford to buy your first home, it's tempting to rush to the nearest estate agent and start making appointments to view lots of properties. But before you do this, consider exactly what it is you are looking for. Given that a home is one of the biggest and most important purchases you will ever make, it's important to get it right and having a vague idea of what you want is not enough.

Although you need to have a clear picture of what you want, it's important to be flexible or you may dismiss a great property that meets most, but not all, your requirements. When your budget is tight, you have to be more flexible than you would if money were no object. That doesn't mean you can't have what you want: You may just have to scale down your ambitions a little and be prepared to compromise. In this chapter, I focus on the factors to take into account when deciding what sort of property you require. The only way an agent can help you find what you want is if you know yourself.

Establishing Your Property Criteria

When you first start property hunting you may have a vague notion of what you want. But you can save yourself a lot of time and energy if you pinpoint your requirements *before* arranging any viewings. Some of the basic issues to address include:

- ✔ **The number of bedrooms you need:** If you're buying on your own, you may not even need a bedroom and be happy with a studio flat. A studio is cheaper than a flat with a separate bedroom, but studios can be more difficult to sell (which you will be doing eventually) because they appeal to a limited number of buyers. You may decide that two bedrooms are necessary so that you can rent one to help pay the mortgage (see Chapter 14 for information on taking in a lodger). If you're buying with a partner, you probably need a couple of bedrooms – maybe three if you're starting a family. And if you're buying with a friend or sibling, you need two bedrooms in order to avoid driving each other mad.

- ✔ **Whether you want a flat or house:** Houses are usually bigger and more expensive to buy, maintain, and insure, while flats are cheaper but noisier because you live in closer proximity to your neighbours.

  As well as the day-to-day practicalities, in England, Wales, and Northern Ireland you also have to contend with freehold and leasehold. Flats tend to be leasehold so you pay rent and service charges to a landlord, while houses are usually freehold so you don't have a landlord to answer to. (See Chapter 10 for more details on freehold and leasehold.)

- ✔ **Where you want to live:** Whether you want to live in the country, town, or city is a matter of personal preference as well as finances. Some people feel oppressed living in a big city while others are bored by the countryside. If you work in the city, it doesn't necessarily mean you have to live there: As long as you are near good transport links you can live in the country and commute. Property prices in desirable parts of a city can be much higher than in the suburbs, although most cities have their rough parts where property prices are relatively cheap because they are undesirable. Don't write these off immediately: The area might not be as bad as it is painted and you may be able to pick up a bargain close to your workplace. Try not to be guided wholly by price (although it is difficult not to be when you are on a budget): Look for an area you can be happy living in. The countryside tends to have a slower pace of life and the air is cleaner. But the roads can be inaccessible in winter, the shops miles away, and the social life limited. The city is more glamorous, with plenty to do. But your money might not stretch as far and there's more pollution. The choice is yours.

✔ **Whether you need a garden:** Gardens can be lovely, particularly in summer when you can invite your mates round for barbecues. But it takes a lot of work to keep them inviting. Consider whether you can be bothered with the upkeep and if not, whether you can afford to hire a gardener. A garden is more important if you have children or pets than if you don't. Gardens also tend to bump up the price of a property, so you may have to reconcile yourself to the fact that you can't afford one – no matter how much you want one.

✔ **Whether you prefer a garage or off-road parking:** If you have a car, you may prefer to park it off-road rather than struggle to find a space in the street when you get home from work. Keeping your car in a garage at night lets you pay lower motor insurance premiums. But again, such luxuries add to the price of a property so you may have to compromise and opt for a property in a street with safe on-road parking.

✔ **Whether you want a new home or an old one:** Often this decision is a matter of personal taste and finances. Some people prefer a property in perfect condition with brand new fitted kitchen and bathroom with all the mod cons. Others prefer the history and character of an older building. Keep in mind that if it's in perfect condition, an older home will cost you a fortune, and if it isn't, there may be more work to do than you can deal with. (See Chapter 12 for information on renovating property or building from scratch.)

Getting the Lowdown on the Area

Even if a property meets all your criteria in terms of size and whether or not it has a garden, if it's in the wrong location it's of little use to you. That's why when deciding what you want from a property you also need to consider what you want from the locality.

You can find out a lot about an area without traipsing the streets. The Internet is a great place to start: Try www.upmystreet.com, which has details of schools, crime rates, the council tax rates, what issues currently concern the local council, as well as the lowdown on restaurants and pubs. The Yellow Pages Web site at www.yell.com provides similar information.

After you have the basic information about an area, check it out for yourself: Don't rely on the Internet search. If you travel by car, get out and walk around to get a feel for the place.

Finding a smaller place in a well-established neighbourhood

Location, location, location is a bit of a cliché but it is one of the most important considerations when buying property. The trouble is you're not the only one who wants to live in a nice area with a low crime rate – so do most people – and this bumps up the price of houses in those areas.

Location costs. A pretty cottage in the picturesque Cotswolds, for example, is going to set you back far more than a similar-sized new build property in less desirable Milton Keynes. Properties in city centres tend to cost more than those on the outskirts, while one area in a city may be much more desirable than another. In London, for example, Hampstead is more fashionable than Lewisham and the housing prices higher.

However, this doesn't mean you have to write off every desirable neighbourhood. Not every property is a swanky five-storey townhouse with a large garden and off-road parking for four cars or a chocolate-box cottage with roses growing round the front door. Every area has its budget accommodations; your challenge is to find them. You have to be extremely realistic in your ambitions though: If your budget would get you a two-bedroom flat in a cheaper part of town, you may have to settle for a studio if you want to buy in a highly desirable location.

Be prepared to spend longer looking for a property you can afford in an extremely desirable area. Contact local estate agents and tell them what your budget is (resist the temptation to lie even if they laugh at you). One friend who bought a fairly cheap flat in Highbury, north London – a very desirable area – found it easier to e-mail estate agents with her requirements and put her name on their property lists rather than wander into their swanky offices, which were rather daunting. Be upfront about what you're looking for: Tell them you love the area, have set your heart on it, and are prepared to compromise on the accommodation. The odd studio or rundown property is likely to come onto their books from time-to-time so you may be in luck.

Coming up with an up-and-coming area

Your money goes a lot further if you buy in an area that hasn't yet become established. The important element here is *yet*. If you can spot an area that's going to be desirable before it actually is, you stand to make a mint on your investment. And you should be able to get a bigger property for the same price as a cramped one in a more fashionable location.

Most people cotton onto up-and-coming areas long after the trendy types have moved on to the next edgy neighbourhood and property prices have already gone up. If you are looking for the next trendy area, don't underestimate the *ripple effect* of a hot, new living area springing up right next door to a well-established area. People who can't quite afford to live in the established neighbourhood often buy property just outside it. It is often only a matter of time before gastro pubs and restaurants follow suit. Check out cheap areas next to expensive ones: Hackney in east London, for example, is the choice of many who can't afford neighbouring Islington.

Getting a room with an elevated view

There's something rather romantic about looking out onto grass, trees, or water. But what about across a city? Views don't come much more breathtaking than those from high-rise flats. Some of London's tower blocks offer superb views that you'd struggle to find on the London Eye. The other advantage of high-rise flats is that they tend to be ex-local authority, so are cheaper than other properties.

But you'll find it impossible to get a mortgage on anything above the fifth floor of a tower block constructed from reinforced concrete as lenders don't want the extra risk: Some 1960s blocks were built from substandard material which hasn't weathered well. If you are interested in buying a high-rise, contact a mortgage broker for advice as to which lenders you should approach. (See Chapter 4 for details on finding a broker.)

Easy access to public transport and plans for new transport links are another pointer towards an up-and-coming part of town. Regeneration plans are also worth looking out for, as these tend to encourage people and businesses to move to the area – local authority Web sites often have this information. To find the Web site of your local authority, check out www.ukonline.gov.uk, which has a list of every local council in the UK and provides a link enabling you to click through to the one you want. Keep an eye on the papers as well. For example, the London bid for the 2012 Olympics, if successful, will lead to extensive regeneration of the east end of London. Although property prices in the area are cheap at the moment, that won't remain the case for long.

It is all well and good moving into a really affordable area that hasn't been gentrified and doesn't have nice restaurants or bars but remember, you have to live there, possibly for several years, so only buy in an area that is convenient, where you will be happy and feel safe. Making a profit when you sell your home shouldn't be your primary aim but a bonus.

Beware of an area that is always up-and-coming and never actually arrives. King's Cross in London is one example of unfulfilled promise. If you bought there 15 years ago when it was deemed the next big thing, you're still waiting for the area to become desirable. That's why you must choose somewhere you can happily live – and any gentrification of the area is seen as a bonus.

If the trendy wine bars and bistros have opened up on the high street, you may have missed the boat. Do your research and get in ahead of the crowd. But be prepared to put up with the boarded-up shops until the restaurants have had a chance to open.

Looking into Local Amenities

Depending on your personal interests, certain local amenities may appeal to you more than others. These may include:

- ✔ **Doctor's surgery or dentist's:** A good local NHS doctor or – increasingly rare – dentist is always useful in case of emergency.

- ✔ **Place of worship:** If you regularly attend church, the synagogue, or the mosque, you may prefer to have one nearby.

- ✔ **Public library:** Although these are sadly under-funded in many areas, some excellent ones lend CDs and DVDs as well as books.

- ✔ **Pubs and restaurants:** This may seem trivial, but if you like a drink after work or at weekends, you may prefer a local populated with familiar faces to a pub miles away. Good takeaways can be a godsend when you don't feel like cooking.

- ✔ **Shops:** A local newsagents, corner shop, and Post Office are all useful, as are a pharmacy and a large supermarket.

- ✔ **Sports centre or health club:** If you do a lot of sport or have kids who need occupying at weekends and in the school holidays, it makes sense to live close to a sports centre or gym.

The following sections talk about other issues you may wish to take into consideration.

Linking to transport

If you rely on public transport, you'll regret buying a house in a village where a bus comes through once an hour if you're lucky. And if you buy a property miles away from your workplace, it's important that there are good train, tube, or bus links – particularly if you work shifts at unsociable hours.

Try out the journey yourself at the time of day you commute to work before buying a property in an out-of-the-way area. Never trust a train timetable!

Educating yourself about schools

A good catchment area with excellent local schools is likely to bump up the price of the property – if it is a family-sized home, with three bedrooms, say. But if you're buying a studio or one-bed flat the price shouldn't be affected by the proximity of a good school.

If you have children, or plan to in the near future, research the schools in an area by checking the performance tables on the Department for Education and Skills' Web site at `www.dfes.gov.uk`. For more information on a school, look at the Office for Standards in Education (OFSTED) Web site (`www.ofsted.gov.uk`). Contact the school itself for more information on the catchment area.

Casing the crime rate

Many parts of the country have high crime rates. Properties in these areas are likely to be cheaper than in areas with low crime rates – with good reason! And even though you are on a budget, I urge you to avoid such areas if you want to live happily and securely in your new home. Don't forget that there will come a time when you want to sell the property and you may find it difficult if you bought in such an area.

If you're planning to buy in the area you rent in, you already know what the crime statistics are and how safe it feels. But if you're thinking of moving to a new area, do your research carefully first. As well as checking `www.upmystreet.com` to get an idea of the crime rate in an area, spend some time there. I suggest driving round the streets late at night to see whether the streets are well lit and appear safe. Are there gangs of kids hanging on street corners causing trouble? Burnt-out cars are also very revealing, suggesting an unloved area with its fair share of troublemakers. If this is what you see, you should consider buying somewhere else.

Considering environmental concerns

Research suggests that the environment we live in can have quite an effect on our health. When considering where to buy, you may want to look out for:

- **Mobile phone masts:** There has been a lot of criticism surrounding phone masts. Government research shows no general risk to health; although worryingly it says there could be an indirect adverse effect in some cases.

- **Electricity pylons:** Again, scientists say there is no convincing evidence of a public health risk but some people are convinced their health has been affected by living in the shadow of an electricity pylon. Play it safe and buy somewhere else if you are concerned.

- **Airports:** Living under a flight path isn't much fun, particularly if it is connected to a very busy airport, such as Heathrow. Properties are cheaper – but can you live with the noise?

- **Waste incinerators:** Again, these may be something you want to avoid living near as the health risks aren't clear.

- **Air pollution:** Living on a main road in a city results in poorer air quality than if you live in the countryside. This may have long-term as well as short-term effects on your health and your children's health.

- **Smog:** This air pollution is a growing problem in big cities, particularly in the summer.

For more information on contaminated land or pollution, go to www.environment-agency.gov.uk. In the *What's In My Backyard?* section you can search by postcode for landfill sites, flood plains, and air pollution.

Part II
Show Me the Money!

"It's always good policy to have your estate agent on your side – in fact, I'm starting to warm to you both already, Mr & Mrs Hazelgrove."

In this part . . .

Getting your hands on the readies is likely to be your biggest challenge and the chapters in this part show you how. Here you'll find the answers to all your mortgage queries, tips on using a guarantor, and info on what special deals lenders are offering first-time buyers. And even if you're on a low salary, you may be able to use your future earning power to get yourself on the housing ladder sooner rather than later.

Chapter 4

Negotiating the Mortgage Maze

. . . .

In This Chapter

▶ Understanding how mortgages work

▶ Looking at rates

▶ Finding the best mortgage to suit your budget

▶ Searching for a self-certification mortgage

▶ Opting out of unnecessary costs

▶ Buying insurance

. . . .

*F*ew first-time buyers have enough cash to buy a property outright so unless you are a Premiership footballer, film star, or have a sizeable trust fund or inheritance, you need a mortgage.

Finding a mortgage can be daunting because of the vast sums of cash involved but the proliferation in the number of deals available means finding one that suits your circumstances isn't too difficult. And with interest rates at their lowest level in decades, there's something to suit even your budget.

But with so many lenders offering a wide range of different, and often complex, mortgage deals it can be hard to choose between them. Finding the right mortgage is crucial because it is likely to be your biggest monthly outgoing. Yet, many people get it wrong, paying £3.5 billion more than necessary each year, according to independent financial adviser The MarketPlace at Bradford & Bingley. You can't afford to make such a mistake, when money is already tight. In this chapter I guide you through the different mortgages available so you don't spend more than necessary.

The process of finding a mortgage can be scary but with the right advice, coupled with your own careful research, you can find a decent deal you won't regret 10 years down the line.

Choosing the Right Type of Mortgage

Before you can choose the right mortgage, you need to get your head round the different types available and how they work. There are two main ways of repaying your mortgage: paying a slice of the capital (the amount you borrow in the first place), plus interest – what the lender charges you for borrowing this cash – each month (*repayment*); or just paying the interest each month (*interest-only*). With an interest-only mortgage you also need to set up an investment vehicle (see 'Going interest-only' later in this chapter) to pay off the capital at the end of the mortgage term.

You can also go for a third option, whereby you take an interest-only deal for the first couple of years of your mortgage, and then switch to a repayment loan. This enables you to keep the costs down in the early years when you may be struggling to budget.

Whether you choose a repayment or interest-only mortgage largely depends upon your attitude to risk. Although monthly payments are higher on a repayment loan than an interest-only deal, many homebuyers prefer the peace of mind and knowing that their mortgage is guaranteed to be paid off at the end of the term. You must decide whether you are prepared to take a gamble on the roof over your head, which is, in effect, what you do with an interest-only mortgage.

Understanding repayment loans

If you want a guarantee that all the capital you borrow is paid off by the end of the mortgage term, opt for a *repayment loan*. You pay a proportion of the interest on the loan plus a slice of the capital each month. If you keep up the repayments, at the end of the mortgage term you've paid off all the capital and the property is yours.

Going interest-only

With an *interest-only mortgage,* you pay a chunk of the interest on the loan each month, but none of the capital. You don't repay the capital until the end of the mortgage term when you pay it back in full. If you fail to do so, your lender can repossess your home. For example, if you borrow £80,000 on an interest-only basis at 5.65 per cent over 25 years, your mortgage repayments are £376.67 per month, with £80,000 due at the end of the term. In contrast, the monthly amount on a repayment loan is £498.46, with no capital due at the end of the term.

Although an interest-only mortgage may seem risky, the monthly payments are lower than on a repayment deal, which makes them quite attractive.

You must set up an investment vehicle to pay off the capital at the end of the term of an interest-only mortgage. Endowments used to be the first choice for many homeowners with interest-only mortgages, but these are unpopular now owing to a number of mis-selling claims (see the 'Endowments and the bear market' sidebar). Individual savings accounts (ISAs) or pensions are other options – I cover all the choices available to you in the following sections.

Making the most of an endowment mortgage

An endowment combines a savings vehicle with an element of life assurance. An interest-only mortgage is not compulsory before you can take out an endowment but most people who take out a policy do so to pay off the mortgage. An endowment policy tends to run for the same length of time as the mortgage. It matures when the time comes to pay back the mortgage capital – raising enough to clear this debt. The life assurance element pays off the mortgage capital if you die before the policy matures. If you outlive the policy, however, there's no guarantee it will generate enough cash to pay off the mortgage.

If you take out an endowment, you make monthly payments into the fund; the life company invests these in stocks and shares, property, government bonds and cash.

There are two types of endowment policy:

- ✔ **With-profits endowment:** The life company undertakes to pay a fixed sum, known as the *basic sum assured*, plus accumulated profits – known as *reversionary* bonuses, which are declared annually – to you on a fixed date, provided you have paid all your premiums. Reversionary bonuses are based on the investment performance of the fund: once added, these can't be taken away, although you can't get your hands on them until your policy matures. The idea of a with-profits fund is that your investment is subject to smoothing: The life insurer holds back some of the profits – in the form of a lower annual bonus – when the stock market is performing strongly, so that you still get bonuses when the market is not performing well. When the endowment matures, you could get a one-off *terminal* bonus based on the performance of the fund: this can be a large proportion of your final payout but it isn't guaranteed. You may get nothing at all if prevailing market conditions at the time are poor so you mustn't rely on this to help you pay off your mortgage. However, if the policy exceeds the performance you require, you may get a tax-free surplus.

- ✔ **Unit-linked endowment:** This type of endowment is specifically designed to pay off an interest-only mortgage. Your monthly premiums buy units in a managed fund run by a life company and invested in the stock market. The number of units you hold increases over time as you pay more premiums and the value of these fluctuates in line with the investment performance of the fund. There are no annual or terminal bonuses and no smoothing as in a with-profits fund: This is why unit-linked endowments are more risky because your investment is linked 100 per cent to the value of the stock market so its value could drop considerably if the market plummets just when you need the money. If the stock market performs well, you get all the growth – unlike a with-profits endowment when you only get a percentage – but if the market does badly, the full effects are reflected in your investment.

Stocks and shares can go down as well as up. Don't gamble on the roof over your head unless you have enough cash in reserve to cover any potential shortfall in your endowment.

Endowments and the bear market

In 1986, endowment-backed mortgages were at the height of their popularity as a result of the booming stock market. They accounted for 80 per cent of all mortgages, according to the Council of Mortgage Lenders. By 2001, this share had fallen to 10 per cent of the market.

This decline in popularity is linked to the falling stock market, known as a *bear market.* Endowment insurers based their projections on the hope that shares would continue to rise, with likely returns of 4 to 8 per cent per annum. At these rates, endowment holders would be able to pay off their mortgage – and get a tidy surplus, which they could splurge on whatever they wished.

But it was too good to be true. The stock market crashed in April 2000 and has continued to struggle since then. Endowment policies were hit hard, with insurers forced to recalculate policyholders' projections and tell them whether their investment was on track to pay off their mortgage.

Many letters notifying policyholders of revised projections identify a potential shortfall in policies and recommend that the policyholder takes action to address this. Those who face shortfalls may have to conjure up thousands of pounds to pay off their mortgage.

Many policyholders claim that the risks weren't spelt out by the salesperson who sold them the endowment; in other words, they were mis-sold. Many have since said they wouldn't have bought an endowment if they had known it was linked to the stock market and have successfully proven their case and received compensation.

But many people weren't mis-sold. They took out an endowment because they liked having lower monthly mortgage repayments than on a repayment loan and hoped to get a windfall once the policy matured. And they would have done if the stock market had played ball.

Endowment mortgages have been widely criticised during the past few years because there is a strong chance that many will fail to provide enough cash for homeowners to pay back their mortgages. The debate about whether endowment policies were mis-sold continues to rumble on (see the sidebar 'Endowments and the bear market').

Investing in ISAs

Instead of an endowment, you can use individual savings accounts, or ISAs, to pay off the capital on your interest-only mortgage. An *ISA* is a tax-free investment vehicle, which invests in cash, insurance or stocks and shares. For the purpose of paying off your mortgage, you invest in stocks and shares through a pooled investment such as a unit trust: cash or insurance just wouldn't produce enough investment growth to pay off your mortgage. Anyone over the age of 18 can invest in a stocks and shares ISA – you don't have to take out a mortgage to have such an investment nor designate it as a 'mortgage ISA' in any way. However, you are restricted to taking out one ISA per tax year, so if you've taken out an ISA to pay off the capital owed on your interest-only mortgage, you can't start another ISA to raise cash for another purpose.

If you're using ISAs to pay off the capital on your interest-only mortgage, you either invest a monthly sum into an ISA mortgage offered by your lender, or build up a personal portfolio of ISA investments, which you choose yourself. The money (hopefully) increases over time, tax-free. It's probably best to go for the latter option: While your lender may offer excellent terms on its mortgage, the same may not be true on its ISAs. You may be able to get better investment performance if you invest in ISAs run by a professional fund manager.

There are several advantages to investing in an ISA rather than an endowment. Returns from ISAs are tax-free, so your investment should grow more quickly. With an ISA you also know exactly how much your investment is worth, unlike an endowment, which generates annual bonuses and possibly a terminal bonus. Investment charges are lower with an ISA: you simply pay an initial charge of around 5 per cent of the amount invested and then an annual management charge of around 1.5 per cent. With endowments and pensions, there are lots of set-up costs, which eat into investment performance in the early years. ISAs are also more flexible. It's easy to switch investments if your fund is under-performing and stop or re-start payments. You also have more say over where your money is invested.

When it comes to repaying a mortgage, too much flexibility is a bad thing if you end up with less money than you need. Also, ISAs are as vulnerable to stock market fluctuations as endowments, so there's no guarantee they'll raise enough cash to pay off your mortgage. ISA mortgages are therefore extremely high risk – so don't take one on unless you are an experienced investor and higher rate taxpayer, so you get the most from the tax breaks available.

There is a limit to the amount you can invest in an ISA each tax year (6 April to the following 5 April), whether you are using it to pay off the capital on your mortgage or not. You can invest up to £7,000 in a stocks and shares maxi ISA this tax year. This will be slashed to £5,000 from April 2006, which could make it difficult to generate enough capital to pay off your mortgage. However, if you buy your home with your partner, sibling, or a couple of mates, each of you can utilise your personal ISA allowance and invest up to £7,000 each.

ISA mortgages are linked to the stock market. So the bear market that has had such a crippling effect on endowments also affects ISAs. In fact the volatility of the stock markets since March 2000 has been so bad that the popularity of ISA mortgages has dropped dramatically and many lenders no longer offer them.

Don't forget to insure your investment contributions in case you lose your job or have an accident and can no longer work. Any of the usual protection products (see the sidebar 'Investing in optional insurance' later in this chapter) is suitable.

Pursuing a pension mortgage

Backing your interest-only mortgage with a pension is a good way of maximising available tax breaks. However, if you are a member of your employer's occupational pension scheme, you can't have a pension mortgage.

In a *pension mortgage*, you invest money each month in a personal pension fund and pay premiums into a life assurance scheme.

When you retire, you get a tax-free lump sum – up to 25 per cent of your pension pot – which you use to pay off the capital you owe. The rest purchases an *annuity* – a guaranteed income for life – which forms your pension. Because you can't get hold of your cash lump sum until you retire, pension mortgages tend to run for a lot longer than endowment home loans – sometimes as long as 35 or 40 years.

A pension is a highly tax-efficient way of saving. For every 78p a basic rate taxpayer invests in his pension (60p for higher rate taxpayers) the Government tops this contribution up to £1 (for example. it contributes 22p to a basic rate taxpayer's pension and 40p to a higher rate taxpayer's). This tax relief leads to higher investment returns than you can get from investing in an ISA or endowment simply because more money is going into your pension fund.

Pension mortgages are extremely tax-efficient but they are stock market-linked and highly complicated so really only suit sophisticated, self-employed higher rate taxpayers. If this doesn't sound like you, give them a wide berth.

There are no guarantees with a pension mortgage – market performance, and the skills of the fund manager handling your investment, decides the amount of cash you end up with, so it can be risky. Keep a close eye on the performance of your fund to ensure it's on track to pay off your mortgage: If not, you'll have to consider alternative arrangements to cover the shortfall. Pension rules also tend to be highly complicated so you need professional advice.

Combining repayment with interest-only

Some lenders try to make life easier for first-time buyers on tight budgets by offering mortgages that are interest-only for the first couple of years before switching to a repayment mortgage.

This combination loan means cheaper monthly payments for the first two years of your mortgage – when money tends to be exceptionally tight – because you pay only the interest and none of the capital. After two years, when things have settled down a bit, you start paying back the capital. The lender calculates your monthly payments so that at the end of the mortgage term you will have paid back all the capital. Watch out for a big jump in the cost of your monthly payments from year three onwards and budget for it accordingly.

Understanding Rates

Once you've decided on a repayment or interest-only deal, you're ready to choose a mortgage rate. The rate you choose should depend on your circumstances and attitude to risk. Before I discuss the different rates available, I run through the main terms referred to in this section. Understanding these will help you find the most suitable mortgage.

- ✔ **Base rate:** This is the benchmark interest rate, set by the Bank of England's Monetary Policy Committee (see below). All mortgage lenders set their key rate, known as the standard variable rate (again, see below) by the base rate. If the base rate moves up, lenders raise their rate accordingly, usually by the same amount: If it moves down, they also lower their rate (although not always by the full amount).

- ✔ **Standard variable rate (SVR):** This is the lender's key rate, from which all its other rates, such as discounted deals, are calculated. If you take out a discount mortgage, for example, it's usually one or two per cent off the lender's SVR for a number of years. At the end of this time, the rate reverts to the SVR. And if the SVR moves up (or down), your discount rate moves accordingly.

- ✔ **Monetary Policy Committee (MPC):** The Bank of England body that meets once a month to decide whether the base rate should be raised, cut, or remain the same. This decision depends on factors such as inflation, consumer spending and the state of the housing market. If there are signs that inflation is rising, for example, the MPC will raise the base rate to curb consumer spending but if the economy is slowing, it will cut rates to boost consumer borrowing.

- ✔ **Offer period:** Lenders provide a number of deals – including fixed, capped, discount and tracker rates – for a set amount of time, otherwise known as the *offer period*. At the end of the offer period, the rate reverts to the lender's SVR and you should switch to another deal, as it is bound to be cheaper.

Avoiding the standard variable rate

The SVR is the lender's benchmark rate from which all its offers or deals are calculated. Because it is variable it can move up and down, with no notice at all – if the Bank of England raises or cuts the base rate, most lenders adjust their SVR accordingly within minutes. You can take out a mortgage on your lender's SVR but it won't be the cheapest rate available. You are better off opting for a deal, such as a fixed or discounted rate, which tends to be a couple of percentage points below the SVR.

When these deals come to an end, the rate reverts to the SVR, so you should switch to another offer. Stay on the SVR, and your mortgage payments will increase dramatically. Remortgaging is straightforward: you switch to another deal offered by your lender or move your mortgage to a different lender – if it offers a more competitive deal. You will have to pay a lender's valuation fee, legal fees, and may have to pay an arrangement fee, depending on the lender.

SVRs vary among lenders, and it's worth keeping an eye on them as they're a useful indicator of the competitiveness of the lender's other mortgage deals. If the SVR is high compared to the base rate and other lenders' standard rates, that lender is unlikely to have competitive fixed or discounted rates either. Find a lender with a low SVR and you are likely to find a cheaper deal.

Calculating interest

Some lenders still charge interest on an annual basis, which costs you more money than if interest is charged daily. Make sure you find out how a lender calculates interest on the mortgage you're interested in before you take it out.

Whether interest is calculated daily or annually can make a big difference in how much interest you pay. The differences between these methods follow:

✔ **Daily calculation:** Your lender calculates how much is outstanding on your mortgage at the end of each day. So when you make a mortgage payment, your money starts working straight-away to reduce your mortgage

debt – and the interest you pay over the term of the loan.

✔ **Annual calculation:** Your mortgage payments are knocked off your outstanding balance just once a year, rather than when you make them. If your interest is calculated on 1 January, the payments you make during the rest of the year don't reduce your outstanding balance until the following January. Thus, you pay interest on a larger sum than you actually owe throughout the year and end up paying much more over time.

Calculating interest on an annual basis is an arcane, outdated method. Avoid lenders who still adhere to this practice.

Fixing on a fixed rate

A *fixed rate mortgage* is exactly what the name suggests – your mortgage payments are guaranteed to stay the same, no matter what happens to the base rate, for a set period of time. For example, if you take out a five-year deal fixed at 3.99 per cent, for five years you'll be charged interest at 3.99 per cent.

A fixed rate brings certainty and protects you if the base rate rises, but if the base rate falls you won't benefit. And if you fix for five years or more, there may be significant rate cuts during this period.

Because your mortgage payments are fixed, budgeting is a lot easier than if you're on a variable rate. When you're on a tight budget, a fixed rate deal is ideal.

Mortgages tend to be fixed for 2, 3, or 5 years, but it's also possible to find deals for 10, 15, 20, 25, or even 30 years. Relatively few homeowners are keen to fix their mortgage for this long though because circumstances can easily change over so many years and you may have to pay a penalty to get out of the mortgage before the end of the offer period.

The longer the fixed rate you opt for, the higher the rate of interest: A two-year fix is cheaper than a five-year deal because it's less of a risk for the lender. If the base rate is likely to fall within the next couple of years, it's worth opting for a two-year fix and then taking out another fixed rate afterwards because fixes will probably be cheaper then. But if rates are more likely to go up than down and five-year fixes are currently attractive it may be a good bet to fix for longer. Even if rates do fall slightly, you still get a cheap deal.

Don't fix your rate for longer than you are absolutely certain about. Most fixed rate deals carry stiff penalties if you try to get out of them before the offer period ends – sometimes as much as several thousand pounds. To avoid paying a penalty, don't fix for five years, for example, if there's a chance you may want to move within three.

When the fixed rate comes to an end, the interest rate automatically reverts to the lender's SVR at that time for the remainder of the mortgage term. So, the end of the fixed rate deal means it's time to shop around for another offer because rarely is the SVR the best deal available.

If you are worried about budgeting, opt for a fixed rate. Be prepared to move quickly, however, as some lenders offer competitive rates for a very limited amount of time. Delay – and you could miss out.

Choosing a discount rate

Discount rates are often attractive to first-time buyers as they're usually the cheapest rate available. They are discounted off the lender's SVR and tend to be a percentage point or two lower. They also tend to be cheaper than fixed rate deals because you don't get any certainty. Lenders usually offer discount rates over two or three years – as with fixed rates, the shorter the term, the lower the rate. Discount rates are variable, moving up and down in line with the SVR. If the Bank of England cuts the base rate, your mortgage rate is reduced accordingly.

But herein lies the problem: If the base rate goes up, your monthly mortgage payments increase accordingly. And if there's a lot of volatility in the base rate, your mortgage payments can fluctuate dramatically from month to month, making it hard to budget.

Opt for a discount rate only if you can afford to be wrong. In other words, if you can cope with an increase in your mortgage repayments. If you can, you'll get a better deal than on a fixed rate – at least initially – plus you can benefit from any cuts in the base rate during the discounted period.

Limiting risk with a capped rate

A capped rate works along the same lines as a fixed rate in that you know the absolute maximum you have to pay each month. It also works like a variable rate mortgage in that it can fall, allowing you to take advantage of cuts in the base rate. This makes a capped rate attractive because you can benefit from the best of both worlds. Your initial mortgage rate is set lower than the cap and can rise only as high as the cap. If the base rate rises after you reach the cap, your mortgage repayments aren't affected.

Capped rate deals are usually offered over three, five, or ten years. The interest on capped rates tends to be higher than for fixed rate deals. You also have less choice because fewer lenders offer them.

Tracking the base rate: index tracker mortgages

An *index tracker mortgage* follows movements in the base rate. These mortgages usually follow or *track* the base rate at a *set margin*: this is the percentage that is added onto the base rate to give the tracker rate. So, for example, if the mortgage tracks the base rate at a margin of 1 per cent, this means that no matter what the base rate happens to be, your mortgage rate will always be 1 per cent above that. So if the base rate is 4 per cent, the interest rate on your tracker mortgage will be 5 per cent until the base rate changes. The big advantage is that your lender can't widen the margin and charge you more than 1 per cent above the base rate, in this example, so you always know where you stand. The lender decides at what premium the mortgage is going to track the base rate: Shop around for the most competitive rate.

Many lenders offer substantial discounts on tracker deals for the first six months or more of the mortgage, which can result in a very attractive rate. Given that tracker deals don't carry penalties you have an added advantage in that you can switch to another deal when the discount runs out or at any other time.

As with a variable deal, tracker mortgages go up and down – there is no certainty. And as they usually track *above* the base rate, you pay more than if you opt for a fixed or discounted deal. They are really only attractive when the base rate is particularly low, and you want the flexibility of being able to change your mortgage at short notice, because you don't pay a penalty for doing so. However, most homebuyers are better off opting for a fixed or discounted rate.

Going for flexibility

A number of lenders offer flexible mortgages, although terms and conditions vary considerably. But you no longer have to opt for a deal which is specifically packaged as flexible because many standard mortgages now come with flexible features.

Many standard deals are also now fully portable, which means you can take the mortgage with you if you move to another property during the fixed or discounted offer period. This enables you to hang onto a competitive rate and avoid paying redemption penalties for switching.

Flexible mortgages allow you to overpay, underpay or even take a payment holiday. However, there may be restrictions, depending on the lender when it comes to missing payments or making reduced payments. You can arrange with your lender not to pay your mortgage for several months only if you have built up a reserve that covers the amount due during this time. You build up this reserve by making overpayments when you have spare cash: if you don't take a payment holiday, you end up paying off your mortgage more quickly because you reduce the interest that you owe.

Some lenders impose further restrictions, insisting that you must hold your mortgage for a certain amount of time before you can take a payment holiday. Other lenders won't let you take a payment holiday for longer than several months – even if you have got the required funds to take a longer one.

A flexible mortgage is only worthwhile if you are going to take advantage of all the flexible features because you usually end up paying for flexibility: These deals can be on the same rate as the lender's SVR and are therefore more expensive than fixed or discounted deals. Some are on fixed rates however, so shop around if you want all the flexible features. If you don't need so much flexibility, steer clear of such a mortgage.

If you're primarily interested in being able to make overpayments to reduce the mortgage term, most standard mortgages now enable you to overpay up to 10 per cent of your outstanding loan, per annum, without penalty. Opting for one of these mortgages tends to get you a cheaper rate than on a flexible deal.

Some lenders won't let you claw back overpayments at a later date on standard loans, unlike a flexible mortgage. If this is the case, be certain that you won't need that cash again before you hand it over.

A flexible mortgage is a good choice if you're self-employed or your income fluctuates a great deal. When you're flush, you can pay more than you need to so that when finances are tight you can miss a payment or two – and not incur a penalty.

Interest is calculated daily on flexible deals, making a huge difference to the amount of interest you pay over the term of your loan.

Opting for offset and current account mortgages

A relatively new innovation is the offset or current account mortgage (CAM). These two mortgages are fairly similar, although they differ slightly on a number of points:

- ✔ **Offset mortgages** enable you to use your savings to reduce the amount of interest you pay on your mortgage. You open a savings account and/or current account with your mortgage lender. Although your savings and the balance in your current account are kept separate from your mortgage debt, they're offset against it in order to reduce the interest you are charged. So if you owe £60,000 on your mortgage but have £12,000 in savings and, say, £500 in your current account, you are charged interest at your mortgage rate on £47,500 (£60,000 − [£12,000 + £500]). You can also offset your family and friends' savings against your mortgage (see Chapter 13 for more details).

- ✔ **Current account mortgages (CAMs)** lump together your current account, savings, and even credit cards and personal loans in one account rather than keeping everything in separate pots. It works in the same way as an offset mortgage but instead of maintaining separate balances, all of your accounts are lumped together into one balance – usually a debt.

  Even a small amount of money can make a big difference to the amount of interest you pay: For example, if you take out a £100,000 mortgage over 25 years at 7.5 per cent interest, and spend all your salary every month – except £100, which you leave in the account – you'll pay off your mortgage six years and nine months early, saving £40,263 in interest. The residue of money left in the account every month might not seem much but the key thing is that it eats away at your debt.

Because the interest on offset mortgages and CAMs is calculated daily, you pay what you owe on that day. So if you have just been paid, it doesn't matter that you'll soon spend all that cash; for several days, a chunk of money has been offset against your mortgage. In the long run, this enables you to repay your loan a lot quicker.

Critics of offset mortgages and CAMs argue that they are so flexible that undisciplined borrowers won't pay their mortgages off on time. For example, some CAM providers will lend you the difference between your mortgage (say, for example, £62,000) and the value of your house (say, £150,000). So, in this example, you can get your hands on a further £88,000 to do what you like with. Other CAM providers limit the amount you can borrow. If you aren't disciplined and are likely to give in to temptation, steer clear of a CAM and opt for a fixed or discounted deal.

Another problem with CAMs is that all your finances are lumped together on one statement each month. While it's handy to see all your debts and savings on one piece of paper, there's a strong chance that the grand total will be in the red by a serious amount – you may not be able to cope with seeing that you are tens of thousands of pounds overdrawn. And if you don't want to switch your current account over to your mortgage lender a CAM isn't for you.

Offset mortgages and CAMS are a great way of reducing your interest payments but they have higher rates of interest than fixed or discounted deals as they are often on the lender's SVR. So unless you have several thousand pounds in savings to offset, it isn't worth opting for one of these. Lenders have started offering fixed rates on offset mortgages, making them more attractive. Watch out for penalties though as these are likely to be charged during the fixed rate period, whereas you won't incur one on a variable offset mortgage or CAM.

Being quids in with a cash-back mortgage

When you're short of money, a *cash-back mortgage* can be ideal as it provides you with that commodity you are short of – cash. With a cash-back mortgage, when you take out your mortgage you get a cash lump sum from your lender. The amount varies from a flat fee of a couple of hundred pounds to a percentage of the amount you borrow (as high as 6 per cent of the mortgage). You can do what you want with this cash – buy a new sofa, pay off your credit card, or take a holiday if you need a break from the stress of moving.

You don't get something for nothing – and this is particularly true with a cash-back deal. Cash-back deals tend to be fairly expensive in the long run because the cash you get back is like an advance, which you pay back over the mortgage term. So £6,000 cash back on a £100,000 mortgage is the equivalent of borrowing £106,000 because you pay interest on this additional loan over the entire mortgage term. The rate of interest also tends to be higher on a cash-back mortgage than on a standard fixed or discounted deal.

Early redemption penalties are common on cash-back mortgages, which can effectively lock you in for five to seven years.

Instead of taking out a cash-back mortgage, get hold of some cash and pay a lower rate by picking a competitive standard fixed or discounted deal. Then take out a personal loan with the lowest rate of interest you can find or extend your overdraft or apply for a credit card charging 0 per cent interest for several months. Not only do you get access to a few hundred or thousand pounds, you can pay it back over just a couple of years, rather than 25, so you pay less interest. You can also choose from a wider range of mortgages, rather than limiting yourself to just those offering cash back.

Longer-term fixed rates and the euro

Chancellor of the Exchequer Gordon Brown is keen for UK homebuyers to opt for long-term fixed rate mortgages of 25 or 30 years – rather than the short-term fixed and discounted deals most buyers currently favour. The Chancellor believes that long-term fixed rate loans create more stability in the mortgage market, reducing borrowers' vulnerability to sharp changes in interest rates – both of which will be crucial when (or if) the UK adopts the euro.

Long-term fixed rate deals are nothing new in the UK, with a handful available since the late 1980s. But few homebuyers opt for them because rates are rarely as competitive as those on shorter fixes, and penalties can be stringent. Many 25-year fixed rate deals don't allow you to exit them until year five at the earliest without paying a penalty, so why not opt for a five-year fix, which is cheaper and more flexible?

Shopping for the Best Deal

Mortgages are available from banks and building societies and are also offered by specialist lenders – usually offshoots of major building societies – who concentrate on niche markets. These specialist lenders may be able to offer you a mortgage if you're self-employed or have credit problems. With more than 7,000 mortgages available from over 100 lenders, you should be able to find one you can afford. It just may take a little time.

Many homebuyers apply directly to a lender for a mortgage but that's not your only option – nor necessarily the best one. With so many choices, you may have trouble deciding which mortgage is best for you. In my opinion, you're better off using an independent broker to find the cheapest deal. (See 'How a middleman can save you money' later in this chapter.)

What the income multiple means for you

Lenders decide how big a mortgage you can have according to how much you earn. Most lenders use a standard *income multiple*: the number of times your income they will let you borrow. The income multiple varies between lenders but tends to be anything between three and three and a half times income. If you are buying a property with a partner, sibling or friend, the lender usually lets you borrow two and a half times joint income. So if you earn £25,000, you should be able to borrow anything up to £87,500 on your own (three and a half times income) or £125,000 if you are buying with someone who earns the same as you.

However, with property prices stretching beyond the means of many first-time buyers, many lenders are relaxing their income multiples. It is not uncommon to find a lender prepared to let you borrow four times income (£100,000 on our previous example) or even five, or six times income (£125,000 and £150,000 respectively). However, these higher multiples tend to be decided on case-by-case basis so you might not qualify for a loan this size.

Even if a lender will let you borrow a high income multiple (four times income or higher), it's not always a good idea to take out such a big mortgage. You are in great danger of over-stretching yourself, particularly if interest rates rise, and you may not be able to cope with the increase in your mortgage repayments. Consider what you can afford (see Chapter 2 for more details on how to calculate this) and stick to a mortgage that's within your means.

Why your bank isn't your best bet

Most people are governed by inertia when it comes to their financial affairs, which is why so many stick with the same bank year after year even though they would almost certainly get a better deal elsewhere. And if this is true of current accounts, it's even more so with mortgages.

Don't assume that the bank you have your current account with should be your first port of call when applying for a mortgage. Banks have different strengths: Yours may offer an excellent current account but it doesn't necessarily follow that it also offers the cheapest mortgage.

If you approach your bank for mortgage advice you are likely to end up being offered one of its own home loans. But even if your bank offers mortgages from a panel of providers – and not just its own product – the choice is likely to be limited and you're unlikely to have access to the best deals on the market. Given the amount of money you're spending, it makes sense to shop around for the best deal instead of automatically taking what your bank offers.

How a middleman can save you money

Buying your first home is an expensive proposition and with money tight it's vital to get the cheapest rate you can at this stage to avoid paying over the odds in the long term.

With this in mind, do yourself a favour and use an intermediary to find the best mortgage at the best rate. An independent mortgage broker does the hard work of shopping around for the best deal for you.

Banking on a broker

I recommend an independent mortgage broker as your best bet. Unlike an independent financial adviser who advises on a range of investment products, a mortgage broker spends all his time keeping an eye on the mortgage market, knows the best deals at that particular time (they are ever-changing), and can talk you through the whole process. If you need your hand held, talk to a mortgage broker.

If you use a broker, don't negate your good intentions by using one who is not truly independent. The best broker has access to the entire mortgage market, not just a handful of lenders, and is able to conduct a full search and find the best deal available. Ask the broker how many mortgages he has access to before asking him for mortgage advice: if he mentions a low number, give him a wide berth. You are looking for someone who can sift through hundreds, if not thousands, of mortgages, to find the best deal for you. Similarly, an adviser who works for a bank may only be able to offer the bank's mortgage products or those of a limited panel of lenders: Again, opt for a broker with wider scope.

Some estate agents provide their own mortgage service, which is much more limited than the broad market view offered by an independent broker. Give your agent a wide berth when arranging the financing on your property purchase.

Paying for financial advice isn't necessary

Independent mortgage brokers are paid for their services either through commission from the lender or a fee paid by you. Much debate goes on about which form of payment makes for the most independent broker, but I believe there is little in it. As long as you're happy with the method of payment – and the amount you pay if you opt for a fee – that's all that matters.

If your broker receives commission, you pay nothing for his advice. Your mortgage provider pays several hundred pounds to the broker for arranging the sale. Critics of commission argue that such brokers aren't truly independent, but a good reputable broker has a lot to lose by recommending mortgages simply on the back of the commission he receives.

The trouble with paying a fee is that you'll stretch your already tight budget even further. Expect to pay up to 1 per cent of the mortgage amount to the broker – so, £700 on a

£70,000 loan, for example. If you really can't afford this, I don't think you need worry about using a broker who receives commission as long as you do your research carefully when choosing him in the first place.

For extra peace of mind and to find a truly independent mortgage expert, contact IFA Promotion, the organisation which promotes independent financial advice. Go to www.unbiased. co.uk for a list of advisers in your area.

Saving on the Internet

The Internet is changing the home buying process, with e-conveyancing inevitable at some point and the ability to save time and jump the queue by applying for a mortgage online.

The Internet is the most comprehensive source of information on mortgages, and can provide you with a wealth of information. Even if you don't actually apply for your mortgage online, it can't hurt to research the various loans and deals available before contacting a lender or broker.

Researching online

Several Web sites provide free calculators that enable you to quickly calculate how much you can borrow and what your monthly repayments will be. These calculators are only general guides – there is no guarantee a lender will let you borrow the cash – but they're a great place to start.

Many big mortgage brokers also have tables of 'best buys' on their Web sites so you can see the best available deals at a glance. When you're ready to sign your mortgage application form on the dotted line, it's worth double-checking these tables to ensure you are getting the best deal.

Some of the best sites, all from independent brokers, follow:

- ✔ **Charcol:** www.charcolonline.co.uk
- ✔ **Chase De Vere Mortgage Management:** www.cdvmm.com
- ✔ **London & Country:** www.lcplc.co.uk
- ✔ **Savills Private Finance:** www.spf.co.uk
- ✔ **The MarketPlace at Bradford & Bingley:** www. marketplace.co.uk

Another excellent independent Web site is www.money supermarket.com. The site enables you to compare over 7,000 mortgages and provides a guide that explains mortgage terms. You are requested to supply some basic information about your purchase and finances to enable you to find the best deal. Such questions include the price of the property you are interested in buying; the size of your deposit (if you have one); and your earnings and outgoings. If you have this information to hand before you begin, the process takes just a couple of minutes. Moneysupermarket.com then provides details of all the deals that might suit you, along with links to the lenders' home pages so you can click straight through if you want to apply.

The Internet is a great way of saving money. By doing your own research using brokers' Web sites and applying online – if you feel confident enough to do so – you increase your chances of getting the best deal. And you save yourself any broker's fee when applying online because you haven't had a face-to-face consultation.

Applying for a mortgage online

An increasing number of homebuyers are applying for mortgages via the Internet, with mortgage broker Charcol revealing that one in three customers applies via its Web site (www. charcolonline.co.uk).

You may not realise that you can apply online for a mortgage, but if you're confident that you have found the right deal and don't need advice, applying online is simple. You fill in an application form on screen and submit it to the lender.

Applying online is faster than filling out a hard copy and posting it to the lender because your application is processed as soon as it's received. Not long after you submit your application electronically, the lender sends you an e-mail confirming that your application is being processed. You know whether you qualify for the loan within a day or two, or even hours, depending on the lender. Some lenders waive their application fee if you apply online so you can also save yourself several hundred pounds.

In contrast, if you apply by post, the envelope has to be opened and your application processed when someone is available to do so. If you are applying at a busy time of year, finding out whether you qualify may take several days instead of a few hours.

Filling in a mortgage application form online isn't for everyone, particularly a first-time buyer. These forms are complicated and many homebuyers prefer to be guided through them by a lender or broker. If you don't feel ready to fill out a form online, there is no shame in sticking to pen and paper and asking for advice.

Seeking a Self-Certification Mortgage

Mortgage lenders require proof of income when you take out a home loan to satisfy themselves that you are capable of meeting your monthly mortgage repayments: three months' worth of wage slips and a letter from your employer. If you are self-employed, you usually need to produce two or three years' worth of accounts to prove your income.

But if your business hasn't been running for at least two years, you won't have enough accounts to satisfy a mainstream lender. And even if you have been going longer than two years, many self-employed business owners' accounts don't adequately reflect their income. If you employ an accountant, her job is to ensure you don't pay more tax than is absolutely necessary. This is perfectly legal but means you may have a problem convincing a lender that you can actually afford to repay more than your accounts indicate.

If you fall into this category, a self-certification mortgage may be your best bet of buying a home. A *self-certification mortgage* enables you to certify your own income by signing a document stating how much you earn. You don't need to prove audited accounts but if you're a first-time buyer you need a reference from your landlord detailing how much rent you pay. This gives the lender an idea of whether you can afford your mortgage repayments.

If you're self-employed a specialist lender may be your best bet in getting a mortgage, as they tend to be more sympathetic to your situation. These include: Bank of Ireland, Birmingham Midshires, Bristol & West, Kensington Mortgages, Mortgage Express, Platform Home Loans, The Mortgage Business, and

UCB Home Loans. A broker can also point you in the right direction and know those lenders worth approaching – and those where you'll be wasting your time.

Miaow! Scratching the Cat-mark

The Government introduced *Cat-mark* (also known as Cat-standard) mortgages to highlight the most straightforward products on the market. To earn a Cat-mark, a mortgage must be low cost, easy access, so it is available to everyone, and have simple terms. No Cat-mark mortgage can charge mortgage indemnity guarantee (see 'Steering clear of mortgage indemnity guarantee' later in this chapter), for example, and interest has to be calculated daily rather than monthly – both of these mandates save you money. The lender must also mention all other fees up front so that you know exactly what the mortgage is going to cost.

Many borrowers wrongly think that a Cat-mark mortgage is guaranteed or recommended by the Government, and therefore one of the best available. This isn't so. A mortgage earns a Cat-mark by meeting certain criteria, including:

✔ You can keep your mortgage when you move, provided the lender is happy to lend on your new property.

✔ You can choose which day of the month you pay your mortgage.

✔ You can pay your mortgage off early and not be penalised. There are no tie-in periods so you don't have to hold the mortgage for a minimum length of time.

✔ The maximum variable interest rate is no higher than 2 per cent above base rate.

✔ If you get in arrears equivalent to three months' repayments, you pay standard interest charges only on the outstanding debt: there are no extra penalties or fees for being in arrears.

✔ If you take out a fixed or capped rate mortgage, redemption fees must be no more than 1 per cent of the loan for each remaining year of the fixed or capped period and reduce each month.

There is no redemption charge once the fixed or capped rate offer period has finished.

Cat-mark mortgages are few and far between as there isn't much incentive for lenders to offer them. And they don't suit homebuyers looking for a discount mortgage or cash back home loan as these deals don't qualify for Cat-marks. They sound great in theory but have largely been a failure because rates aren't competitive. If you pick a standard mortgage with a good rate, no MIG and no extended redemption penalties after your offer period ends, you won't go far wrong and don't need a Cat-mark deal.

Most specialist lenders judge each case on its own merits and affordability rather than using strict income multiples to decide how much you can borrow. But as a general guide, many let you borrow up to three and a quarter times your stated income: So if you state that your earnings for last year were £40,000, the lender will let you borrow up to £130,000.

It may be tempting to exaggerate your income in order to get a bigger mortgage, but resist this temptation. You may have problems meeting your repayments if you overstretch yourself.

You have to stump up a bigger deposit for a self-certification mortgage – some lenders require as much as 25 per cent of the purchase price. However, some specialist lenders accept a 15 per cent deposit, so all is not lost if you can't afford such a substantial down payment. You just have to shop around for a deal you can afford.

You can choose between the same types of deal with a self-certification mortgage as for a standard mortgage – fixed, discounted, capped, tracker, and so on – although a flexible loan may be most suitable because if you are self-employed your income is likely to fluctuate.

Rates on self-certification mortgages used to be much higher than on standard deals because of the perceived extra risk of lending to the self-employed, but they have come down a bit in recent years. Some lenders even offer mainstream loans to self-certifiers. However, in the majority of cases expect the interest rate to be a couple of percentage points higher than on standard loans.

Avoiding Unnecessary Costs

Mortgages can be a minefield because many products have a sting in the tail, usually hidden deep in the terms and conditions. And if you don't spot it, you can end up with a deal that's not as competitive as it first appears. Make sure you read the small print.

If you use a broker, he should point out potential nasties but if there are major concerns, he shouldn't be recommending that deal in the first place. But you can also help yourself by keeping a look out for the main problems.

Steering clear of mortgage indemnity guarantee

Mortgage indemnity guarantee (MIG) is a one-off insurance premium charged by some lenders – paid for by you – which protects the lender if you default on your mortgage repayments. Some lenders charge MIG to borrowers who have a small deposit, or none at all, because they are seen as being an increased risk. If you do default on your mortgage repayments and the lender has to repossess your home and sell it to cover what you owe, the MIG policy will pay out if there is a shortfall.

Not all lenders charge MIG: Some impose it if you borrow more than 80 per cent, while others charge it if you borrow 95 per cent of the purchase price. It's not cheap – the one-off fee is worked out as a percentage of your mortgage and usually costs a few thousand pounds.

Given that money is tight, the last thing you want to do is pay MIG. But the good news is that you don't have to. The best way round it is to get a bigger deposit, so if you can borrow the necessary cash from relatives, this can save you a lot of money. If this isn't possible, shop around for a lender who doesn't charge MIG – there are plenty who don't.

Dodging penalties for early redemption

Most mortgage deals carry redemption penalties if you cash in your mortgage during the offer period. If you take out a five-year fixed rate deal, for example, the only way the lender can offer those terms is if you stick with that mortgage for at least five years. If you switch mortgage sooner, the lender loses out so it imposes a penalty to dissuade you from switching and to cover its losses if you switch regardless. The penalty is a percentage of the interest on the loan. Most lenders charge redemption penalties during the term of the offer period on fixed or discounted deals, although not all do.

Never take out a mortgage with an *extended redemption penalty* (also known as an overhang because it runs for longer than the offer period). The rate will undoubtedly be more attractive than loans without overhangs but there is a good reason for this: You are stuck on a higher rate (the lender's SVR) for what can seem forever after your offer period has come to an end.

For example, some lenders offer two-year discounts at startlingly good rates. But the payback is you are tied to that mortgage for not two but five years, or longer. If you switch to another lender after your two-year discount period ends, you incur a substantial penalty – often thousands of pounds. Yet you no longer benefit from a cheap deal as the rate reverts to the lender's SVR after the offer period ends. To make matters worse, these lenders often have the highest SVRs. Any of the earlier savings you made tend to be lost because you pay higher interest for years after the offer period has ended.

There are plenty of loans available where you aren't tied in after the offer period and have to pay a penalty if you want to switch mortgages. Some lenders don't impose a penalty at any time. Such deals are cheaper in the long run. Don't be dazzled by the headline rate: Look beyond it and think longer term.

Casting off compulsory insurance

Some lenders force you to buy their buildings or home contents insurance when you take out a mortgage. This tends to be a rip-off – avoid it at all costs. Certain forms of insurance are essential when taking out a mortgage, such as buildings insurance (see 'Insuring Your Home' later in this chapter), but the only way to get the best deal is to shop around. Your mortgage lender may offer the best insurance deal but there is a strong chance that it may not.

Many lenders, particularly building societies, offer two mortgage rates: a really cheap deal and a more expensive one. The catch with the cheap deal is that you have to take out the lender's buildings insurance (and in some cases contents cover as well). If you take the higher rate, there are no such restrictions. Yet in the long term you're better off opting for the higher rate and shopping around for cover. This enables you to find cheaper insurance and to change your insurer when your premium comes up for renewal if you can find a better deal – harder if your cover is linked to your mortgage.

It's easier than ever to get insurance quotes. The Internet is a great resource, with plenty of Web sites such as www.insure supermarket.com, www.moneyextra.co.uk, and www.the-aa.com providing quotes from a range of insurers within minutes. If you don't have Internet access, phone a few brokers to compare prices.

Some lenders don't impose compulsory insurance but because insurance is such a money-spinner they make it as easy as possible for you to take out their cover. Often, the lender provides a box on its mortgage application form for you to tick if you want to take out its buildings cover. A reminder next to this box states that buildings insurance is compulsory. Lenders count on the fact that you're likely to be stressed by the whole home buying process so one less thing to worry about is welcome – a bit like buying overpriced travel insurance from the travel agent or tour operator you purchase your holiday from. Even though some lenders offer competitive insurance rates, don't assume this is the case. Shop around for the best deal.

Some mortgage lenders charge you a fee – usually around £25 – if you don't take out their buildings cover. Lenders claim this covers the cost of the check they have to do to ensure you have taken out cover elsewhere. Even if you have to pay this fee, you're nearly always better off doing so as you are likely to find more competitively priced insurance elsewhere.

Completing the Mortgage Application Form

Once you've decided which mortgage you want, you need to complete an application form and supply several items to prove you are who you say you are. This is to crack down on fraud and lenders take this very seriously.

As soon as you start looking at properties, start gathering together the information your lender will want to see. Keep hold of wage slips, your most recent P60, bank statements, and some recent utility bills. Getting them ready now saves you time – and stress – later.

Every lender has its own version of the mortgage application form so it isn't possible to predict exactly what information you may be required to provide. But most lenders follow the same pattern, so I can give you a very good idea of what they're looking for. Most forms run to several pages and require the following information:

- ✔ **The name, current address, and date of birth of each applicant.** If you haven't lived at your current address for at least three years you must provide the address(es) of anywhere else you lived during that time.

- ✔ **The address of the property you intend to buy and how much you want to borrow.** You'll also be asked for a contact name and number for someone who can give the lender access to the property to arrange the valuation. This is usually the estate agent handling the sale, unless the owner is selling privately.

- ✔ **Your solicitor's name, address, and contact number.** The lender will want evidence that you have instructed a solicitor as it will deal with her during the application process. If you're doing your own conveyancing, tell your lender.

- ✔ **The size of your deposit and where you got it from.** Again, the source of your deposit is important to reduce the risk of money laundering. Acceptable sources are savings, a present from a relative, or a loan.

- ✔ **Each applicant's job title, employer's name and address, salary, and length of employment.** These convince the lender that you and those applying for the mortgage with you earn enough to meet the monthly repayments and aren't overstretching yourselves.

- ✔ **Each applicant's bank account details, including name and address of the branch, sort code, account number, and number of years you have banked with them.** This information enables the lender to check each applicant's creditworthiness.

- ✔ **Whether any applicant has county court judgements (CCJs) against them or has ever been declared bankrupt.** The lender wants to know whether you have defaulted on any loans or mortgages in the past: and therefore whether you are likely to meet your repayments each month.

- ✔ **Details of any personal loans, outstanding credit card debts, or other monthly outgoings.** By finding out about your current commitments the lender can establish whether you can afford to finance your mortgage.

✓ **Whether you want to take out the lender's buildings insurance.** If you do, tick the box. But I recommend that you don't until you have shopped around to check whether your lender offers the best available deal (see 'Casting off compulsory insurance' earlier in this chapter). If the premiums aren't competitive, buy your insurance elsewhere. But make sure you do so before you exchange contracts or your solicitor won't let you go ahead with the property purchase.

✓ **Each applicant's signature and the date.** The signature is an important declaration that all the information you have provided is correct, so don't forget to sign the application form.

Once you have completed the form and signed it, return it to the lender (or broker, if you're using one) along with the application fee. Then sit back, cross your fingers, and await the decision.

Insuring Your Home

Only one type of cover is compulsory when it comes to your home – buildings insurance. Your lender won't let you have a mortgage if you don't have buildings cover, which insures your home (and anything you'd leave behind if you moved, such as a fitted kitchen or bathroom) if it's badly damaged by fire, flooding, subsidence, or a tree falls on it.

Your home is covered for the cost of rebuilding it if it's completely destroyed – not the market value. You must be properly covered: If you are under-insured, your insurer may not be able to meet the full amount of any claim you make. This can leave you with a shortfall – and as rebuilding work can cost thousands of pounds, you may struggle to find the cash to cover it.

The valuation commissioned by the mortgage lender (see Chapter 9 for more details) includes an amount for the cost of rebuilding the property, which you can use for building insurance purposes. However, if your lender refuses to disclose this figure (there is no obligation for it to do so) and you commissioned a homebuyer's report or full building survey (see Chapter 9), the surveyor should calculate the rebuild cost of the property. If you didn't opt for a full survey, most insurers supply quotes on the basis of information you provide regarding the size and age of the property. If you want to work out the rebuild cost yourself, try using the calculator on the Association of British Insurers' Web site (www.abi.org.uk).

If you buy a freehold property rather than leasehold (see Chapter 10 for the difference between these), you own the building and the land it stands on so you are responsible for taking out buildings insurance. But if you are a leaseholder and pay annual rent and service charge to a landlord – the freeholder – he is responsible for arranging this cover. Your service charge covers the premiums.

Investing in optional insurance

As you are buying your home on a budget, you may be loathe (or simply not able to afford) to splash cash on insurance. There are several forms of insurance that are very useful and wise to have, but if you really can't afford to take them out at the present time, you won't be breaking the law for not doing so. It just means that life can be quite uncomfortable for you if anything does go wrong – if you are burgled and don't have contents insurance, for example, or lose your job and don't have any form of mortgage payment protection insurance (MPPI) to cover your monthly payments.

✔ *Home contents insurance* covers your belongings in case of burglary, flood, fire, or accidental damage. Replacing all your belongings is likely to be expensive so if you can afford to take out home contents cover, you may save yourself a lot of heartache. Reduce your premiums by shopping around for cover and beefing up security with a British Standard BS 3261 five-lever mortice lock on external doors and window locks. A BS 6799 burglar alarm will also help, as will joining your local Neighbourhood Watch scheme – if there is one.

✔ *Life assurance* is important if you have a partner or children who won't be able to pay the mortgage if you die: It pays out a lump sum that covers the mortgage debt. If you're single with no dependants but want to leave your property to someone, you need life assurance to ensure they receive it mortgage-free.

(continued)

(continued)

- *MPPI,* also known as accident, sickness, and unemployment insurance (ASU), covers your mortgage payments for up to a year (in most cases) if you can't work due to accident, sickness, or loss of job. But if you are sacked for misconduct or you resign, your policy won't pay out. The premiums are expensive but you can reduce the cost by taking out one or two of the elements (you don't have to take out all three): If your employer already covers you for accident or sickness, for example, there's no point taking out extra cover for this.

- *Critical illness cover* can also be used to pay off your mortgage if you contract a serious illness and can't work. A range of conditions are covered, including strokes, cancer, and heart attack, but instead of a monthly payment direct to your lender (as with MPPI) you get a lump sum.

- *Permanent health insurance (PHI)* provides an income for people unable to work due to ill health. You get a proportion of your gross income – usually 50 to 65 per cent – until you retire. You can reduce your monthly premiums by opting for a longer deferral period (how long you wait before the policy pays out), so you need to strike a balance between affordable premiums and a deferral period you can comfortably cope with.

Chapter 5

Getting a Mortgage with a Guarantor

*Y*ou may be keen to buy your own home so that you no longer have to live with your folks (I mean this in the nicest possible way of course!). But even if getting away from your parents is your motivation, it's worth remembering that they may be able to help you realise your goal – even if they aren't extremely wealthy and haven't got thousands of pounds lying around which they can give you for a deposit.

In this chapter, I explain how your parents can help you qualify for a mortgage in the first place or get a bigger mortgage than you could get all on your own.

Understanding How Guarantor Mortgages Work

Rising property prices are putting home ownership beyond the reach of many first-time buyers. If your income simply isn't high enough to generate a big enough mortgage to get you on the property ladder, you could try asking your parents to sign up as guarantors. Not all parents can afford to hand over thousands of pounds in cash to put towards a deposit but they may be able to help you get a guarantor mortgage.

With a guarantor mortgage, a third party guarantees the repayments for the mortgage-holder. This third party is usually a parent, although sometimes it can be another blood relative or a close family friend. Lenders have different rules on who can be a guarantor so shop around if a particular deal doesn't suit.

With a guarantor mortgage, most lenders use the guarantor's income, rather than yours, when calculating how much they'll lend you. If your dad, who earns £50,000 per annum, is your guarantor, theoretically you may be able to borrow up to four times his salary – £200,000. But his outgoings – such as his mortgage – are taken into account and deducted from his salary before the income multiple is calculated, so you may not be able to borrow this much.

Some lenders charge a hefty mortgage indemnity guarantee (MIG) (see Chapter 2 for more information on MIG) if you don't have a deposit or much of one – even on a guarantor mortgage, which is ludicrous when you consider what MIG is for. MIG protects the lender (but is paid for by you) in case you default on your mortgage and the lender has to repossess your property and sell it at a loss. Yet this clearly isn't going to be a problem with a guarantor home loan as the whole point is that you have someone guaranteeing to pay your mortgage if you can't. Not all lenders charge MIG on their guarantor deals so look for one that doesn't.

Differentiating between guarantor mortgages

Most lenders insist that the guarantor covers the whole of your mortgage as well as her own. So if your guarantor has an outstanding mortgage of £30,000 on her property, for example, and you want to borrow £130,000, her salary needs to be high enough to cover a mortgage of £160,000. In other words, she has to earn at least £40,000 if the loan is calculated at four times income, which is often the case. This can be a tall order unless your guarantor is on a good salary or has already paid off her own mortgage and is relatively free of debt.

Some lenders require only that the guarantor cover the short-fall between what you can afford and the home loan. So if you earn £20,000 and can get a mortgage for £80,000 but the property costs £125,000, the guarantor only needs to cover the shortfall, or £45,000 in this example.

Normal income multiples apply with guarantor mortgages so if your lender normally loans up to four times income, that's how much you'll get on a guarantor deal (the difference being it is usually four times the guarantor's earnings).

Thinking twice before overstretching yourself

Just because you *can* borrow tens of thousands of pounds more by using a guarantor than you could on your own doesn't mean that you *should*. I can't stress enough that you shouldn't take on a much bigger loan than you can realistically afford to repay. Remember, your income hasn't increased, just the amount you can borrow. Even though you are lucky enough to have some-one willing to act as your guarantor, this doesn't mean you don't have to bother about paying your mortgage each month. You owe it to your guarantor, who has helped you get your mort-gage in the first place, to aim to pay the whole amount and ensure that this is feasible. If you find it a struggle from the start because the repayments are simply too high to manage on your income, it doesn't bode well. Consider how you'll cope if interest rates double. Your guarantor will obviously have to help out if you can't afford the full amount yourself, but calling on your guarantor's funds should be a last resort.

If paying your mortgage is going to be a struggle, think twice about taking out a guarantor home loan – or at least one of that size. If the figures just don't add up when you try to work out how big a property you can afford, borrowing more money won't solve the problem: It will only make things worse. Do your sums before committing yourself (see Chapter 2 for details on working out what you can afford to pay).

Guarantors are rarely called upon to pay the mortgage they have guaranteed, which means most first-time buyers aren't overstretching themselves and taking on bigger mortgages than they can afford. Make sure you do the same. You could even pass this statistic on to your parents to reassure them that they are doing the right thing acting as your guarantor!

Cutting the guarantor short

The guarantor doesn't have to guarantee your mortgage repayments for the entire mortgage term – usually 25 years. If this were the case, your parents would still be promising to pay your mortgage when you're in your forties!

Instead, what usually happens is that the guarantor agrees to pay your mortgage, if necessary, during the early years of the loan when you're on a particularly low income and struggling to cope on your own. Once you get a pay rise or two under your belt – and can take on full responsibility for your mortgage – you should inform your lender of this and the guarantor can be relieved of her duties.

The guarantor should be able to plan ahead and buy that holiday home in the sun in a few years' time, if that's what she wants. When you no longer need a guarantor, you switch to a standard mortgage and take on the entire responsibility of paying it yourself.

Positioning yourself as a candidate

To qualify for a guarantor mortgage, you must be in permanent full-time employment (although you can qualify if you're a student). Some lenders insist that you earn at least £15,000 a year and are over 21, but not all of them do. Terms and conditions vary. When you apply for a mortgage, your guarantor has to go through a similar application process, supplying details of her income and outgoings. Most lenders require that the guarantor is not over the age of 60 so an elderly relative will be rejected.

Because guarantor mortgages assume that your income will rise over time – perhaps fairly significantly – many lenders offer them only to young professionals (see Chapter 7 for more on loans aimed at professionals). Typically, 'professionals' include medical doctors, dentists, accountants, solicitors, and vets – people who tend to be on a low wage initially but have accelerated earnings potential. If you are in one of these professions, you'll find it much easier to obtain a guarantor mortgage.

Even if you aren't classed as a young professional you may be able to find a guarantor mortgage. For example, some lenders offer them to students even though they have no income, because they take the guarantor's income into account not the applicant's (and they assume that once you graduate you will earn a reasonable salary).

If you aren't a professional or a student, you may have to shop around for a guarantor mortgage. Ask an independent broker for advice: She will know all the ins and outs of available deals (see 'Finding a Guarantor Home Loan' later in this chapter).

Explaining Guarantors

An increasing number of first-time buyers are calling on their parents to act as guarantors who agree to pay the mortgage in the event that the mortgage-holder (their child) isn't able to. If your parents are your guarantors and you default on your mortgage repayments, your parents are obliged to meet the shortfall (or the full amount, if necessary).

The advantage of having a guarantor is that you can get a bigger mortgage than you could on your own because lenders consider you to be less of a risk.

If your low income means you don't qualify for a big enough mortgage to get a foot on the property ladder, a guarantor mortgage can help. If you earn £20,000 a year, for example, most lenders will let you borrow a maximum of £70,000 (three and a half times your income), which won't get you far when you consider that the average property in the UK costs more than £150,000.

Your guarantor has to sign a legal agreement saying that she agrees to guarantee your mortgage repayments and under-stands exactly what this involves. Any potential guarantor needs to consider the situation carefully – and take legal advice – before committing herself.

Your parents need to be aware that if they commit themselves to covering your mortgage it may restrict them from doing what they want. For example, if they wish to buy a holiday home on the Costa del Sol, they may not be able to get a mort-gage because lenders regard them as being over-committed. It doesn't matter that your parents may not actually be repaying your mortgage – while there is a chance they could be it will affect their ability to get further credit.

Finding your guarantor

Most first-time buyers have a parent as their guarantor but you may be able to use another blood relative if you prefer. Some lenders even let you use a close friend. Check the lender's requirements before submitting your mortgage application.

Your guarantor doesn't have to be wealthy but she does need to have the funds available to cover your mortgage as well as her own home loan and other outgoings. To make this a more realistic prospect, opt for a mortgage that requires the guarantor to cover just the shortfall between what you can afford and the mortgage amount – rather than the full sum. See 'Differentiating between guarantor mortgages' earlier in this chapter for more details.

Given the financial commitment involved, the best guarantor is someone who has paid off her own mortgage and has a reasonable income.

Not every parent or close friend is cut out to be a guarantor. It's a big responsibility and may have dire financial repercussions if you suddenly can't afford your mortgage any longer. Your guarantor needs to not only understand the risks involved but also be in a financial position to guarantee your mortgage payments.

Your guarantor must fill in an application form providing details of her income and outgoings. If she has her own mortgage, for example, she must state how much she owes and when it will be paid off. Likewise, any outstanding debts or loans must be disclosed. The lender then decides whether the guarantor is in a strong enough position to service her own debts as well as your mortgage. If she is, she'll be approved as your guarantor and you'll get your mortgage; if not, your application is rejected.

Steering clear of unsuitable guarantors

Being a guarantor is quite a responsibility and lenders don't consider everyone to be suitable. A guarantor can't simply make a throwaway remark such as 'Yeah, I'll guarantee your mortgage if you can't cope'. She has to endure a rigorous screening process to ensure her finances are good enough to back her promise.

Consider the suitability of your guarantor carefully before you go to the trouble of making a mortgage application. Otherwise, you will just be wasting the lender's time, as well as your own and the potential guarantor's, and it may affect future applications for a guarantor loan to that lender. Get it right the first time and save yourself a lot of effort and hassle.

Not everyone willing to help you qualifies as a guarantor. There's no point putting forward your best mate as your guarantor if she hasn't got the funds to cover your mortgage as well as her own – even if you are confident she'll always be there for you. The whole point of having a guarantor is that she can guarantee to repay your mortgage if you can't.

Read the list below to get an idea of what makes someone unsuitable to be a guarantor:

- **People who are already mortgaged to the hilt:** Your mortgage lender will want to reassure itself that, if necessary, your guarantor can afford to pay your mortgage as well as her own. If your prospective guarantor only has a couple of hundred pounds left over each month after paying her own mortgage, it's unlikely this is enough cash to cover your home loan as well.

- **Elderly relatives:** Lenders tend not to accept guarantors over the age of 60 because if they haven't already retired, it won't be long before they do. And if your guarantor isn't working, this could affect her ability to repay your mortgage, if she is required to do so. Even if your elderly parents have a sizeable disposable income from their pensions or other investments, which will more than cover your mortgage, it is unlikely that a lender will consider them to be suitable guarantors.

- **People who have never had a mortgage of their own:** If you have a relative who's offering to be your guarantor because she's got the cash to spare – mainly because she hasn't got round to buying her own place yet – she may not be suitable. She may change her mind next year and decide she does want to buy – only to find she can't because she has committed herself to covering your mortgage repayments if you default. You are better off choosing someone who has already repaid her mortgage or will do so in a few years' time.

- **People who want to buy a holiday home:** If your parents want to buy another property within the next couple of years, they may find they can't get a mortgage if they have committed themselves to covering your home loan. If they are prepared to delay their purchase a few years, they can still be your guarantor because you won't need them to be guarantors forever – just until your salary increases and you can cope with the full responsibility yourself. Your parents will then be free to buy their holiday home.

✔ **Anyone who doesn't understand the implications of being a guarantor:** Your guarantor has to sign a contract confirming that she understands what she's letting herself in for. If she doesn't fully understand all the implications, recommend that she take legal advice before committing herself. The last thing you want is her complaining to you at a later date that you didn't explain it all properly.

Finding a Guarantor Home Loan

Several lenders offer specialist guarantor mortgages so you should be able to find one that suits you and your guarantor. They have differing conditions and requirements as to how much of your mortgage is covered by the guarantor, your profession, the amount you can borrow, and the size of your deposit. As with any mortgage, you'll find the best deals by using an independent broker. (See Chapter 4 for more details on finding a mortgage broker.)

You don't have to opt for a specialist guarantor mortgage. Most high-street lenders will consider letting you use a guarantor when you take out any of their standard mortgages, although they may require a 25 per cent deposit instead of the smaller deposit you normally need on a standard home loan. This is worth investigating because it enables you to choose between a wider range of rates and deals, so it may well work out cheaper for you in the long run. Again, a broker can advise you on this.

Being Prepared If It All Goes Wrong

Even the best-laid plans can go awry. When it comes to repaying your mortgage, a lot can go wrong: You can lose your job, become ill and be forced to give up work, or interest rates may rise dramatically so you simply can't afford it. And if you don't pay your mortgage your home is at risk. With a guarantor mortgage this shouldn't be a problem for you because the guarantor is obliged to cover your home loan if you can't. But this could be a problem for your guarantor, particularly if her circumstances change.

When you miss repayments

If you miss a mortgage repayment, your lender won't contact your guarantor the following day demanding that she stumps up the cash. Although your guarantor is ultimately responsible for paying your mortgage if you can't, your lender first makes every effort to recover the money from you.

The guarantor is the last resort – not the first one.

Your mortgage should be your priority every month – the first thing you pay so you don't find yourself in this position – but these things do happen. If you haven't got enough cash to pay the mortgage one month, do something about it as soon as you realise you're coming up short. If it is a one-off – perhaps you've run out of cash because you had to replace the boiler earlier in the month – you may just need enough money to tide you over for a week or two.

The easiest and cheapest way of arranging some short-term financing is to get an overdraft or extend an existing one. Ask your bank for permission before you do so to avoid being stung by extortionate unauthorised overdraft rates, which can be as high as 30 per cent. Alternatively, you can get a cash advance on your credit card, although the rate of interest is higher. Avoid a personal loan – it's not suitable for a small amount of money borrowed over a short period of time because you'll pay so much interest.

If this shortfall isn't a one-off blip – perhaps you have lost your job or fallen ill and can no longer work – and you don't have mortgage payment protection insurance (see Chapter 4 for more on this cover), you must make alternative arrangements. If you believe that finding another job fairly quickly won't be a problem, you may be able to arrange short-term credit to cover the shortfall until then. But if there is a chance that you may be unemployed for many months, you must inform your lender and your guarantor.

Although it's tempting to cover up your difficulties, you need to keep your guarantor well informed if you get into financial trouble. If there's a chance that she'll have to stump up a few thousand pounds to cover your mortgage for several months, she may need to do some budgeting for this. Although she should be able to make the repayments – the lender's credit checks when you applied for your mortgage should see to that – it's not quite the same as actually having to hand over the cash. She may need to juggle her finances first.

Your guarantor is unlikely to thank you if the first she hears about your financial problems is when your lender contacts her demanding she pay several months' worth of mortgage repayments you've missed. Out of courtesy keep your guarantor in the loop. Your lender may also be more sympathetic if you keep it informed about what is happening.

When your guarantor can't stump up the cash

If you haven't paid your mortgage for several months, it's ultimately down to your guarantor to cover what you owe. But even though your lender will have screened your guarantor to ensure her income is high enough to cover not only your mortgage but her own (if she has one), she may not be able to get her hands on the cash. Her spare cash may be tied up in savings or investments that don't allow withdrawals without notice. Or her circumstances may be different: She may have lost her job or gone part-time, for example.

If the guarantor can't raise the cash needed to cover your mortgage, she has a problem – and so, ultimately, do you. She has the same options as you have of raising the cash in the short term: extending her overdraft, getting a cash advance on her credit card or taking out a loan. If she can't raise the cash, she must inform the lender immediately.

Don't panic. The last thing the lender wants is the hassle of repossessing your property and trying to sell it to raise the cash to recoup what it lent to you. And there is no guarantee that it will raise enough money to pay back what you owe. Take advantage of this fact – you may be able to come to some agreement with your lender (and guarantor) to pay a reduced amount for the time being until you are in a position to make the outstanding mortgage payments in full – just as you'd do on a standard mortgage.

If the lender does end up repossessing your home and selling it, and there is a shortfall between what you borrowed and the sale price, the lender is likely to pursue your guarantor to make up the difference. But your guarantor's home is not at risk, unless it was offered to the mortgage lender as security, which is highly unusual and not to be advised for this very reason. But if the guarantor hasn't got the cash to hand to pay back what you owe, she may need to raise the funds against her own property.

If your guarantor is paying your mortgage because you are out of work, you need to go all out to find reasonable employment to reduce her burden. But if this just isn't possible you may have to consider selling your home. Whether you have to take such extreme action depends on your circumstances and the financial position of the guarantor. If your parents act as guarantors and have lots of spare cash they may be able to bail you out for the foreseeable future. But if this isn't the case, you may need to consider selling up. Regard this as your last resort, however, and don't make a decision before talking it through with your guarantor.

Making Sure It Doesn't All Go Wrong

There are very few instances of people with guarantor mortgages defaulting on their repayments but it is not unheard of. To make sure it doesn't happen to you, ensure the following:

- ✔ **Don't overstretch yourself:** Avoid taking on a bigger mortgage than you can comfortably afford to repay each month. If you are not sure how much your repayments are likely to be, ask the lender to work this out for you. Make sure you can afford that repayment.

- ✔ **Make a budget and stick to it:** When you're on a low income, it's easy to spend more than you earn from time to time. But the one thing you mustn't skimp on is the mortgage – it should be your priority every month and you should pay it before anything else. I recommend setting up a direct debit so your mortgage payment is transferred to your lender the day after your salary is paid into your bank account. That way you won't get a chance to spend it. If you arrange to pay your mortgage three weeks after you get your monthly salary you're asking for trouble.

✔ **Opt for a fixed rate deal for the first few years of the mortgage, at least:** When money is tight, budgeting can be difficult so the advantage of a fixed rate is that you know what your monthly repayments will be for the next two, three, or five years (depending on how long you fix for). I wouldn't advise fixing for longer than this as you don't know for certain what you will be doing in say, ten years' time: there is a strong possibility that you may want to move before then. With a fixed rate deal, even if interest rates rise, your repayments aren't affected. (See Chapter 4 for more information on fixed rate mortgages.)

✔ **Take out insurance to cover your mortgage payments:** There are several types of cover you can buy to ensure your mortgage repayments are met (or the loan paid off in full) should you lose your job or fall ill and not be able to work. The main types of cover are life assurance; accident, sickness, and unemployment insurance (also known as mortgage payment protection insurance); critical illness cover; and permanent health insurance. (See Chapter 4 for more information on these.) This cover can be expensive but it buys you (and your guarantor) peace of mind.

✔ **Build up your savings:** It's a good idea to save up the equivalent of at least three months' salary in an instant-access savings account for emergencies. For good measure, ensure these savings are earning the highest rate of interest you can find. These savings act as a buffer to cover a shortfall for a little while so if you lose your job you have several weeks' grace to find another one before you need to worry about how you are going to pay your mortgage. Savings are particularly important if you don't have any form of mortgage payment protection. And if you do have this cover, you can opt for a longer deferral period (the length of time that passes before the insurer pays out) because you'll have savings to cover you until then. This results in cheaper monthly premiums.

Chapter 6

Making the Most of Being a First-Time Buyer

*A*s a first-time buyer you may despair of ever being able to afford to get on the housing ladder. You may also think you are going to have a hard time getting lenders to take you seriously because of your limited budget. But the opposite is the case: First-time buyers are important to lenders because they make up such a large proportion of their business. Or at least they used to – the number of first time buyers fell to an all-time low in 2003.

This decline is prompting lenders to offer products tailored to people like you, to give you a leg-up onto the property ladder. As well as making their standard mortgages more attractive by introducing special offers for first-time buyers – such as no legal, valuation, or arrangement fees – many lenders also offer specialist first-time buyer mortgages. There are around 2,000 of these deals being offered by some 60 lenders, aimed at helping those on low budgets become property owners.

In this chapter I run through the main incentives lenders are offering and assess which ones are worth taking advantage of. Not all first-time buyer mortgages are that attractive, however: I also look at those circumstances where you are better off opting for a standard loan.

Offering Perks Aplenty

As a first-time buyer, you're attractive to lenders because they need people like you to help them make money in the long term. And with the number of first-time buyers continuing to fall as property prices move ever upwards, lenders are coming up with innovative ways of trying to tempt you back into the marketplace.

It is worth taking a look at first-time buyer mortgages as they usually come with lots of sweeteners, designed to make your life a lot easier and your finances stretch further. The three main ways in which lenders are trying to make life easier for first-time buyers are:

- **Reducing upfront costs:** Raising the property purchase price is difficult enough without taking into account all the other costs you have to consider. Ideally, you will have a deposit of 5 to 10 per cent of the purchase price. You also have to pay for a survey, stamp duty, solicitor's fees, charges for local searches and the Land Registry fee, mortgage arrangement and valuation fees, and mortgage broker fee (where applicable). These charges can easily add thousands of pounds to your final bill. To make life easier for you, many lenders pay some of these costs, such as your legal fees.

- **Including upfront costs in the mortgage amount:** Some lenders let you add the cost of the application, arrangement or completion fee onto your mortgage. This doesn't reduce the cost of those fees, but at least means you don't have to drum up a lump sum all at once. Instead, you pay the money back over a number of years.

- **Giving you cash to play with:** Most lenders offer first-time buyers a cash handout on completion, which you repay over the term of the loan. This cash back is many first-time buyers' idea of heaven because money is so tight at this time. You can do what you like with it – buy furniture, for example, so you won't have to sleep on the floor for six months while you save up for a bed.

While first-time buyer mortgages can offer plenty of incentives to help you out in the early years, they may not be so attractive over the long term. If you get cash back or add fees to the mortgage amount, you pay back a lot more than the original sum because you are charged interest on it over the term of the mortgage.

Even though you may be offered any number of first-time buyer packages, you don't have to take out such a deal. Do some investigation on your own. You may find that one of the lender's standard mortgages suits your circumstances better.

Whatever deal you go for, study the small print before you commit yourself. And ask an independent mortgage broker for advice if you don't understand something (see Chapter 4 for more details on finding a broker).

Getting a free valuation

Many first-time buyer mortgages include a free valuation or refund this fee. Normally, the £150 to £200 valuation fee is unavoidable. The lender insists that a qualified surveyor value the property you want to buy before it makes you a formal mortgage offer. You, the borrower, usually pay the valuation fee to the lender upon completion.

Waiving the valuation fee is a relatively small deal for the lender, but as you are on a tight budget, it's one less thing to worry about if it does.

Scrapping the application fee

Many lenders charge you a fee for arranging your mortgage – known as an application, arrangement, or completion fee (depending on when the lender requires you to pay for it). But many lenders refund this on their first-time buyer deals, usually saving you between £200 and £300. Some lenders charge as much as £600 for a completion fee so you can save quite a bit if it is prepared to scrap it.

Forgiving legal fees

You almost always need to instruct a solicitor when you purchase a property, and the solicitor's fees may well be the largest expense aside from the deposit and purchase price itself. So a mortgage deal that pays your legal fees may be worth looking into.

Why sellers also love first-time buyers

First-time buyers are not only popular among lenders. Sellers are also interested in the fact that you haven't got to flog a property before you can buy theirs.

If you were already a homeowner looking to buy a bigger property, you would probably have to sell your home to raise the cash to buy another one, and thus be part of a chain that may be broken if any one of the people involved pulls out. The fact that you aren't part of a chain puts you in a strong position. As long as you get your finances agreed in principle, whereby a lender agrees to let you borrow a certain amount, the seller will see you as someone who is not going to drag his heels or cause a break in the chain. All the seller has to worry about is making sure his purchase doesn't fall through.

Conveyancing fees are payable to a solicitor or licensed conveyancer for transferring the property from the seller to you. Conveyancing can be a long, laborious process, which is reflected in the price: The legal fees for the transfer of a £100,000 property from one person to another tend to be in the region of £545 (including VAT). Expect a bigger legal bill if you are buying a more expensive property or a leasehold flat in England, Wales, or Northern Ireland, because the solicitor has to work his way through the lease, which can be complicated.

Your lender's offer to pay your legal fees may mean that your choice of solicitor is restricted. You may not be able to use any old solicitor who takes your fancy to do your conveyancing. Your lender won't foot the bill for an expensive City law firm, for example. You are expected to use one of the solicitors on the lender's select panel, all of which are registered with the Law Society. The lender gets a preferential rate because it passes on so much business to these solicitors, so it won't pay as much for your conveyancing as you will if you use your own solicitor.

You may be worried about the independence of a solicitor recommended by your mortgage lender. But don't be overly concerned – these solicitors belong to the Law Society so if you have any problems, you can take your complaint up with this body. (See Chapter 10 for details of the Law Societies in England, Wales, and Northern Ireland, or Chapter 11 for

Scotland.) The lender is risking a lot of cash in letting you have a mortgage so wants to ensure that your property transfer is handled properly – it's not in the lender's best interests to recommend a biased or shady solicitor. Your solicitor has a duty of care and obligation to the mortgage lender, as well as to you.

You're not obliged to use the solicitor your lender recommends, but remember that if you use your own, you have to pay his bill. Consider whether you can really afford to do this.

On top of your legal bill, you have to pay your solicitor for the local searches he carries out on your behalf (also known as disbursements) and the Land Registry fee.

If the lender has agreed to pay your legal fees, it won't pay your solicitor for the disbursements carried out on your behalf, however: You pay for these. The lender only covers the cost of the basic conveyancing. If you instruct the solicitor to do anything else you pay the extra. So if you decide to write a will at the same time as you purchase a property (a very good idea, incidentally) you pay a fee to the solicitor for this.

A lender may not be prepared to pay your legal fees but may let you add the cost onto your mortgage instead to reduce your upfront costs. While adding the legal fees onto your mortgage may make life a little easier initially, remember you'll repay this sum over 25 years so will pay quite a bit of interest as well in the long run.

Even if your lender is paying your legal fees, it won't cover your stamp duty so you must remember to budget for this.

Discounting rates early on

One of your main problems is probably a limited income, making it hard to repay your mortgage in the early years. To make life easier for you, many lenders offer *discount mortgages*, which require lower payments in the early years of the loan. A discount rate is usually cheaper than a fixed rate – at least initially – because with a fixed rate deal you pay for the certainty of knowing what your monthly repayments will be for several years.

Choosing the best incentive

Some lenders offer first-time buyers a choice of incentives on their specialist mortgages, so you can pick the perk that suits you best. But how do you decide whether cash back is better than having your valuation fee refunded or your conveyancing paid for?

Check first how the mortgage rate is affected by opting for one over the other: Lenders tend to tailor interest according to what incentive you opt for. So if you decide to have your legal fees paid for (costing, say, £550), this obviously saves you more money than if you choose to have your valuation fee (£150) refunded. As a result, the mortgage rate on the valuation fee deal is higher. It can be difficult to compare the true cost of different rates so ask a mortgage broker for help if you are confused.

Discount mortgages guarantee to charge a set amount below the lender's standard variable rate (SVR) for a specified amount of time. The SVR goes up and down but the discount remains fixed. Lenders offer discounts ranging from six months to five years: the shorter the period, the higher the discount. So if you opt for a two-year discount you may get 1 per cent off the SVR, but if you opt for a one-year discount, you may pay 2 per cent below the SVR.

If interest rates seem to be moving upward, you may want to take a short discount; if rates tend to be moving downward, a longer discount may be a good idea.

Discounted rates are initially cheaper than fixed rates but this is because your repayments can fluctuate. If the Bank of England base rate moves upward so do your repayments. Of course, the opposite can happen. The base rate can be cut and your mortgage rate can go down accordingly, resulting in lower payments than you pay on a fixed deal.

Only opt for a discount if you can afford to be wrong – if interest rates go up, make sure you can cope with the higher repayments. See Chapter 4 for more on discounted mortgages.

After the discount period ends, your rate reverts to the lender's SVR so if you don't have to pay an extended redemption penalty for switching, look around for another discounted deal if this worked well for you. And try not to opt for a loan charging extended redemption penalties in the first place.

Choosing cash back

A shortage of cash is likely to be a problem when you're buying a home for the first time. To get round this, many lenders hand over some cash on completion, which you can spend on anything you want – furniture, paying back your parents, or even for a holiday if the property purchase has all been too much for you.

Lenders usually offer 5 to 8 per cent of the mortgage in cash back. Be warned that this sum is added onto the loan and repaid over the term.

A cash handout is attractive, particularly if you can't afford to furnish your new home because you are putting all your savings towards the deposit. With cash back, you get several hundred pounds to do exactly that. But cash back doesn't come cheap: You end up paying well over the odds for it. Because you repay the money over the term of your mortgage you can end up paying interest on the amount for the next 25 years. Cash back is, in effect, the same as taking out a bigger mortgage.

As well as costing you more in the long run, a cash-back mortgage also carries stiff early redemption penalties for the first six years or so of the loan. If you try to remortgage to another deal during this time, you pay a heavy penalty – possibly a few thousand pounds – for doing so. You are also unlikely to get the cheapest mortgage rate, because many of the best discounts aren't available on cash back deals.

Some lenders charge a significant arrangement fee if you plump for cash back, while other lenders don't charge anything at all. Watch out for such a fee as it can vary significantly: One lender charges a whopping £595 for letting you have cash back, for example, while other lenders charge nothing at all. Shop around to avoid paying an extortionate fee.

If you need several hundred pounds in cash there are more cost-effective ways of getting your hands on it than a cash-back mortgage. I suggest you take out the most competitive standard mortgage, with the best rate and lowest fees available (and no redemption penalties), to buy your home. To get your hands on the extra cash, opt for a cheap personal loan – try www.money supermarket.com, a Web site that enables you to compare loans. You may pay a higher rate of interest on the loan initially than if you opt for cash back, but only in the short term. Aim to pay it off within five years at most – not 25 years. And because you aren't tied to a standard mortgage for as long as you are with a cash back deal, you can remortgage sooner and not pay a penalty. This may enable you to opt for a lower mortgage rate, saving you even more cash – a win-win situation.

Buying without a deposit

If you are typical of many first-time buyers you don't have much of a deposit to put down on your property. Whereas in the past, saving up for a deposit was commonplace, rising property prices mean first-time buyers just don't have enough time to raise enough cash.

To solve this problem, a handful of lenders offer 100 per cent mortgages, which don't require any deposit. The rate on 100 per cent mortgages tends not to be as attractive as on standard deals – which you need a deposit to qualify for – because lenders regard you as being higher risk. As you haven't got a deposit, you aren't putting any of your own cash on the line (just the lender's) so you have less to lose if you default on your mortgage repayments and your home is repossessed and sold.

While advertising the fact that they don't require a deposit, some lenders suggest you spend your savings on furnishing your new home instead. Don't do this. Aim to put down the biggest deposit you can afford. Having a deposit widens the choice of mortgages available to you and you can get a cheaper rate than if you use the cash to buy wooden floorboards instead.

If you don't have a deposit, you may be charged MIG (also known as a higher lending fee). This can work out as much as 3 per cent of the mortgage so may cost you thousands of pounds. (See Chapter 2 for more details on MIG.) MIG is usually charged upfront but watch out for lenders who offer to add it to the mortgage to 'help with your cash flow'. As with legal or survey fees added to the mortgage, you have to repay these over the term so will end up paying back significantly more than if you paid upfront.

If you just don't have a deposit and it's a choice between delaying your purchase while you save up for one or buying now using a 100 per cent mortgage – buy sooner rather than later and opt for the bigger home loan. If you put off the purchase for much longer you may be priced out of the market entirely. Realistically, it's unlikely that you'll be able to save enough for a decent deposit in a year or two on a low income. So bite the bullet, accept the higher rate, and buy now.

Watching Out for Problems

Although most lenders are prepared to offer you a sweetener or two – such as a refunded valuation fee or help with your legal fees – to help you get on the first rung of the property ladder, be wary of paying too high a price for being desperate to buy your first home.

There are several things you must be aware of when taking out a first-time buyer mortgage:

- ✓ **Higher rates of interest than on standard mortgages:** You end up paying for those benefits you get on a first-time buyer deal (which aren't always that brilliant) in the long run. If you really can't stump up the cash to pay your legal fees or the lender's valuation, you may welcome the lender's offer to cover these. But if you can pay these fees yourself, or your parents can help you out, you are better off doing so and opting for a cheaper standard loan.

- ✓ **Mortgage indemnity guarantee (MIG):** You don't need to pay this expensive insurance, which covers the lender if you default on your repayments, because many lenders no longer charge it. But quite a few lenders do charge MIG, and they are particularly likely to pick on you because you are a first-time buyer and seen as more of a risk. If you are charged MIG because you don't have a deposit, this can add thousands of pounds onto your mortgage, so avoid it at all costs. Shop around for a lender that doesn't charge MIG, using a mortgage broker if necessary (see Chapter 2 for more on MIG).

✓ **Expensive redemption penalties:** Many lenders tend to tie you into a first-time buyer deal for longer than if you were taking out a standard mortgage. And if you decide to switch your mortgage regardless, you can get charged stringent penalties – particularly if you take out a cash-back mortgage.

Keep your options open. In a couple of years' time you may be in a much stronger financial position and able to pay back your cash back or put down a deposit. Don't tie yourself into a mortgage with stiff redemption penalties.

Don't sign up for any mortgage until you understand all the implications involved and know how much it's actually costing you, once the price of the incentives has been factored in. Your lender or an independent mortgage broker can work this out for you.

Chapter 7

Using Your Future Earning Power to Get a Mortgage

*I*f you're a university graduate or young professional and don't earn very much, lenders are likely to look upon your mortgage application with more sympathy than if you aren't. Lenders see your future potential: You're expected to earn more in the long run than someone who didn't go to university or doesn't have a profession. You're exactly the type of customer a lender wants to attract because you are likely to take out a bigger mortgage in the future – when you move up to your next property – so your business may be extremely valuable to them.

To capture your business, many lenders offer specialist graduate mortgages or home loans for professionals designed to suit your particular circumstances. But they aren't always the best deal on the market, so you need to consider them in the context of what else is available at the time. In this chapter, I look at the range of professional and graduate mortgages available and what you need to watch out for when choosing one.

Understanding the Benefits of Having Potential

The advantage of being a graduate or young professional is that lenders are likely to take you seriously: You may not be earning much now but chances are that you'll take home a good salary in the future. You are a good risk and if the lender helps you out now with special deals and offers, you may well decide to stay put once you are earning a bigger wage and prove to be an extremely valuable customer.

You aren't tied to a particular lender for life. Lenders can only *hope* you'll stick with them – you don't have to. Make sure the mortgage you choose doesn't have extended redemption penalties (so you end up having to pay a fee for switching your mortgage, even after the offer period has ended) and shop around for another deal when the fixed or discounted rate comes to an end. You don't owe the lender any loyalty at all.

Borrowing on the basis of a higher future income

Most lenders allow people applying for graduate and professional mortgages to trade on their future earning power by borrowing more than they can on a standard home loan.

With a standard loan, most lenders let you borrow between three times and three and a quarter times your annual income or two and a half times your joint income if you are buying with a partner or friend. With a graduate or professional loan you may well be able to borrow more.

The idea is that while your current salary may not be high enough to justify the size of the loan you need, your income will increase (possibly fairly soon). So you are less of a risk for the lender than someone in a low-paid job with no prospects.

Lenders treat professionals and graduates differently, with professionals regarded as being lower risk:

✔ **Professionals** are usually able to borrow up to five times their basic salary from certain lenders. Some lenders require that you currently earn at least £25,000 a year, although not all demand this.

Other lenders let professionals borrow up to four times their income, or three times joint income if you are buying a property with someone else (who doesn't have to be a professional).

✔ **Graduates** tend to be offered lower income multiples than professionals. Three and a half times your basic annual salary is typical if you buy on your own; or three and a half times your salary, plus your partner's salary, if you are purchasing your property with someone else. The lender may also impose a limit to the size of the loan: HSBC lets you have a mortgage no bigger than £250,000 on its graduate deal, for example.

A bigger income multiple can make quite a difference to the size of the mortgage you can get and thus the size of the property you can buy. For example, if you earn £26,000 a year, the absolute maximum you can borrow on a standard mortgage is £84,500 (three and a quarter times income). But on a professional deal, you may be able to borrow £130,000 (five times income) – quite a difference.

 Terms and conditions can vary considerably between lenders, so shop around to see whether there's a deal out there for you (see 'Finding a Professional or Graduate Mortgage' later in this chapter).

Doing without a deposit

Most lenders let professionals and graduates borrow 100 per cent of the property purchase price on specialist deals. This is good news because you don't have to spend years saving up for a deposit.

 Some lenders let you borrow even more than 100 per cent of the purchase price, depending on their lending criteria. For example, Scottish Widows Bank allows professionals to borrow up to 110 per cent of the purchase price of the property: The extra 10 per cent can be used for any purpose whatsoever.

If you're a graduate you needn't feel too left out, although you're not treated quite so favourably as professionals. Scottish Widows Bank lets graduates borrow 102 per cent. The idea is that the extra 2 per cent can be used to cover stamp duty or legal costs. The valuation fee on this deal is also refunded – up to a maximum of £250 – and the lender contributes £150 towards legal fees.

Although most lenders offering professional or graduate mortgages don't charge mortgage indemnity guarantee (MIG), some do if you don't have a deposit. You may have to pay a fee of more than £1,000 (depending on the lender's individual charges) for the privilege of taking out a 100 per cent loan. Make sure you don't pay this. Shop around for another loan, where you won't be charged MIG. Money is too tight to pay this unnecessary charge. (For more details on MIG, go to Chapter 2.)

Taking out a bigger mortgage than the property is worth can be asking for trouble. Over time, property tends to increase in value so it should be worth more than you paid for it when you come to sell it – if you don't move for several years at least. But if you take out a 110 per cent mortgage and spend the extra 10 per cent on furniture and a holiday, in effect this puts you into negative equity from the outset – meaning that you owe more than the house is worth (see Chapter 2 for more on this). If you decide to sell your property in a couple of years' time, and property prices have fallen since you bought, you may find your property is worth less than your mortgage. You'll have a shortfall between the selling price and what you owe your mortgage lender and will have to find this cash from somewhere.

The only alternative is to stay put until property prices recover and the value of your home rises above your outstanding mortgage, which may take several years.

If you take out a 110 per cent mortgage and use the extra 10 per cent to pay for improvements to the property, you should increase its value – thus avoiding the prospect of slipping into negative equity right from the start.

Paying less in the early years

Because it's generally accepted that you'll earn more in the future than you do now, lenders may let professionals and graduates make lower repayments in the first few years of the mortgage, when money is particularly tight. Your payments increase – so they are higher than they would have been on a standard mortgage – once you are earning more and are better able to cope.

By making reduced payments for the first three years or so of your mortgage, you are paying only the interest on the loan – none of the capital. When this period ends, you switch to a repayment deal, so you pay back a slice of the capital each month along with the interest. Your lender calculates your payments so that by the end of the mortgage term you'll have paid back all the capital, plus interest, and owe nothing – you don't have to take out an investment vehicle, such as an endowment, to pay off the capital at the end of the term. See Chapter 4 for more details on the difference between repayment and interest-only mortgages.

Expect quite a hike in your monthly payments when you switch to a repayment deal, particularly as you'll be playing catch-up for those years when you paid only the interest on your home loan. Remember to allow for this hike when budgeting.

Mixing and matching mortgage rates

With standard mortgages borrowers tend to choose between a variety of rates: fixed, discounted, capped, tracker, and standard variable. But with professional or graduate deals you can often mix and match rates to better suit your circumstances.

Some lenders offer the same incentives to professionals and graduates as they provide to other first-time buyers, such as refunded mortgage valuation fees or a contribution towards your legal fees (up to a certain amount). See Chapter 6 for more information on first-time buyer offers.

Fixed rate

The fixed rate on a professional or graduate mortgage is likely to be higher than the cheapest fixed rate standard home loans, so if you're not taking advantage of any of the other aspects of the deal – such as the higher income multiple – and you have a deposit, you may be better off opting for a standard fixed rate deal. See Chapter 4 for more on fixed rate mortgages.

Part fixed, part variable

Some lenders offer a combination of fixed and variable rates: Part of the loan is fixed so you know exactly what your monthly repayments will be for two, three, or five years (depending on the length of the fix). The remainder is on the lender's variable rate, which can go up or down, depending on movements in the base rate.

The advantage of this deal is that your circumstances may change in the short term – you may get a big pay rise sooner than you thought. Thus you may have more cash to put towards the mortgage but if your whole home loan is on a fixed rate, there may be restrictions on overpayments during the offer period (although most lenders will allow you to overpay up to 10 per cent of the outstanding mortgage balance per annum without penalty). If you have a variable portion of the loan, however, you can overpay on this without penalty, enabling you to pay off your mortgage more quickly.

A variable deal also enables you to hedge your bets against movements in interest rates: If the base rate falls, for example, you pay less on the variable portion of the mortgage. But if rates rise, part of your mortgage is fixed so you don't need to worry about your repayments increasing too dramatically.

Stepped fixed rate

A stepped fixed rate mortgage means your rate is fixed but rises over time at set intervals. You pay less in the early years when money is tight, and more later on when you're (hopefully) on a higher wage. And you have plenty of notice before the increase (the dates and rate rises are fixed when you take out the loan), giving you plenty of time to budget.

Say, for example, you could take out a five-year stepped fixed rate deal, with an initial rate of 5.29 per cent until 30 June 2005. The rate then rises to 5.39 per cent until 30 June 2006; 5.49 per cent until 30 June 2007; 5.59 per cent until 30 June 2008; and 5.69 per cent until 30 June 2009. The deal then switches to the lender's standard variable rate, which is likely to be less competitive, and it's time for you to shop around for another deal. See Chapter 4 for more on mortgage rates.

The advantage of a stepped fixed rate is you know exactly what your repayments will be over a period of time – you just have to remember that they increase on a yearly basis. However, the rate may look less competitive at the end of five years than at the start, so work out the average rate over the length of the offer. Your lender or mortgage broker can help you do the sums.

Discounted base rate tracker

Another way of ensuring you pay less in the early years of your mortgage is to opt for a base rate tracker, which has a discount for the first few months. Typically, lenders offer this discount for six months so your mortgage tracks the base rate – at a discount initially and then at a premium. So, for example, you may get a 0.25 per cent discount for the first six months, say, giving you a payable rate of 3.75 per cent (if the base rate is 4 per cent). After this period comes to an end, your mortgage could track 1.25 per cent above the base rate, giving a payable rate of 5.25 per cent.

While there's no certainty with a tracker rate because it moves up and down in line with the base rate, the advantage of this deal is that it should remain competitive because your lender is committed to track the rate at a set premium – it can't suddenly decide to charge you 2 per cent more than the base rate. You tend to get a very good deal initially on the discount, and there are usually no penalties for switching your mortgage at any time (even during the discount period on some deals) so you can switch to another deal if the rate becomes uncompetitive. A discounted base rate tracker is a very flexible option, which is great given that your circumstances are likely to change considerably.

If you're no good at budgeting, stick with a fixed rate deal – at least in the early years of your mortgage when money is likely to be tight.

Seeing Who Qualifies

Lenders offering professional mortgages disagree as to what makes someone a professional. Not all graduates are equal, either. So while you think you may qualify for one of these loans, you may find that in the lender's eyes you don't, or you may have to shop around for a deal that you are considered to have the right qualifications for.

Passing yourself off as a professional

Lenders tend to have fairly strict criteria as to who they regard as being a professional – and who they don't:

- ✔ Most lenders agree that doctors, dentists, accountants, and solicitors are professionals. You need to be fully qualified, practicing, and registered with the appropriate professional body.

- ✔ Teachers and vets are also professionals in the eyes of Scottish Widows Bank, but not all lenders offering professional mortgages consider them to be.

- ✔ Other lenders consider anyone with a good job with career prospects, so you may be in luck even if you haven't chosen one of the previously listed professions.

Lenders have different age restrictions when lending to professionals – one lender insists that you're over 21, another that you're 23 or over, and a third that you are aged between 25 and 35. Shop around if you don't fit one lender's criteria.

The lender may have a minimum earnings requirement – one lender insists that you earn at least £25,000 a year.

Making the grade for a graduate mortgage

Most lenders consider anyone with a degree a graduate (after all, it is the generally accepted definition).

Don't be tempted to lie and pretend you did graduate if you dropped out halfway through your course. Most lenders require evidence in the form of a copy of your degree certificate.

Graduate mortgages are available to a wider pool of borrowers than professional home loans but there are still restrictions you need to be aware of:

- ✔ Many lenders require that your degree be from a recognised UK university.

- ✔ You must be 21 or over. Child prodigies who graduate at a younger age will have to wait to get on the housing ladder via a graduate mortgage!

- ✔ You must have a job – permanent students are out of luck. Generally, the lender wants evidence that you have been permanently employed in the UK for at least 12 months prior to making your mortgage application and that you are not on a probationary period.

  Some lenders have even more stringent criteria, and require that you are employed by one of the largest 100 or 250 companies by market capital as listed on the London Stock Exchange: the FTSE 100 or the FTSE 250. But this is the exception rather than the rule, so don't lose any sleep over this if it isn't the case for you.

- ✔ You must be a fairly recent graduate. Some lenders may reject your application if they feel that you graduated too long ago. HSBC Bank, for example, only considers applications from those who have graduated from university within the past five years. Scottish Widows Bank provides a bit more leeway: It will consider your application if you graduated within the past seven years.

Finding a Professional or Graduate Mortgage

Several lenders offer professional or graduate mortgages, so there's a choice available at fairly competitive rates. But there isn't anything like as much choice as there is with standard mortgages, so you may well find a more competitive rate on a non-specialised loan. And if you don't match the quite strict criteria for professional or graduate mortgages, you may find you can't get one anyway.

Most lenders assess applications on a case-by-case basis so the lender may be flexible if you can put up a convincing case as to why you need to be considered for one of these home loans. But that also means that there are no guarantees that you'll be accepted for such a mortgage. You'll have to shop around for the best deal, and if you can't get one, you may have to settle for a standard loan – if you can borrow enough on such a deal.

A broker can give you a good idea of which lender to try first, taking your particular circumstances into account. (See Chapter 4 for more information on finding a broker.)

You may be a professional or a graduate but you don't have to take out a specialist professional or graduate loan. Particularly if you have a sizeable deposit, you may well be able to find a cheaper mortgage rate if you shop around and take out a standard deal.

Making Sure You Don't Over-Stretch Yourself

Just because you can find a lender who's prepared to let you borrow more than your salary because you are a graduate or professional, doesn't mean you should borrow this much. While you may be able to cope with the repayments now, what happens if interest rates increase in the coming year – before you get a pay rise? And if you are struggling now, chances are you won't be able to cope at all if this happens.

Follow the tips in the following sections to keep your financial future secure.

Knuckling down to good old-fashioned budgeting

You can't beat budgeting, even though it's boring to think about how much you're spending all the time. But as your income is limited, budgeting is vital.

One of the first steps is to keep track of your monthly outgoings: I advise keeping a diary of your spending for a few weeks so you can see exactly where your cash goes. Analyse this diary carefully: Are there any areas where you can economise? Perhaps you buy expensive brands when you go food shopping whereas supermarket own-brand items are often just as good. Or maybe most of your cash goes on a pint or two every night down the pub: Staying in one night a week could slash your outgoings considerably.

After you've identified the areas where you can save money, continue to make a note of what you spend. This will make you think twice before frittering your cash away on items you don't really need.

Looking for a safety net

You can't stop the Bank of England from raising interest rates, but you can protect yourself from the impact of such a decision by opting for a fixed or capped rate mortgage. With a fixed rate you know what your monthly mortgage repayments are going to be for the next two, three, five, ten years, or even longer, depending on how long you fix for.

A capped rate means you know the absolute maximum you have to pay for a set period of time.

Protecting yourself by yourself, or why you can't rely on the government

'Your home is at risk if you don't keep up the repayments on a mortgage or other loan secured on it' is an oft-quoted saying that's worth remembering.

The government offers little help if you can't afford your mortgage because you have lost your job or overstretched yourself. Although you get Jobseeker's Allowance if you lose your job, you have to wait *nine* months before you can get help with your mortgage re-payments. Even then, state support is capped and means tested so you must receive Income Support or Job-seeker's Allowance to qualify, which means you mustn't have savings of more than £8,000. Benefits cover only the first £100,000 of the loan anyway,

so if you meet all the above conditions and have a bigger mortgage than this, you'll still have to meet the shortfall yourself.

The government now encourages homeowners to take out mortgage payment protection insurance (MPPI) to protect themselves. MPPI cover ensures that after a deferral period of 30, 60, or 90 days – whatever you choose when you take out the policy – your mortgage repayments are covered for a fixed period of time (usually up to a year), by which time you'll hopefully have found another job. The longer the deferral period, the cheaper your premiums (see Chapter 4 for more details on MPPI).

The mortgage rate on a capped deal is usually higher than a fixed rate so such deals tend to work out more expensive. If you need some security, a fixed rate may be a better bet, particularly over a shorter time scale such as two or three years.

Protecting your income

Redundancy can play havoc with your finances, particularly if you have overstretched yourself by taking out a much bigger mortgage than your salary justified. You may not have any savings, for example, because everything goes towards paying the mortgage every month. And you may have made all the sacrifices you can so there's no room for further cutbacks to your monthly expenditure.

To make matters worse, you can't rely on the state for help with your repayments until you find another job (or indefinitely, if you can't work any longer because of illness). See the nearby sidebar 'Protecting yourself by yourself, or why you can't rely on the government' for more details.

The only way to protect your mortgage repayments is to buy insurance, preferably when you take out your loan. There are several forms of insurance available, from life assurance – which pays off your mortgage if you die – to mortgage payment protection insurance (also known as accident, sickness, and unemployment cover) – which covers your repayments for up to a year if you can't work. See Chapter 4 for more details on insurance.

Changing Your Career and the Effect on Your Mortgage

If you're a graduate or professional, lenders treat you more favourably than someone who started working in a factory at the age of 16 – because of where your career is headed. But what if your career doesn't go there? What happens if you get sick of being a lawyer or discover that being a teacher isn't all it's cracked up to be? If you drop out, what does that mean for your graduate or professional mortgage? The answer is not a lot, depending on what happens next.

Once you qualify for the favourable rates and conditions on a professional mortgage – a higher income multiple or lower repayments in the early years – you don't have to tell your lender if you change career. (And you don't have to tell your lender with a graduate mortgage either, as it isn't granted to you on the basis of what job you're doing.) As long as you pay your mortgage every month your lender is unlikely to be interested in what you do for a living. So if you can find another job that pays enough to enable you to pay the mortgage, you have nothing to worry about.

However, if you opt for a new career with an even lower salary and no chance of it increasing as significantly as it would if you'd stuck at being a doctor, this can make paying the mortgage difficult. Remember: Your mortgage was granted with your future earnings in mind – but if your income never reaches these predicted levels you'll continue to struggle. Talk to your lender about remortgaging if you're struggling with your repayments: If you extend the mortgage term, you can pay less each month. But get advice from an independent broker before you do this, because you'll commit yourself to your mortgage for longer.

If you're struggling with your mortgage, inform your lender. You may be able to come to some arrangement whereby your lender accepts lower monthly repayments for an agreed period until you get back on your feet.

Don't bury your head in the sand if you get into financial difficulty: It will make life that much harder for you and your home can be at risk.

Part III

Finding the Right Property and Making an Offer

"The high ceilings, the wooden beams, the leaded windows – this old house is absolutely <u>steeped</u> in history."

In this part . . .

The chapters in this part guide you through the process of dealing with estate agents and what to look out for when viewing properties. There's also guidance on making an offer and negotiating a deal to ensure you don't pay over the odds. You can even find tips if you are interested in building your own property from scratch or gutting and renovating a house.

Because a property transaction involves a considerable amount of money, you want to make sure that it is all done legally and above board. In the chapters in this part, I make conveyancing easy to understand. There's also a separate chapter for the legal process in Scotland. So for all issues legal, read on.

Chapter 8

Dealing with Estate Agents and Handling Viewings

*E*state agents are often the butt of plenty of jokes. You may even have an unkind word to say about them yourself (unless you're related to one). Although some agents rightly earn a reputation for being untrustworthy, many more honest ones are out there doing a good job. More importantly, they can be vital in helping you find your dream home.

The viewing process is one of the most important – and fun – parts of buying a home. Getting this right is vital if you're going to find the best property for you. You can't make an informed decision about whether you want to buy a property – or not – by looking at photos or reading the property particulars. It's essential to have a good poke about and ask the seller, or agent, all sorts of questions. You'll also have the opportunity to discover whether you can imagine yourself living there.

When you buy your first property the viewing process can seem rather daunting. But, as I point out in this chapter, as long as you know what questions to ask, how to interpret the answers, and what problems to look out for you shouldn't go far wrong.

Finding Out about Estate Agents

Finding a good agent with plenty of properties that you might be interested in and who won't mess you about is a bit hit-and-miss. If the record number of complaints against agents is anything to go by, many buyers get it wrong. In 2002, some 6,462 homebuyers and sellers complained to the industry Ombudsman about the service they received from their agent – 16.2 per cent more complaints than in 2001.

An increasing number of homebuyers may be able to find their new home on the Internet or advertised in their local paper but they are in the minority. Most people buy through an estate agent. Your local estate agent's window could be your first port of call when house hunting, or you may spot an estate agent's 'For Sale' board outside a property and call the advertised number.

Using an agent doesn't have to be an unpleasant or unfruitful experience: You can get what you want out of her – the property of your dreams – while ensuring she doesn't play you off against another buyer. As long as you bear in mind that estate agents act for the seller, not you, and simply want to make as much money as possible as quickly as they can, you'll minimise the chances of problems cropping up.

Reviewing certain realities about agents

Every high street seems to have at least one office of estate agents (and usually many more) packed full of eager young things who drive flash cars and thrive on making the sale. But while they have a bad reputation for being pushy and underhand, estate agents can help you successfully buy your new home – as long as you remember a few things:

- **The seller pays the agent and calls the shots.** The estate agent works for the seller because the seller pays the commission for successfully selling her property. So the agent's aim is to get the best price possible for the seller, which means getting as much money as possible out of you.

- **The agent must pass on all offers to the seller.** Even if the seller has accepted your offer, the agent is legally bound to pass on every offer – even those made after an offer has been accepted – to the seller. This means you have no guarantee. *Gazumping* – a situation in which the seller accepts another, higher, offer after she has already accepted an offer from another buyer – is all too common. Have a look at Chapter 9 for help with how to avoid being gazumped.

✔ **Agents are legally obliged to treat you fairly.** Although you aren't paying the agent commission, they have a duty of care to you and you're entitled to be treated honestly and fairly. If you feel you have been deliberately misled or that the agent has been economical with the truth in the property particulars, you can complain and may be due compensation (see the nearby sidebar 'Complaining about an estate agent').

✔ **Estate agents are the best source of properties for sale in your area.** You could try buying privately, surf the Internet or hunt through the private ads for properties for sale in your local paper. But the quickest and easiest way to find a property is via an estate agent. Why make life harder on yourself?

Finding a good agent

Personal recommendation is the best way to choose an agent, so ask friends and family whether they can suggest one (or one you should avoid). Remember that not all agents sell all types of property so ensure the agents you register with offer the sort of property you are interested in.

To reduce the risk of using an estate agent who deliberately misleads you, I suggest only using those who are members of the main professional body – the National Association of Estate Agents (NAEA) or are registered with the Royal Institution of Chartered Surveyors (RICS). This should bring you some extra peace of mind. The NAEA is a voluntary organisation with 10,000 members so it only represents about 60 per cent of the industry. These members follow a Professional Code of Practice and Rules of Conduct; if they breach these they can receive a formal warning, a fine, be suspended or expelled. For a list of NAEA-registered agents, go to www.naea.co.uk. If you opt for a RICS member, you can be confident that the agent under-stands and employs best practice. You can also get access to independent redress, if anything goes wrong.

For extra protection, opt for an agent who also belongs to the Ombudsman for Estate Agents (OEA) Scheme, which has more teeth and can award compensation against agents who breach the rules (see the 'Complaining about an estate agent' sidebar nearby). Membership is also voluntary and many agents, including well-known high-street names, haven't signed up. It's worth picking an agent who is a member of the scheme though as most complaints are made against estate agents who aren't members. To contact the OEA, telephone 01722 333306 or visit its Web site at www.oea.co.uk.

Registering with several agents

You don't usually pay the estate agent for her services, so my advice is to take advantage of this and register with as many *suitable* estate agents as possible. If you stick with one agent you drastically reduce the number of properties you get a chance to consider – perhaps missing out on the one that is perfect for you.

Notice the emphasis on *suitable*. Make sure that the agents you select offer the type of property you want to buy in the areas you are interested in. For example, if your budget is £110,000 and you're after a studio flat in Bristol city centre, there's no point registering with an agent who specialises in rural properties in the southeast.

Check your local newspaper and estate agents' windows to see the type of property each estate agent offers. Log onto your estate agents' Web sites, particularly if you are buying in an area some distance from where you live and it's not convenient to visit the local agent.

Register with as many agents as possible while remaining wary about those who aren't affiliated to one of the official trade bodies. Cost isn't an issue, as you don't have to pay the agent. You have no loyalty to any of them and can view as many properties from as many different agents as you like.

Don't lose sleep about which agents you register with. This issue isn't nearly as important for you as it is for the seller. A seller can waste serious time and money by placing her property with a useless agent.

Complaining about an estate agent

If you feel that an agent has treated you unfairly, you can try to sort the problem out with her directly, or failing that, her head office if the company she works for is part of a chain. If this doesn't resolve the problem, contact your local trading standards service (details in the *Yellow Pages*). If you live in Northern Ireland, you can contact the Northern Ireland Executive (www.nics.gov.uk). The Citizens Advice Bureau (again, check the *Yellow Pages*) is another useful port of call.

If your estate agent is a member of the NAEA or belongs to the OEA Scheme, they may be able to help. But remember that they won't be able to unless you've already tried to resolve the problem with the agent first. When you contact the OEA, you'll receive a complaints form and some guidance notes to help you complete it. You must also sign another form consenting to allow the Ombudsman to gather information about your dealings with the agent. Once these forms have been received, the Ombudsman will appoint a case officer to review your complaints.

If the Ombudsman supports your complaint, it may award compensation: The estate agent will be informed of this beforehand and has 14 days to appeal. Any appeal will be considered and the Case Review amended as necessary. The Case Review is then sent to you: You have 28 days to accept the decision or make your own appeal. The Ombudsman will only reconsider her decision in exceptional circumstances. Any award of compensation in your favour is binding on the estate agent. And once you accept it, you do so in full and final settlement of your complaint against the estate agent.

Contact the NAEA at www.naea.co.uk or on 01926 496800. The Ombudsman can be reached on 01722 333306 or www.oea.co.uk.

Getting the Best Out of Your Estate Agent

When you register with an estate agent you'll be asked what type of property you want to buy and the all-important question – how much you can afford to pay for it. Be as honest as possible on both counts or you'll waste everyone's time. Once the agent knows your requirements she may be able to show you details of suitable properties straight away. If not, as suitable properties come onto her books, she'll contact you to arrange a viewing.

Avoiding mortgages offered by agents

The estate agent's strength is in negotiating sales, not arranging financing. Yet many agents offer mortgages, either through an in-house specialist or referring you to a lender with whom it has an agreement. I advise you to steer clear of these. It may be more convenient than shopping around, but you'll restrict your choice to a tiny panel of lenders and are unlikely to get the best deal. And as money is tight you may require a particular type of mortgage – family offset or rent-a-room scheme – that the estate agent simply doesn't offer. The best place to find a mortgage is through an independent broker (see Chapter 4 for more details on brokers).

You are not obliged to take a mortgage from an estate agent so don't allow yourself to be pressured into it.

On the other hand, you may be wise to go with an agent-recommended surveyor or solicitor to handle your conveyancing (see Chapter 10 for more on this). Rates are often competitive because of the volume of business the estate agent is able to pass on. But again, don't feel bullied into using the surveyor or solicitor recommended by an estate agent and don't commit to anything until you have shopped around for quotes.

Be straight about how much you can afford: If the agent laughs when you tell her your maximum budget is £80,000, resist the temptation to pretend you can afford more. You'll get found out in the end and you'll have wasted everyone's time. You are also likely to feel rather depressed viewing lots of properties that are well beyond your means.

Getting the agent on your side

You might not be paying the agent but there are ways of making sure you get what you want out of her – the property you desire at a price you can afford.

Because money is tight, you need to be cute. At the risk of sounding repetitive, be unashamedly upfront about what you can afford. Then, when the agent does call you with details of a property in your price range, be ready to act immediately. Arrange a viewing as soon as possible if you like the sound of it to show you're serious and encourage the agent.

Be ready to befriend the agent. No, this doesn't mean cosy drinks after work every night, but make sure she thinks of you first when a property comes onto her books that meets your requirements.

What estate agents like more than anything are serious buyers who arrange their finances before they start looking at properties so they know what they can afford – this is particularly important when money is tight. It demonstrates that you can move quickly and won't drag your heels. Estate agents also like buyers who are flexible: If you're realistic about what your money can buy and don't have too many conditions, such as the property must have a garden, garage, *and* be on a particular street, you'll make life much easier for yourself. The agent is also likely to act more favourably towards you.

Being specific about your demands

Hundreds of properties come onto an agent's books every week and most of them won't suit you at all. To avoid wasting your time (and the agent's) try to be as specific – and accurate – as possible about what you want. If your budget only stretches to a small studio flat, there's no point saying you are interested in four-bedroom family homes. Not only will you waste your time traipsing around properties you can't afford, the agent will quickly pick up on this – and you won't get the call when a property comes up that you can afford.

Make sure you have a clear idea about what you want, what you can live with, and what you can't. Chapter 3 has tips to help you decide what's essential for you and what's not. Because you're on a tight budget it's important to be realistic about what you can afford.

Living in the real world

Buyers often have unrealistic expectations about what sort of property they can get for their money. After chatting it through with an estate agent, you may hear a recommendation that you revise your expectations: that is, if you want a two-bedroom house with a garden in central London but only have a budget of £150,000, you aren't going to find one. Listen to the agent: If she thinks you will only get a one-bedroom flat for your money you will have to downsize your demands or choose a cheaper location in order to afford a bigger place.

Using Estate Agents' Web Sites

Most agents have extensive Web sites listing details of hundreds of properties for sale. There are several advantages to using one of these:

- ✔ **It saves trawling round agents' offices.** You can search the Web sites of several agents in the time it would take you to visit your local estate agent's office.

- ✔ **You can take a virtual tour.** As well as property particulars, many sites include several photos of a property rather than just the single bog-standard shot taken from the front garden that appears in most estate agents' windows. Many also offer virtual tours so you can look round the inside of a property – and if it isn't what you are looking for, it saves you a wasted visit.

- ✔ **Regular e-mail updates save you time.** Once you register your details and requirements, many agents will alert you by email as soon as a property comes onto their books that fits your criteria. This means you are notified as soon as a property becomes available, saving you the time and effort of trawling through details of hundreds of unsuitable properties.

There are far too many Internet sites to mention here but it's worth starting with www.ukpropertyguide.co.uk, which offers a comprehensive list of the best sales databases in the UK. In Northern Ireland, try www.4ni.co.uk for details of Web sites of nearly 300 estate agents.

Seeing Past the Hype: Checking the Property Particulars

Estate agents provide *property particulars* – a description of the property for sale – which they write. These give you an idea of what the property is like; the number of bedrooms, the dimensions of the rooms, and whether there's parking and a garden, for example. The Property Misconceptions Act 1991 forbids an estate agent to make false or misleading statements about a property. So if the property particulars mention that the flat is double-glazed, then it should be.

Take the adjectives used to describe properties with a large pinch of salt. Agents are well-practised at making something sound a lot better than it actually is: they have to be if they're going to shift some of the properties that come onto their books. Try reading between the lines: 'traditional' could also mean old-fashioned and in need of some renovation; 'landscaped garden' could denote the presence of a few shrubs here and there; 'contemporary' may be a bit radical for some tastes; 'cosy' may more realistically be described as poky, and so on.

The property particulars may include terms you don't understand. If you are unsure about anything, ask. Don't worry about looking stupid; if it isn't clear to you, chances are it will be confusing for many buyers. And if you don't ask, you could end up making a costly mistake.

Most of the complaints received by the Ombudsman concern sales literature, with many buyers feeling that it didn't accurately describe a property. Some descriptions are clearly wide of the mark: one complainant bought a flat that had been advertised as having a garage, for example, but when he moved in he discovered it hadn't. This also underlines how important it is to have a good look round the property and check the particulars against what is actually before your eyes. If you like the sound of a property, you must arrange to take a look for yourself to help you make up your mind.

Arranging a Viewing

As soon as you come across a property you like the look of, make an appointment with the estate agent or seller (if it is being sold privately) to view it as soon as possible. It's important to move quickly, particularly if the property has just come onto the market – if it's desirable, other prospective buyers will also be interested. There is more demand for cheaper properties than expensive ones at the top end of the market so they tend to be sold more quickly.

You want to view as many properties as possible, which is fair enough, but it's a waste of time viewing those that aren't suitable. The trick is to eliminate unsuitable properties *before* arranging a viewing – the house hunting process is exhausting enough as it is without wandering round properties that don't meet your requirements at all. Drive or walk past a property before arranging a viewing. Quite often a picture in an advert doesn't tell the full story – such as how busy the road is or whether you can park your car nearby if the property doesn't have a garage or driveway. A quick drive-by, without stopping to go in and look round, will give you a preliminary impression, which might be enough to cross it off your list. But if you don't see anything that puts you off and you actually like what you see, you should arrange a viewing as soon as possible.

Take someone with you to viewings: for safety reasons, this is particularly important if you are female. But even if you aren't, it can be really helpful to take someone along for a second opinion. There is also someone there to stop you getting carried away and making an offer, there and then, without thinking it through first. But try not to take the kids or the dog along as they'll just get in the way and distract you from the task in hand.

Knowing when to view

Most people view properties in the evening, after work, or at weekends (usually a Saturday as most estate agents don't work Sundays). Arrange to view the property during daylight hours so you can see how much natural light it gets. In winter the weekend is better for viewing than an evening after work.

Work out how many properties you can comfortably view in one evening or day. Try not to book in more than a handful or you'll get tired and irritable and be less capable of making the right decision. When I was flat hunting, the maximum number of viewings I could handle in one day was five and that was exhausting enough: any more and I'd have keeled over. If your employer owes you some holiday, it's worth taking a day off and arranging to view several properties in one go. The advantages of doing this are that the agent will be less busy than at weekends, you'll be able to get a good number of properties out of the way in one hit, and it won't cut into your leisure time.

The earlier in the day you can view a property, the better. If a flat in a desirable area goes on sale on a Thursday, for example, and you can't see it until Saturday evening you are likely to have missed the boat. If you really can't arrange to view the flat before the weekend, at least arrange to see it first thing Saturday morning. That way, you'll get to look round before the majority of your rivals who also can't make a viewing until the weekend. If you like it, you can make an offer before they've even put a foot over the threshold.

If you want to enjoy an unhurried viewing, avoid looking round properties on a Saturday when estate agents are likely to be very busy and pushed for time. But if you have no alternative than to view on a Saturday, remember that estate agents get booked up quickly so arrange a viewing as soon as you can: Don't leave it to the day itself to call the agent because she is unlikely to be able to fit you in.

Be wary of tactical viewing. Estate agents often show you a property that is in poor condition, overpriced, and even unsuitable for you in order to make the next one you view – a property the agent really wants to sell – appear even better. Avoid being sucked in by sticking to your list of requirements for a property and don't be swayed by the agent's persuasive arguments.

If you're interested in more than one property on an agent's books, you may be able to persuade her to show you them in one go – perhaps during an afternoon or evening – saving you time. If she's willing to drive you round the properties as well, you'll also save money on transport.

When I was flat hunting, I managed to persuade one agent to drive me round several properties in one evening. As we viewed one dingy flat after another I began to despair of finding my dream home. But it was while we were viewing the unsuitable properties that another flat she was selling popped into her mind as a possibility for me. It hadn't even been advertised at that point and was below my budget as it only had one bedroom (I wanted two). It was also in an area I hadn't considered even though it was only a mile from the flats I had viewed. But as she had the car and could drive me there, I agreed to give it the once over. As you may have guessed already, I fell in love with it and offered the full asking price on the spot (there was a lot of competition for flats in the development). Sometimes it pays to be flexible.

Realising that once isn't enough

If you're still interested in a property after the initial viewing, revisit it several times. Don't be afraid to make as many appointments to view it as you need to help you make up your mind – and ask to look round without the agent or seller watching your every move. This will make you feel less harassed. You're unlikely to have a load of questions to ask on follow-up viewings, and you'll know your way round by this point, so the presence of the seller or agent is not as necessary.

If the property is reasonably priced, beware of dithering too long. It's important not to rush into a property purchase without thinking it through carefully but you also don't want to take so long making your mind up that you miss out. Try and gauge the level of interest in the property; if it has languished on the market for several months with no buyer making a firm offer, you can probably afford to take more time than if it's just gone on the market. Ask the estate agent for this information.

Listening for alarm bells

A friend of the family recently bought a two-bedroom cottage in an old-fashioned market town. He viewed the property five times but the only problem he encountered was the viewing times: The seller seemed to work such long hours that she couldn't show him round before 7 p.m. on weekdays and not at all at weekends because she said she was usually away on work trips.

However, he liked the cottage, couldn't see anything wrong with it, and made an offer, which the seller accepted. It was only after he moved into the property with his family that he finally realised why the seller had been so inflexible over viewing times. The road was a nightmare during the day: The school directly opposite meant the road was impassable between 8 a.m. and 9.30 a.m. and again between 3 p.m. and 4 p.m. If he'd known this beforehand, my friend wouldn't have bought the cottage as the traffic is a real hassle during term-time.

Be suspicious if the seller is inflexible as to when you can look round. It is essential to view properties at different times of the day and evening to assess traffic and noise levels and anything else that the seller may be trying to hide from you.

The second viewing is useful for measuring up and checking whether your sofa will fit into the lounge or your curtains are long enough for the dining-room windows. Feel free to take a tape measure and notebook to jot down these details. Double-check that there's enough storage for your needs: many purpose-built flats have limited storage space, which can prove to be a problem if you've got a lot of belongings.

Arrange follow-up viewings at different times of the day and night (within reason) so you can assess how noise and traffic levels affect the property. For example, if the house is opposite a school the road will get very busy around 9 a.m. and 3.30 p.m. This might not bother you if you leave for work at 8 a.m. and return after 6 p.m. But if you work from home, the noise from the school at playtime and all that coming and going might be too much hassle. It's worth arranging a second viewing during the day, perhaps just before home time, to see whether it's going to be a problem.

Time follow-up viewings to nose out any potential problems:

- ✔ **If the property is on a major road:** Make sure your second viewing is during the rush hour. If the noise is incessant, it might be difficult to open the windows on a warm summer evening and still be able to hear the TV. And if you have cats or small children, you should see the road at its busiest to assess whether it's too dangerous for them.

- ✔ **If the property is close to a train station:** Make an appointment to view the property during the day to see whether commuters clog up the street with their cars and will make it difficult for you to get in and out of your drive, or park in the street if the property doesn't have off-road parking. If a train track runs near the property you should also be wary of the potential noise (see 'Not forgetting the exterior' later in this chapter).

- ✔ **If the property is next to a pub or above a shop:** Visit during opening hours and chucking out time to judge whether the premises are noisy or intrusive. Be particularly wary of off licenses, nightclubs and 24-hour corner shops where gangs of kids might congregate outside and cause a nuisance.

Making the Most of Your Viewing

Before you even make an appointment to view your first property it's important to be clear about what you're looking for.
This may seem obvious, but until you ask yourself what features
a property *must* have and what features you'd quite like but
aren't essential, you can't work out whether it's suitable for you.

I recommend writing a list of must-haves and would-likes
before viewing any properties. As long as you can tick off all
the must-haves, the property is suitable. And if there are several ticks next to the would-likes as well, that's a bonus.

Not forgetting the exterior

Your viewing of the property starts before you even set foot
inside the front door. Before entering, check the exterior and
make sure you are satisfied with the answers to the following
questions:

- Do the neighbouring flats or houses appear clean and
well cared for? Are neighbours' drives clear of old
bangers and rubbish? This could be an important factor
when you come to sell the property – even if it's years
before you get round to doing so.

- Is the road noisy and busy? Is there room for parking if
the property doesn't have a drive or garage? How easy
was it for you to find somewhere to park? Would you feel
happy leaving your car in the street at night? Would it be
safe for children (if you have any) to play in the street or
for the cat to wander about outside?

- How safe does the street appear? Is it well lit at night?
Would you feel safe walking home late at night?

- Does the roof of the property appear sound or are there
tiles missing? Don't forget to check the condition of the
guttering and drains, particularly if it's raining.

- Does the exterior of the property need a lick of paint?

- If there's wood on the front of the property, is it in good
condition or does it need replacing?

- Have any extensions been added to the property?

Walk round the exterior of the property if possible, and check out the garden, if there is one. You may have to do this at the end of your viewing but make sure you have a good look. If it is night time, come back during daylight.

Although selling the property on is likely to be the last thing on your mind, this is likely to happen at some stage so you should consider how easy this would be. Look out for anything that may make it difficult, such as mobile phone masts or electricity pylons in the immediate vicinity, planes roaring overhead, or Intercity trains hurtling past at all hours of the day and night. Check train timetables and arrange several viewings at different times to make sure the noise from aircraft isn't intrusive.

Poking about in the cupboards

Once inside the property, the agent or seller will usually take the lead and guide you round, pointing out certain features. Go along with this but don't allow them to rush you no matter how busy they are. You are on a tight budget, which the agent might think doesn't qualify you for the red carpet treatment, but it is a lot of money to you, so take as long as you need.

If you want to poke about in the kitchen cupboards you should be able to do so without feeling you have made an unreasonable request. In fact, opening and shutting kitchen drawers and fitted wardrobes will quickly reveal whether they are solid and of good quality – or not. It may be clear that they will need replacing as soon as you move in, which could be reflected in your offer to the seller. Likewise, have a good look at the boiler and consumer unit or fuse box; if you need to replace the former or have the property rewired, this will cost thousands of pounds. Again, if such work is necessary it will give you ammunition for negotiating the asking price.

Aim to have a really good look round and see whether you can spot anything that might pose a problem. Use the checklist in Figure 8-1 (make several copies and take one to each viewing) to ensure you don't forget anything and, if you are looking at several properties, make notes as you go round each one – otherwise you'll forget which was which and the details will merge into one other. It's also a good idea to take photos.

Property Checklist

Date of viewing: _____

Property address: _____

_____

_____

Asking price: _____ Negotiable? _____

Age and type of property: _____

Freehold/leasehold? _____

Seller's name: _____

Is seller part of chain? _____

Estate agent: _____

(Put a tick next to room that exists, plus add comments as to general condition or anything striking about property)

❑ Kitchen: _____

❑ Lounge: _____

❑ Dining room: _____

❑ Bedroom one: _____

❑ Bedroom two: _____

❑ Bedroom three: _____

❑ Bathroom: _____

❑ Downstairs toilet: _____

❑ Car parking: _____

❑ Garden: _____

❑ Central heating: _____

❑ Double-glazing: _____

❑ Fixtures and fittings included? _____

❑ Has the seller made any structural changes? _____

Running costs

Gas: _____   Electricity: _____

Water: _____   Council tax: _____

Score the following out of 10 (10 is excellent; 0 is poor)

Traffic: _____   General noise: _____

Condition of paintwork: _____   Guttering:_____

Roof: _____   Wiring: _____   Windows:_____

Repairs needed? _____

_____

Does the area feel safe? _____

Time to get to work: _____

Local amenities

Schools: _____

Pubs, restaurants, takeaways: _____

Cinema/theatre:_____

Swimming pool/leisure centre: _____

Shops/newsagent:_____

Comments: _____

_____

_____

Date of second viewing: _____

Look out for damp patches, mould, or any cracks in the walls indicating subsidence. Although it's wise to commission a survey before buying a property, it's worth seeing if you can spot anything during the viewing that might pose a problem. Ask the agent or seller what is likely to be the cause of it, how long it has been like that, and whether any work has been done to try and rectify it. Be suspicious of new paint or wallpaper as the seller could be trying to hide a problem, particularly damp.

Take a torch and go up into the loft and down into the cellar, if possible. Check for any holes, leaks, or running water and make sure the roof is properly insulated.

Unless the property is vacant, it's likely to be full of the seller's belongings and decorated to her taste. There's a strong chance you won't like the furniture or décor but try not to get too hung up on the velour armchairs or blood-red walls. The seller will take the furniture with her and you can always repaint the walls or throw out the flower-power style carpet if she leaves these behind. You'll have to use your imagination and try to see beyond the dodgy furniture to the property's potential because you'll really struggle to find something exactly as you'd like it, particularly on a tight budget.

Asking All the Right Questions

You probably have a hundred and one questions for the seller or agent. I suggest jotting them down before the viewing so you don't forget them. Remember to make a note of the answers, particularly if you are viewing several properties. Questions you might want to ask the seller include:

> ✔ **Why are you moving?** People move for many reasons: if you are buying a bed-sit or one- or two-bed flat, there's a fair chance the seller is moving to a bigger property, perhaps because they've got kids and have outgrown it. Other people move because they have to relocate for their job or simply fancy a new life abroad or in another part of the country. But if the seller is moving because the neighbours are so noisy she's made an official complaint, you need to know this as it will affect your decision to buy the property.

✔ **What are the neighbours like?** The seller has to declare any problems with the neighbours if she has made a formal complaint to the council or the police. Ask this question when viewing the property, even though your solicitor will also ask the seller this. If the seller doesn't tell you about a complaint she made and you experience your own difficulties with the neighbours once you move in, you can take the seller to court for withholding this information. But remember that if the seller hasn't formally complained about the neighbours she doesn't have to tell you whether they are noisy or disruptive. Try to read between the lines and work out whether the seller is withholding information. If she isn't forthcoming, be suspicious and give the property a wide berth.

✔ **How long have you lived here?** Moving house is so stressful that if the seller has only lived at the property for six months or a year, alarm bells should ring. There may be legitimate reasons for this: She may be moving because she's been offered a great job in another part of the country or she's a property developer and bought the property in a dilapidated state, spent thousands of pounds doing it up, and is now selling it on. Also be wary of sellers who have lived in a property for 20 or 30 years: there's a good chance that a lot of work will be required to update the property. Many people put up with problems over the years and learn to live with them. You might not be able to.

✔ **How long has the property been on the market?** If it's only been on sale for a couple of weeks, you may have to make a quick decision before another buyer snaps it up. But if the property has been on the market for months (or even years) there is likely to be a problem (or several) with it. It could be too expensive, there might be major structural problems, or the property could be at severe risk of flooding, making it difficult for a buyer to get a mortgage and insurance. Or it may be that the seller is just very difficult and continually messes people around. Think carefully about whether you want to buy a property that someone else has had trouble selling, as you too may experience difficulties when you come to sell up.

✔ **Have you had many prospective buyers view the property and has anyone made an offer?** You need to know how much competition there is for the property and how quickly you will have to move if you are interested. But watch out for sellers and agents who exaggerate interest from other buyers in order to encourage you to make an offer.

✔ **Is the property freehold or leasehold?** If the property is a freehold property, as most houses in the UK are, there is no problem: If you buy it, you own it outright. Many flats are leasehold, though, which means you simply purchase the right to live there for a set number of years. You must pay service charges and ground rent annually to the freeholder or landlord, and abide by certain rules. The freeholder is also responsible for repairs to the communal areas of the property (see Chapter 10 for more details on the differences between leasehold and freehold.) Ask the seller for her most recent service charge bill from the landlord and ask what the landlord is like: Is she reasonable or has the seller had problems with her?

✔ **Are you in a chain and when do you want to move?** Most sellers are also buyers. The seller of the property you are after may also be buying another home – the seller of which, in turn, is also buying somewhere. This is known as a *chain* and the longer and more complicated it is (with lots of buyers and sellers), the more chance there is of something going wrong. A hiccup with one property can break the chain, resulting in a knock-on effect for several people. What's more, it could take months to rectify: If a buyer pulls out, the seller of that property will have to find another buyer, which may not be easy. Avoid complicated chains if possible: The advantage of being a first-time buyer is that you aren't part of a chain because you aren't selling a property. So try not to get caught up in one.

✔ **How much are utility bills and council tax?** Ask to look at the seller's gas, electricity, and water bills. Ask what council tax band the property comes under and, if possible, look at a recent council tax bill as well.

✔ **Has any work been carried out on the property?** If so, find out when, how extensive it was, and ask to see receipts or guarantees. Mention it to your solicitor so that she can check that any necessary permission was obtained from the local planning authority beforehand.

✔ **Which fixtures and fittings are included in the sale?** Some sellers prefer to leave carpets or curtains because they are buying new or can't face the hassle of taking them: others strip the property to the bare bones. Find out what the seller is planning to do so you don't get a nasty shock when you move in and find it empty when you were expecting to find carpets and curtains. If there is anything you'd like to keep, try to negotiate with the seller to leave the items for an extra sum.

✔ **Has the property ever been burgled or your car stolen from outside?** If the seller is honest and answers 'yes, my car has been broken into several times', you might think twice about moving to the area – even if you don't own a car. But if there was an isolated incident, where her car or home was broken into, it may not be such a big problem. This is particularly true if the seller was burgled but has since tightened up on security so you'll benefit from secure locks and maybe even a burglar alarm. Find out whether the property is in a Neighbourhood Watch area; if so, the neighbours will look out for each other's homes, which can act as a deterrent to burglars. It also means you'll qualify for lower premiums on your home contents insurance.

✔ **How easy is it to find a parking space?** This is a concern if you have a car and the property doesn't have a garage or off-road parking. Ask the seller how much you have to pay for a residents' parking permit (if required). Look at the other cars parked in the street: If they are valuable and their owners are happy enough to park them there, it should be fairly safe for you to do the same. But if you can only see old bangers and a burnt out car or two, you may think twice. It may be possible to tarmac over the front garden to provide a driveway, particularly if the neighbours have done so (and you will save yourself the time and effort of mowing the lawn).

✔ **Where is the nearest school/hospital/shop?** The questions you ask about local amenities will partly be determined by what is important to you: If you don't have children or a car, good public transport links nearby will be more of a priority than the location of the nearest primary or secondary school. You are also likely to want to know where the nearest corner shop, newsagent or supermarket is.

Making the Decision

Once you've viewed a property several times and don't think you'd gain anything more from seeing it again, it's time to make a decision. Make sure you don't buy the property just because you've had enough of house hunting and want to purchase *anything*. You'll only end up regretting your decision in years to come.

If you decide to make an offer, it needs to be handled carefully. If you are really excited about a property, you must try curbing this in front of the seller or agent if you think there is room for negotiation over the asking price. If they can see how thrilled you are, they will also be delighted as it means you are more than likely to offer the asking price because you're so desperate to buy.

While you may be able to save some money by containing your excitement and haggling over the asking price, you also need to convince the seller of your seriousness. Tell her that you are a first-time buyer, you aren't in a chain, and that your finances are all arranged (see Chapter 9 for more on this). These details can convince the seller you are not a timewaster and she is likely to take you more seriously, even if you make a lower offer, than a prospective buyer who hasn't arranged a mortgage.

Be friendly towards the seller: It won't cost you anything and may help if it comes down to you and another buyer competing for the property. Even if your offer is lower, the seller may decide to let you have the property if you have built up a rapport with her.

Chapter 9

Looking at the Ins and Outs of Offers

*B*uying a property is a nerve-wracking experience: It's no wonder it is rated as one of the most stressful things you are ever likely to do. And making an offer on a property is a major contributor to stress levels. You have to decide how much to offer and go through a tense waiting period and possibly negotiations, and even after the seller accepts your offer, you have a long way to go before you can actually move in. You need to instruct a solicitor to handle the legal transfer of the property to you and commission a survey to ensure there are no unwelcome surprises in store, such as dry rot or subsidence.

This chapter takes you through all the phases of making an offer and tells you how to get from fantasising about the new furniture you plan to buy to throwing a big housewarming party after you move in.

Working Up Your Offer

Once you find the home of your dreams – or at least the home of your budget – the next step is to make the seller an offer.

An offer declares the amount you're prepared to pay for the property. It may not be the same as the asking price, which is what the seller hopes to get for the property. You can offer less, if you think it's worth haggling, or you can even offer more than the asking price if you face a lot of competition for the property from other buyers.

As well as buying the property itself, you may be interested in purchasing certain furniture and/or curtains from the seller. Mention this when making the offer and be prepared to pay extra for these.

You make the offer verbally to the estate agent handling the sale or directly to the seller if the property is being sold privately. You can put your offer in writing but it isn't strictly necessary. However, you may want to keep a diary of your conversations as the sale progresses.

You should make it clear that the offer is subject to survey and contracts though – you are not obliged to proceed with the purchase until you are happy with the findings of the survey (if you commission a surveyor to examine the state of the property) and contracts (the legal documents transferring property ownership from the seller to you) have been exchanged. Stating that the offer is subject to survey and contracts covers your back and makes sure there is no confusion.

If an agent is handling the sale, he puts your offer to the seller and acts as go-between, letting you know whether the seller is prepared to accept it or not.

Keep in mind that the estate agent works for the seller, not you. The seller pays the agent commission for achieving a sale, so the more you pay for the property, the bigger the agent's commission. Be wise and treat the estate agent's advice about how much to offer with a healthy dose of scepticism.

Your offer is not legally binding unless you're in Scotland (see Chapter 11). It merely demonstrates your interest in purchasing the property.

Crafting the amount

Most properties are advertised along with an asking price – the amount the seller is hoping to get – but this is not set in stone.

In many – but not all – cases the seller expects you to try and knock down the price a bit so he puts his home on the market for a few thousand pounds more than he realistically expects to receive. You need to consider several factors – covered in the following sections – before deciding how much to offer.

Check what price similar properties in the area are fetching by keeping an eye on your local estate agent's window. If a similar-sized flat further down the street was recently sold for £10,000 less than the asking price of the flat you're interested in, there's a strong case for trying to knock £10,000 off the asking price and citing this as your reason. If the vendor is serious about selling, he will have to be reasonable about this. If he isn't prepared to reduce the asking price accordingly, you can try arguing the toss (which might not get you anywhere) or carry on looking for another property. Don't be drawn into paying over the odds, no matter how much you like the property.

In an ideal world you would pay less than the asking price for a property, even if it were fairly priced. As you are on a tight budget, the more you can save at this stage the less stretched your finances will be and the more cash you will have to spend on bits and pieces for your new home. The most important thing is not to pay more than you absolutely have to and certainly not more than you can afford.

Once you set your budget, make sure you stick to it, unless stretching yourself by a few hundred pounds more will get you the property you've set your heart on. But know when to stop: Committing yourself to paying thousands of pounds more than you can afford is extremely foolish.

Sizing up the market

Assess the current state of the housing market before making an offer. Otherwise, you risk losing out on the property of your dreams or getting sucked into paying well over the odds without justification. The housing market gives you a good idea what you can get away with – or not. The housing market is governed by supply and demand and whether there's more supply than demand or vice versa at the time you want to purchase property plays a large part in how much you offer and ultimately pay for your home.

In an ideal world, you look for a property during a *buyer's market*, which is when there are more properties for sale than people willing to buy them. In this situation, you can try offering below the asking price and have a good chance of getting your offer accepted.

The opposite of a buyer's market is a *seller's market,* in which there are more buyers than properties for sale. A seller's market is bad news for you because the seller calls the shots. You may need to offer close to the asking price or even higher if you want to be the successful buyer.

To find out whether the market is favouring buyers or sellers, you have to do some research. Chat to estate agents to find out how long properties are taking to sell and keep up-to-date with house price movements by reading the national press, which is always full of tales about that great British obsession: the housing market!

Even during a buyer's market, it isn't always sensible to offer below the asking price. If there's a lot of competition for the property and plenty of prospective buyers prepared to pay the full asking price, for example, you are likely to miss out. But it is up to you to negotiate a deal that suits you – at a price you can comfortably afford.

If you have the misfortune to be purchasing in a seller's market there is a strong possibility that another buyer has an eye on the same property. If this is so, it makes it harder to knock much, if anything, off the asking price. In fact, you could end up paying more than the asking price in order to secure the property.

Trying to get the seller to accept less than the asking price isn't always a good idea. In June 2000, the height of the most recent housing boom, there were 12 buyers to every property for sale in the south east of England, according to Bradford & Bingley's HOME report. This demand was not reflected to quite the same extent across the country, but in the north and west of England there were still three buyers for every property. Offering less than the asking price got you nowhere as there were other buyers ready to pay what the seller wanted.

Beware of trying to time your purchase by waiting for a buyer's market. You could find yourself waiting years for a property crash that never comes. If you're ready to buy, my advice is to get on and do so. By waiting, you risk pricing yourself out of the market further. Just make sure you don't overstretch yourself.

Considering the property's particulars

Thankfully, you don't face cut-throat competition for every property. Sometimes, quite the opposite in fact. If a property is taking a while to shift, for example, the seller runs the risk of having to wait weeks, or even months, for another buyer to come along if he rejects your offer. Find out how long the property has been advertised for by asking the estate agent handling the sale.

Calling the seller's bluff

A property had been on the market at £200,000 for four weeks, with no viewers. My father viewed it with the aim of buying it and renting it out to tenants. He realised it was perfect for his purposes – in a good location with the right number of reasonably-sized rooms and in excellent condition with very little work needed – in other words, ideal for the tenants he had in mind.

He made an offer of £190,000, which reflected the slowdown in the property market and the fact that nobody else had been round to view it. He was also aware that the estate agent was busy reducing other, similar sized properties on his books. The agent said that he thought the seller would accept £192,000 but that my father's offer was too low. Indeed, after speaking with the seller, the agent came back to my father and said that the seller would only accept £192,000. It is likely that he had advised the seller that he might be able to get this amount out of my father, demonstrating to the seller his importance in the negotiating process. Of course, the added incentive was that the extra £2,000 would have boosted the agent's commission.

My father stuck to his guns. While he liked the property, he saw it as a hard-headed business purchase and while it suited his needs he was prepared to go elsewhere if it meant paying the correct price. He instructed the agent that he wasn't going above £190,000 and asked if the agent had anything else on his books. Later that day, the seller accepted my father's offer of £190,000.

Sometimes it pays to stand your ground. But you need the confidence to make sure you are doing the right thing and aren't going to regret it. Research the market carefully and get a good feel for what you can get away with – and what you can't.

Depending upon the market and the house itself, you may be able to try knocking several thousand pounds off the asking price:

- ✔ If the property has been on the market without attracting much interest from potential buyers, it may be overpriced.

- ✔ If the seller calls your bluff and refuses to reduce the price, you have to decide how much you want the property. If you firmly believe it is overpriced and are not too bothered about buying it, stick to your guns. There will be another property around the corner. And chances are the seller may well decide to lower the price anyway once he realises that you aren't going to budge.

- ✔ The seller wants to move quickly. He may already have put his plans on hold for a while – so he may be prepared to accept less than the asking price in exchange for a quick sale. This may also be the case if he has found another property on which he is itching to make an offer, or face losing out.

- ✔ The property needs a lot of work and the asking price doesn't reflect this. Go ahead and offer less and give this as your reason. If problems are unearthed in the survey, and they are not so great as to put you off the property completely, this will increase your bargaining power. Obtain estimates for repairs to further strengthen your case and make it hard for the seller to disagree with your reasoning.

Meeting the asking price

If you want to buy a property that is fairly priced and has several other potential buyers interested, haggling over the price is foolish. One of the other buyers will no doubt be prepared to pay what the seller wants and by the time the agent informs you of this, the seller may have already accepted that offer. If you like the property and can afford to buy it, it's foolhardy to start messing about. My advice is to offer the asking price – and quickly.

Instinct can be a useful tool when purchasing a property. If you go with your gut feeling, you end up making the right decision a lot of the time.

Going on instinct

My first property purchase was a one-bedroom flat in a new development in the East End of London. I arrived for the viewing having psyched myself up to offer £5,000 below the asking price, not because I felt it was over-priced but because that's what everyone told me you did when buying a property.

I instantly fell in love with the flat and decided to make an offer. The agent told me that there were only four flats left for sale in the block (out of 42), so if I didn't put a non-refundable £500 deposit down within 24 hours to demonstrate my interest, chances are by the weekend they'd all have been sold.

Faced with this demand, I realised there wasn't much point in trying to haggle and had to make a quick decision: Was I prepared not only to pay the asking price but also to stump up a deposit? The answer was 'yes' and I agreed to go to the agent's office the next day to pay the deposit to secure my flat. By the time I got there, the other flats had already been sold. My decision turned out to be the right one.

Offering below asking price

If you are haggling with the vendor and have offered below the asking price, there may be a delay before you hear whether you have been successful or not, especially if the seller is prepared to accept some reduction but doesn't want to appear too desperate.

Once you've decided to offer below the asking price, try not to panic and bombard the estate agent with calls, saying you've changed your mind and will pay the asking price after all. Wait for the agent to report back: Showing your desperation plays right into his hands. You can kiss goodbye to any bargaining power you thought you had.

Assess the situation rationally. If you have thought it through carefully, firmly believe the property to be overpriced, and are not prepared to pay over the odds, stick by your decision. If you came to it rationally, it's the right one. But if you aren't sure because you didn't really think it through properly in the first place and subsequently think you may have made a mistake, holding your nerve is a darn sight harder.

Entering Negotiations

If you're blessed, you make an offer and have it accepted immediately. If your offer is accepted, insist the property is taken off the market and look for confirmation of this on the memorandum of sale issued by the agent.

In many cases, an offer isn't accepted immediately. And if this is the case for you, some negotiation may be necessary.

If several buyers are interested in one property, a bidding war could break out – every seller's dream and every buyer's nightmare because it bumps up the price.

Going back and forth

If the seller rejects your offer, the estate agent usually comes back with a suggestion as to what price the seller may be persuaded to accept. You can try negotiating this if you decide it's worth your while. For example, if the original asking price was £150,000 and you offer £140,000, the estate agent may tell you that the seller will accept £142,000 but no less. As this isn't that far off your offer, you should accept this if you can afford the extra £2,000. It's not worth haggling over relatively small amounts.

However, if the agent tells you that the seller won't accept less than £148,000 – considerably more than you offered – the seller has clearly not made much effort to meet you halfway. In such a situation, I suggest that you bid £145,000. The agent may come back and say the offer is too low but the seller might accept £146,500 and so on, until, hopefully, a price is agreed. How much negotiating goes on depends on how flexible both parties are prepared to be.

If the seller also wants to offload their furniture or curtains, he may be persuaded to consider your offer more favourably if you tell the agent you're prepared to pay a few hundred pounds for these.

Engaging in a bidding war

If another buyer (or several) is interested in the same property as you, the estate agent may ask you whether you want to increase your offer in order to beat the rival buyer, which could lead to a bidding war. The problem is that when you make a higher bid, the estate agent is likely to go back to the other buyer and inform him of your increased bid. That buyer may, in turn, increase his bid and you'll then be invited by the agent to do the same. It is easy to end up offering much more than you originally intended.

Don't get caught up in a bidding war. Your mortgage lender won't loan you more cash simply because you got caught up in the excitement of bidding for your dream house. And your lender certainly won't let you borrow more than the property is worth, as determined by the valuation. I strongly advise against trying to raise thousands of pounds extra to secure a particular property. You might be tempted to take out a personal loan from your bank, or tap your parents for extra cash. But you will only overstretch yourself, which could be a problem later on if interest rates rise. Plus, you will be living in a property that cost you more than it was worth. It could take several years for the value to rise above the purchase price, and until then you're trapped, unable to move.

If several buyers are interested in the same property, the estate agent may insist upon sealed bids, which are standard in Scotland and becoming increasingly popular everywhere else. Sealed bids speed up the process and ensure the seller gets as much as possible for his property, although the highest offer is not always the successful bid. If you have a buyer for your home and your finances arranged, for example, the seller may go with your bid – even if it isn't the highest one – because you're able to move quickly.

With sealed bids, all interested buyers submit an offer and details of their employment and financial status in writing to the estate agent by a certain date. Make sure you meet the deadline for bids: if you miss it, you miss out. If you can move quickly because you are a first-time buyer and not part of a chain – you don't have to sell an existing property before you can buy – you should indicate that this is the case as it counts in your favour.

Even if the seller accepts your offer, there are still no guarantees that you'll end up the successful purchaser. If someone offers more at a later date, the agent is still required by law to inform the seller, and it isn't unheard of for the seller to accept another offer. There is no guarantee of your success until contracts are exchanged.

Having Your Offer Accepted!

When your offer is accepted, you receive a letter from the seller's estate agent confirming the purchase price you agreed to, the address of the property, and the name, address, and contact number of the agent handling the sale, the seller's solicitor, and your solicitor – so line up a solicitor in advance.

Once a price has been agreed, it is time for conveyancing to begin. *Conveyancing* is the legal process of transferring ownership of a property or land from one person (the seller) to another person (you). I cover the intricacies of conveyancing in Chapter 10. Several legal documents, such as the title deeds, need to be checked and various documents signed and forms completed. Local authority and land searches are also vital to find out if there are any long-term plans that could affect the value of the property.

Instructing a solicitor

Instructing a solicitor sounds as if it's a very grand process, but be assured that you don't actually instruct the solicitor to do anything – it's just a turn of phrase. Instructing a solicitor just means that you find one to agree to take on the conveyancing involved in your property purchase. Although you may already have a perfectly good solicitor, he will not be suitable to handle your house purchase unless he is also experienced in conveyancing. If you don't know a conveyancing specialist, ask friends, family, or work colleagues for recommendations. And if all you hear are bad reports about various solicitors, at least you will be able to cross them off your list and won't waste time instructing them.

If friends and family can't recommend a solicitor you may be tempted to trawl through *Yellow Pages* and find one for yourself. True, there are hundreds of solicitors listed there but you only get their contact details – you won't have a clue how good they actually are. Rather than pick one at random ask your estate agent or mortgage broker (if you are using one) to make a suggestion. They deal with solicitors every day so are likely to know someone who will be suitable. There is also a strong chance that you will get a discount on the conveyancing or survey fees if you use an agent or broker-recommended solicitor or surveyor.

If you are really stuck, try the Law Society (www.lawsociety.org.uk) or call 020 7242 1222 for a database of solicitors in England and Wales. In Northern Ireland, try the Law Society of Northern Ireland (www.lawsoc-ni.org) or call 028 90 231614. You don't have to opt for a solicitor either: Another option is a licensed conveyancer who specialises in conveyancing and nothing else. Try the Council for Licensed Conveyancers (CLC) on 01245 349599 or www.conveyancer.gov.uk for a list of specialist conveyancers.

Your solicitor doesn't have to be based locally. It is more than likely that you won't ever have to deal with him face-to-face. Modern communications enable you to sort everything out over telephone, by fax, or post. Often, a solicitor will ask to see proof of identity – usually your passport (which can be posted to the solicitor) is taken as proof of this. The advantage of using a solicitor who isn't on your patch is that it could save you money (see Chapter 10 for more on the cost of instructing a solicitor).

Once you instruct your solicitor, keep in close contact with him. Although nobody wants to be a pest, it is worth calling your solicitor on a regular basis, particularly as you approach exchange of contracts, to ensure you aren't holding up the purchase without realising it. Solicitors can get very busy and need chasing up from time to time, just to ensure that everything is going as it should. There may be something you can do to help things along: If the seller is holding up the process in some way, you may be able to find out the reason for this, for example.

Sometimes, even though you have gone to a lot of trouble choosing a solicitor, he just doesn't live up to your expectations. If you are unhappy with the work your solicitor is doing – or perhaps because he doesn't seem to be doing any! – you should first complain to the solicitor. If you get no satisfaction from him, or one of the firm's senior partners, take your complaint higher. All solicitors in England and Wales have to be registered with the Law Society (the Law Society of Northern Ireland for solicitors practicing in Northern Ireland), and these have an established complaints system in place. Contact the relevant society directly. The CLC also has a complaints system and will refer you to the Legal Services Ombudsman if it can't deal with your complaint. If it is upheld, you could be in line for compensation.

Arranging your finances

It is worth ensuring that your finances are arranged before you make an offer so that you are ready to move quickly. Chapter 4 deals with the ins and outs of mortgages to help you get started. If you haven't sorted out your finances before you make an offer on a property, you could find you really hold everything up as you are buying on a budget so may have more trouble getting financing. My advice is to play it safe, and avoid annoying the seller, by getting your finances arranged well in advance.

Finding ways to get round a solicitor

A friend of mine got very frustrated because the purchase of her flat was taking so long. She called the seller to find out what the hold up was.

The seller revealed that his solicitor was waiting for my friend to sign some documents and return them to him, although these hadn't even been passed onto my friend by her solicitor. Convinced of her solicitor's incompetence and fed up of not being able to speak to him personally, my friend took matters into her own hands and befriended the solicitor's secretary.

This worked brilliantly as the secretary always answered the solicitor's

phone and seemed to know more about what was going on in that office – what documents were lying in the in-tray, for example – than the solicitor himself. The secretary also wasn't used to clients being polite to her so she was happy to chat with my friend. As a result, the hold-ups vanished, everything was done promptly and my friend grew to enjoy her daily chat with the secretary who lacked the patronising, hurried air of her boss.

If you can't get the organ grinder to give you what you want, don't write off the monkey.

Getting a mortgage application approved can take a couple of weeks, sometimes longer if yours is not a straightforward case. But many lenders are happy to supply you with a certificate indicating that they are prepared to lend you a certain amount of money, subject to valuation and credit checks. This is known as an *agreement in principle.* You can obtain one of these certificates – valid for up to six months – before you even step foot inside a potential property. This should give you plenty of time to find a property before you have to apply for another agreement in principle.

Doing the full monty or going with the bare minimum – The survey

Before your lender agrees to let you have a mortgage, it insists on a valuation of the property. At this stage you must decide whether you are happy with just this basic valuation or want a more comprehensive survey done, and if so, what type. Your decision will depend on the condition of the property, your own knowledge of buildings, and how much you can afford to spend.

If you opt for a homebuyer's report or structural survey you can often get this done at the same time as the mortgage valuation. This will save time and hassle because only one surveyor will need access to the property. But remember that not all surveyors will be able to carry out both types of survey.

I recommend that you opt for the most extensive survey you can afford. When you compare the cost of a homebuyer's report, for example, to the amount you spend on purchasing the property in the first place, it pales into insignificance. It is true that you are on a tight budget, but ask yourself whether you could afford to put right some extensive (and expensive) problems that emerge only after the property is bought and paid for.

Cheap as chips: The lender's valuation

The valuation report is compulsory. The lender will arrange a local surveyor to carry it out. You have to pay for it – it costs between £150 and £200 – but it benefits the lender. It doesn't tell you anything about the condition of the property, it only reveals whether it is worth what you are hoping to borrow. The valuation ensures that the lender is assigning its money wisely.

If you don't commission a survey of your own and rely solely on the valuation, and serious structural problems are discovered after you have purchased the property, you only have yourself to blame. Yet despite the obvious risks, around 75 per cent of buyers rely on the valuation and don't bother commissioning a fuller survey.

Middle ground: A homebuyer's report

The next step up is the homebuyer's report, halfway between the basic valuation and a full structural survey. As well as telling you whether the purchase price is reasonable, the surveyor gives you a good idea about the condition of a property, whether it's sound or he sees any problems that could need attention, such as damp or subsidence. He'll also suggest what decisions and actions need to be taken, if any, before exchange of contracts.

If you have a specific concern, which is not covered in the homebuyer's report, the surveyor will check this out at extra cost. Make sure you agree the price for this beforehand.

It is worth choosing a homebuyer's report if the property:

- ✔ Is in good condition and doesn't obviously need significant renovation
- ✔ Is conventional in type or of traditional construction

A homebuyer's report will cost from £250 plus VAT for an average-sized property. However, many surveyors call for further specialist reports to cover themselves – to check the electrics or the source of a damp patch, for example. If the surveyor calls for further reports, your lender will insist upon them and you'll have to pay extra for these.

Some surveyors are extremely pessimistic and an inexperienced buyer reading through a surveyor's report may be terrified by its findings. But one advantage of having a proper survey rather than relying on the lender's valuation is that you can chat to your surveyor and ask him to explain any remarks you're concerned about. He'll be able to provide reassurance and advice.

Going over the top: A full structural survey

A structural or building survey is the most comprehensive and detailed. This takes a lot longer than the homebuyer's report as the surveyor examines all facets of the property in great detail from every little crack in the walls to the loft. It's vital if the property:

- Is very old – it was built before 1914
- Is in poor condition and needs a lot of renovation
- Is not of traditional construction; for example, it is a thatched or listed building
- Has been extensively altered
- Is going to be significantly altered by you
- Is very expensive

Expect to pay between £400 and £1,000 plus VAT for a building survey, depending on what you want to know and the size of the property. But it is money well spent if a problem is unearthed. Sometimes the surveyor will recommend that you get a specialist survey done if he thinks a particular issue needs more investigation, such as whether trees growing close to the property will have a negative effect on the foundations and need removing by a tree surgeon.

Conducting searches

Part of your solicitor's job is to find out whether there are any problems that might affect the property and your enjoyment of it. To do this, he will apply to the local authority in which the property is situated to do a local search. This will unearth whether there are any plans for road widening, building a motorway, planning difficulties, tree preservation orders, or compulsory purchase orders in the immediate area. The search also uncovers whether the property received planning permission if any work has been done: This is vital because if not, you may be forced to pull the property down or put it back to it's pre-altered state at a later date.

Searches reveal a lot but they don't reveal everything. If your neighbour is in the process of selling his back garden so that it can be developed into a block of flats, for example, this won't be revealed – even though all the construction noise and coming and going will have an impact on you. You may have to make separate searches of adjoining land, particularly if it's an empty field – ask your solicitor to do this if you're worried as he won't visit the property and see that this may be a possibility.

Local searches can cost you anything in the region of £100 to £150, depending on the local authority and can take a couple of days or several weeks, again according to the local authority.

Lack of cover causes the holiday blues

One of the readers of the newspaper I write for contacted me to warn homebuyers about the perils of not taking out buildings insurance after her own difficult experience. She had made an offer on a house, it had been accepted and everything was proceeding smoothly – or so she thought.

The day arrived when contracts were due to be exchanged: She and her husband thought this would be fairly straightforward so arranged to call into their solicitor's office on the way to the airport (bound for a week's holiday in the West Indies). The tenancy agreement had expired on the property they were renting so their aim was to complete on the purchase the day after they returned from their trip, enabling them to move straight into their new home.

However, all did not go according to plan. Their solicitor asked to see proof of their buildings insurance for the new property but they couldn't provide this as they hadn't arranged cover. As they hadn't bought a property before, they were relying on their mortgage broker to guide them through the process but he hadn't mentioned that they would need buildings insurance before exchange of contracts could take place. With their flight set to leave in a few hours they faced a difficult choice: delay their holiday and stay home to arrange insurance or go on holiday regardless and deal with it when they got back. This they did but it cost them a lot of money: It delayed completion so they had to stay in a hotel for a week while they waited to complete their property purchase.

Remember: arrange your buildings insurance well in advance of exchange of contracts. And try not to leave the country at this critical point in the transaction: otherwise, like this couple, you won't be able to do anything until you get back, which will hold up the sale.

Exchanging contracts

As soon as both solicitors have completed their work, the survey's findings are deemed satisfactory, the searches haven't unearthed any problems, and your mortgage application has been approved, a date is set for completion. You also have to sign the contract. Once this is done, your solicitor will exchange contracts with the seller's solicitor.

This is the point of no return: You can't back out after exchange of contracts unless you are willing to incur significant financial penalties for doing so. If there is any uncertainty in your mind (and if there is, you should have done something about it long before you get to this stage), make sure you don't go any further.

At the point of exchange you electronically transfer your deposit to your solicitor's bank account, along with any outstanding solicitor's fees and stamp duty.

Lining up buildings insurance

After exchange of contracts you are responsible for insuring the property. *Buildings insurance* is the compulsory cover all homeowners with a mortgage must take out on their property to cover the rebuild cost in case the house is destroyed or severely damaged.

Your solicitor will insist that you take out buildings insurance for your new property before you exchange contracts in case anything happens to the property before completion. Often, the seller cancels his buildings insurance at the point of exchange of contracts so if you didn't take out buildings cover, the property isn't insured. If something happens to the property between exchange and completion – such as it burns to the ground – in theory, you will still have to complete on it. It would be a terrible piece of bad luck if this did happen but at least buildings insurance will cover you if such a problem does occur.

Gazumping and How to Avoid It

Even if the seller accepts your offer, you have no legal guarantee that you will end up successfully purchasing the property. Consider this sobering statistic: According to the National Association of Estate Agents, one in three agreed sales in England, Wales, and Northern Ireland does not make it to *exchange of contracts* (where the property is legally transferred from the seller to the buyer). No wonder buying a property is one of the most stressful challenges you ever face.

If you are buying a property in Scotland, your offer is binding (see Chapter 11 for more on the house-buying process there). But in the rest of the UK this isn't the case. Either you or the seller can pull out of the deal right up until contracts are exchanged. *Gazumping* is a situation in which a seller accepts another offer after accepting your offer.

Gazumping is frowned upon but isn't illegal. The Government is hoping that introduction of Home Information Packs (HIPs), otherwise known as seller's packs, will go some way to reducing the risk of being gazumped. This is because HIPs will speed up the house-buying process by making the seller responsible for arranging a survey and local searches before putting a property on the market, so there is less time for another buyer to come in with a higher offer. But no date is fixed for their introduction so you will have to take your own measures to reduce the risk of being gazumped until then.

Being gazumped can be heartbreaking as well as financially costly. You could stand to lose a considerable amount of money because you paid out for a survey, instructed a solicitor, and paid a mortgage application fee. With money tight, you can ill-afford such losses, particularly as you will be back to square one and have to start the house-hunting process all over again.

Because money is in short supply, you have a particularly tough decision to make if you are gazumped: Are you prepared to get involved in a bidding war? You may feel you have to make a higher offer than the rival bidder as you have already invested so much money and can't face losing it. But if you enter a bidding war you end up paying over the odds for a property that probably isn't worth it. And you may have to overstretch yourself to get your hands on the necessary cash if it is over your budget. Either way you are onto a loser from the start: My advice is to step back, assess whether you can afford the extra cash it would take to secure the property and if you can't, cut your losses.

Looking at some reasons buyers are gazumped

When the housing market is buoyant, gazumping is a fairly common practice. The long drawn-out process of buying a property is to blame as it can take as long as 10 to 12 weeks, sometimes longer, to finalise the deal. In a buoyant housing market, where prices increase at an incredible rate, this could mean that a property can fetch several thousand pounds more by the time it comes to exchange of contracts, and if another buyer is prepared to offer this, it may prove too tempting for the seller to refuse.

Under the Estate Agency Act, estate agents are obliged to pass on all offers they receive to the seller of a property, even if the seller has already accepted an offer. So even if the property has been taken off the market because your offer has been accepted, there is still a risk that another buyer who viewed the property before you made an offer will make a bid, which the agent is obliged to pass onto the seller. In some cases, buyers bypass the agent and go straight to the seller anyway. If the seller accepts the later offer, you have been gazumped.

A higher offer can be extremely tempting to a seller, particularly if you have managed to upset him. Don't leave yourself open to being gazumped by giving the seller cause to consider another offer. If you are serious about buying a property, you can't afford to delay.

Avoiding being gazumped

Keeping the seller happy may be the easiest way to avoid being gazumped. You can reduce your chances by ensuring that you don't hold up the purchase in any way. Arrange your finances before making an offer and pre-appoint a solicitor so that you can move forward with the purchase as soon as your offer has been accepted.

Some estate agents have a policy on gazumping and ask clients to sign a contract stating that they will not do it. If you take the trouble to find an agent with such a policy in place, it will increase your peace of mind and could save you hundreds of pounds.

Looking to lock-out agreements

One of the best ways of ensuring that another buyer doesn't outbid you at the last minute is to ask the seller to keep the property off the market for a certain period of time and not accept any offers from other buyers after you have agreed on the price. As part of the deal, you will have to adhere to a strict timetable to complete the purchase.

A lock-out agreement is not an unreasonable request, particularly if you offered the asking price.

If the seller agrees, an 'Under Offer' board should replace the 'For Sale' sign outside the property or in the estate agent's window. Check this has been done and if it hasn't, make sure this is rectified. If the property is advertised with more than one estate agent, make sure all of them know it is under offer and no longer on the market.

Buying insurance

If you are really worried about being gazumped, there are a number of insurance schemes available that pay out if the purchase falls through after your offer has been accepted. For a one-off premium of around £30, you can take out a protection policy providing around £400-worth of cover for legal and valuation costs if the seller causes the deal to fall through.

Several insurers, mortgage lenders, and brokers offer buyer and seller protection policies. If you are interested, ask your lender or mortgage broker for more details. But remember: You must take the policy out before you instruct your solicitor to ensure your legal fees are covered if the sale does fall through.

In a strong housing market, buyer and seller protection policies can be extremely attractive as you get a lot of cover for a relatively small premium. But given that money is very tight, weigh up how likely it is that the sale will fall through. If the market is sluggish or the property you are buying has languished on the market for several months you might think that the risk of being gazumped is minimal and decide the cost is an unnecessary extra.

Paying for a pre-contract deposit agreement

One way of minimising the chances of the seller pulling out once he has accepted your offer is to establish a pre-contract deposit agreement, which you can ask the estate agent to arrange.

The way it works is that you and the seller each hand over a small percentage of the agreed purchase price – typically 1.5 per cent – to a third party such as a solicitor. If either party subsequently pulls out of the deal without good reason, they forfeit this sum to the other party. An example of an acceptable reason to pull out is that the survey indicates that the property is not worth what you offered for it. Acceptable reasons for pulling out should be written into the pre-contract deposit agreement, along with a date by which you agree to exchange contracts.

Both you and the seller benefit from a pre-contract deposit agreement. You know the seller won't accept a higher offer after you have shelled out hundreds of pounds on a survey and legal fees. And the seller knows you are serious about the purchase and not going to change your mind at the last minute after his property has been off the market for several weeks.

Making the seller your new best friend

The best way to ensure you don't get gazumped is to get the seller on your side. There are several ways of doing this:

- ✔ Offer the full asking price; prove you have the cash by getting an agreement in principle *and* that you can move quickly. That way you won't look like a timewaster.

- ✔ Don't fuss over minor points. If the seller won't leave you the lounge curtains that you really like, let them go. Find out where he got them from and buy your own.

- ✔ Instead of imposing a timeframe onto the seller that suits you, make it clear that you are accommodating and will fit in with his plans, where possible. If this means kipping in your brother's spare room for a couple of weeks because you have to move out of your current accommodation ahead of moving into your new home, it's not ideal but it's a small price to pay in the long run.

- ✔ Don't underestimate the power of guilt. It sounds cynical, but attempt to establish a friendly relationship with the seller so that he would feel bad about doing the dirty on you and accepting an offer from a rival buyer.

✔ Keep in regular contact with the seller and/or estate agent so that you know exactly what is going on and whether other buyers are sniffing around the property once your offer has been accepted. Establish a regular flow of information: Tell the agent when your survey has been completed or you've received a formal mortgage offer from your lender. This will inspire confidence in the seller that you are serious and the wheels are turning smoothly.

Completing the Sale

This is it: the day the property legally becomes yours, the keys are handed over, and you can move in. Completion can happen the same day as exchange of contracts or several weeks later, depending on what you and the seller agree. Usually, though, completion takes place between one and four weeks after exchange of contracts.

In the run-up to completion, you should arrange for the meters in the property to be read and ensure that all the utilities – gas, electricity, water, and telephone – are transferred over to your name from the date of completion. You don't want to spend your first night in your new home sitting in the dark, now do you?

Chapter 10

Conveyancing in England, Wales, and Northern Ireland

*O*nce the seller accepts your offer, the legal process of transferring the property to you, known as *conveyancing,* begins. Most buyers use a solicitor to take care of this but you can do it yourself. In this chapter, I help you decide if you have what it takes and how to find a good solicitor if you decide you haven't.

Taking a Look at the Legalities

Conveyancing is the transfer of *good title* – the legal right to possession – from the seller to you. It is not always a straight-forward process. Sometimes a lot of detective work is involved and it can take months to gather together all the necessary information. Even though your solicitor does the bulk of the work, hold-ups, or the impression that he isn't treating your case as a priority, all make for an incredibly stressful time.

Conveyancing can take a frustratingly long time, and HM Land Registry and the Lord Chancellor's office are working on plans to speed it up by introducing electronic conveyancing, or e-conveyancing, over the next decade. This will make the process faster by replacing the endless reams of paper that are passed back and forth between solicitors with contracts and deeds that can be signed electronically. But until e-conveyancing is introduced, you just have to put up with the laborious and time-consuming process.

 Find a solicitor or licensed conveyancer before you make an offer – ideally *before* you start house hunting (see 'Finding a Solicitor or Licensed Conveyancer' later in this chapter). Otherwise you may hold up proceedings. Also make sure that the person you hire isn't the same one the seller is using so that there's no conflict of interest: Your lender will insist upon this. If you have the same solicitor one of you can switch to another partner in the firm. Or, to be absolutely sure, you may prefer to use a solicitor from another practice.

Setting out the solicitor's role

Your solicitor liaises with the seller's solicitor and passes on various documents for you to sign. You need to do this promptly. The process is long enough without adding in delays – it can take 12 weeks between an offer being accepted and exchange of contracts partly because buyers and sellers delay returning documents. Your solicitor must ensure that nothing in the contract or lease (see 'Understanding the difference between freehold and leasehold' later in this chapter) or anything unearthed by the local searches causes you problems. Your solicitor is responsible for

✔ Checking the legal jargon in the title deeds and ensuring that the contract is legal.

✔ Finding out the property's background via planning and title searches to ensure planning permission was received before it was built and that the seller is, in fact, in a position to sell the property to you.

✔ Making sure there is nothing in the lease (if it is a leasehold property) that affects your ownership of the property.

✔ Helping you renegotiate the price if problems crop up.

Deciphering the draft contract

Your solicitor comes into the picture when he receives the draft contract from the seller's solicitor. This is the first version of what will become the final contract, which confirms the transfer of the property from the seller to you. The draft contract typically goes through many changes and alterations before buyer and seller agree to all its terms and conditions. After everything is agreed, the final contract is drawn up for both parties to sign.

The two main parts to a draft contract are:

✓ **Particulars of sale:** A description of the property, and of any fixtures and fittings included, and whether it is freehold or leasehold (see the upcoming 'Understanding the difference between freehold and leasehold' section).

✓ **Conditions of sale:** Details of the proposed completion date and the deposit you must pay when contracts are exchanged.

The draft contract should also spell out whether you have agreed to purchase certain items, such as carpets and curtains, and whether you are paying an extra sum for these.

A copy of the title deeds, a document stating who currently owns the property, usually accompanies the draft contract. Your solicitor needs to check this to ensure that the seller actually owns the property and has the right to sell it.

Your solicitor works through the draft contract and raises any questions with the seller's solicitor. After everything is settled, your solicitor sends you a copy of the draft contract, which you then need to check carefully to ensure that everything you agreed with the seller is included. The draft contract can go back and forth for some time.

If something has been omitted from the draft contract and you don't tell your solicitor, you have no comeback once the contract is signed. So, if the seller promised to throw in the carpets, make sure you get this in writing.

Moving on to local searches and Land Registry

At the same time as the draft contract goes backwards and forwards between solicitors, your solicitor will also conduct a number of local searches and contact the Land Registry to check that the seller is in a position to sell the property to you, and that there are no conflicting rights to the land the property is built upon.

The cost of local searches depends on the size of the property and the local authority where it is situated. These costs are non-negotiable and searches tend to take a couple of weeks, although this can be longer if the local authority is inefficient or busy. The cost of these is payable to your solicitor just before completion, when you pay the solicitor's fees. For the following searches on a property purchase of £100,000, expect to pay in the region of:

- **Local authority search fee:** The local search reveals whether planning permission was given for the property to be built in the first place and whether there are any plans to build a motorway or other roads within 200m of the property: £144

- **Drainage search fee:** Your solicitor applies to the Water Authority for this search to discover whether the waste water goes into a public or private sewer: £30

- **Bankruptcy search fee:** Your lender will insist that your solicitor does a search to ensure that you aren't bankrupt: £2

- **Land Registry search:** This is paid to the Land Registry to check that the property is in the seller's name and identifies any outstanding mortgage to be repaid by the seller: £4.

- **Land Registry fee:** This is charged by the Land Registry for issuing a certificate registering the property in your name once the purchase has been completed. Charges are stepped, rising according to the cost of the property: £100.

If you want your purchase to go through quickly, you can speed up the searches by employing a private search company to gather information for your solicitor. But you'll have to pay an extra charge. Onesearch Direct guarantees to complete a local search within five days for £100 on top of the usual cost of the local searches (www.onesearchdirect.co.uk).

Local searches become invalid after about three months, so your solicitor may need to conduct the searches again if your purchase drags on longer.

Looking at Land Registry

Your solicitor contacts the Land Registry twice during the conveyancing process – once to search whether the property is registered in the seller's name and that he's in a position to sell it, and once to register the property in your name, after the purchase has been completed.

Instigating local searches

If you've set your heart on a house in a quiet, cosy cul-de-sac, you may not be so keen when you discover that there are plans for a motorway to run beside it. Local searches are designed to reveal whether such plans are in existence *before* you buy your new home: If something is planned that would be detrimental to your enjoyment of the property, you may be gutted but at least you can pull out before exchange of contracts so you won't have to put up with traffic roaring past your bedroom window.

Local searches reveal:

- ✔ Whether the council has plans for a motorway at the end of the road or there are planning restrictions affecting your ability to renovate or extend the property.

- ✔ Whether planning permission was received for the property before it was built, or any extensions or conversions in need of consent. If they weren't, the council may insist the property is knocked down or the extension removed.

- ✔ If the water drainage system is working and who owns the drains, via the water authority search.

The location of the property determines whether other searches are necessary, such as commons searches or coal mining.

Local searches aren't comprehensive. They only cover the property itself and roads within 200m of the property – they don't check the surrounding area. Your property may be built on contaminated land but not all councils keep a detailed register of this, so you may not discover it. You won't find out about a waste disposal plant planned for the adjoining land or whether there is planning permission for a block of flats on adjoining land, either.

Revolutionising house buying with seller's packs

The proposed Home Information Packs (also known as seller's packs), will revolutionise the house-buying process and make home buying easier for first-time buyers on a budget. The seller's packs dictate that the seller pay for the survey and local searches, not the buyer. This will speed up the conveyancing process as this will be done before the property goes on the market – and save buyers hundreds of pounds.

Under the proposals, the seller also has to provide details of works carried out and a copy of the lease (if relevant) before he puts his property up for sale. At the time of writing, much detailed work still needs doing on the legislation so it's unlikely the packs will be introduced before 2006.

Get your solicitor to check if anything – such as planning permission for a supermarket – is registered against any vacant land close to the property. Your solicitor won't visit the property himself so you have to tell him if you have concerns so that he can investigate them.

Critics query whether the buyer will be able to rely on information provided by the seller and wonder whether sellers will be dissuaded from putting their property on the market in the first place if they have to spend hundreds of pounds before doing so. And if the property doesn't sell within a set period of time, that money is wasted and the seller has to pay for them to be done again. But seller's packs will make the process less uncertain for buyers and save them money. A buyer gets the complete picture *before* making an offer and so knows there are no potential nasties. This will increase the chances of the sale going through and reduce the risk of being gazumped (see Chapter 9 for more details of this) because completion should happen much sooner.

Understanding the difference between freehold and leasehold

The draft contract states whether the property is freehold or leasehold:

✔ **Freehold** is straightforward – you own the property and the land it is on up to its boundaries. As long as you act within the law, you can do what you like on your property. Most properties in England, Wales, and Northern Ireland are freehold.

✔ **Leasehold** is more complicated. With leasehold, you buy the right to live in the property for a fixed number of years – the length of the lease. Leases vary in length: many run for more than 99 years, while some have 999 years left on them. Mortgage lenders usually don't let you borrow against a lease shorter than 75 years.

Once the lease expires, the property reverts to the landlord. The landlord retains ownership of the building and the land during the lease: He imposes ground rent and an annual service charge. The service charge covers the upkeep of the communal areas of the building, such as cleaning of the entrance hall, stairs and corridors and upkeep of the lift (if there is one). It also covers the cost incurred by the landlord for arranging buildings insurance for the property.

There are two million leaseholds in the UK (except in Scotland), so you may well end up with one.

Conveyancing on a freehold property is more straightforward than on a leasehold property because there are less potential problems. But in the majority of cases, buying a leasehold property doesn't present insurmountable difficulties. As long as your solicitor studies the lease closely to make sure there are no nasty clauses likely to affect the value of your investment, you should be okay.

Finding a Solicitor or Licensed Conveyancer

If you've already got a good solicitor you may think he is the perfect choice to do your conveyancing. But while the legal work involved in transferring a property from seller to buyer is often regarded as one of the more mundane jobs in the legal profession and totally lacking in glamour, it is a very exact science and not one to trust to any but a specialist.

Most mortgage lenders insist that you use a qualified solicitor to do your conveyancing and that there are at least two partners in the practice who are members of the Law Society. The rest is down to you but I suggest you choose a solicitor who specialises in conveyancing. In England and Wales you could use a licensed conveyancer instead of a solicitor if you prefer: These offer the same services as a solicitor but are limited to house purchasing.

The estate agent handling the sale or your lender may be able to recommend a solicitor who can offer you a special rate. You are under no obligation to use this solicitor so don't feel pressured to give in to the agent's insistence. However, if the fees seem reasonable, he may be worth considering.

Find out as much as you can about a solicitor and his practice before instructing him. Nobody can say for sure how long conveyancing will take, but you need to get an idea and if the solicitor is very vague, find somebody else. If he's eager he's more likely to get on with the job. Find out who will handle your case on a day-to-day basis: Quite often it's an office junior but you should find out how involved your solicitor will be – if he will be overseeing this person closely. Try to assess how professional and efficient the solicitor is because you need to deal with him a lot in coming weeks.

Personal recommendation is the best way of choosing a solicitor: A solicitor a friend speaks highly of *after* buying property must be all right. Likewise, if someone tells you they've had a bad experience with a solicitor, give that solicitor a wide berth. If you don't have a personal recommendation, try the Law Society (www.lawsociety.org.uk) or call 020 7242 1222 for a database of solicitors in England and Wales. In Northern Ireland, try the Law Society of Northern Ireland (www.lawsoc-ni.org) or call 028 90 231614. Or contact the Council for Licensed Conveyancers (CLC) on 01245 349599 or www.conveyancer.gov.uk.

Knowing that local isn't necessary

If you use a solicitor who is local to the property, he should know the area well and whether there are likely to be any planning restrictions. You can also speed up the process by popping into his office with documents or to sign paperwork – rather than relying on the post.

However, you don't *have* to use a local solicitor, as there isn't much face-to-face contact, if any. This is good news if your local solicitor is rushed off his feet and unable to take on your business. Conveyancing tends to be done over the phone, by fax, and the post. You need to provide your solicitor with proof of your identity but you can do this by sending your passport via registered post.

Considering legal costs

While the cost of local searches and Land Registry fees are non-negotiable, solicitors' fees vary considerably, so get a couple of written quotes before instructing one. Solicitors tend to calculate their fees as a percentage of the purchase price, so the more expensive the property you buy, the more you pay to the solicitor. As a general rule, expect to pay about £550 plus VAT if you are purchasing a £100,000 property. If it is leasehold, expect to pay another £75 plus VAT to cover the extra work involved in checking the lease. Don't forget that you will probably also have to pay stamp duty upon completion: The amount depends on the purchase price (see Chapter 2 for details on stamp duty).

Solicitors with swanky offices in prime locations tend to charge higher fees than those with basic offices in suburban towns. As it's not necessary to instruct your local solicitor, shop around.

While you don't want to pay over the odds for conveyancing because money is tight, beware of paying too little. It's tempting to opt for the cheapest quote but this solicitor may not charge much because he doesn't offer a good service. He may cut corners in order to offer this price, or take on more work than he can cope with in order to make his money up. Yet a very expensive solicitor isn't necessarily better: That bustling, pricey City firm may be too busy to treat your case as a priority and you can end up at the bottom of a very big pile. A small practice dedicated to conveyancing may produce much better results.

A number of Internet sites offer a fixed price for conveyancing, and these prices are cheaper than using a high-street solicitor. But this is a little like sticking a pin in the list of solicitors who specialise in conveyancing in the *Yellow Pages*: You take potluck. Stick to recommendations from family and friends to minimise the chance of problems down the line.

Do-It-Yourself Conveyancing

If the thought of legal fees sends a shiver down your spine because of the cost involved, consider joining an increasing number of buyers who do their own conveyancing. Not every lender let's you do this, however, unless you have legal experience. Check with your lender first and consider doing your own legal work only if you are buying a vacant freehold property: Leasehold properties are too complicated.

If the seller is doing his own conveyancing, you should think twice about doing the same. If two of you do your own conveyancing on the same transaction, a whole host of legal problems can arise that neither of you can deal with.

Doing your own conveyancing is labour-intensive as the work is very detailed but it saves you time in the long run. You are likely to move faster than a solicitor as it's in your interests to do so. You can respond to letters and requests from the seller's solicitor quicker if you're not reliant on your solicitor to pass them on to you. Let's face it: The conveyancing on your house purchase ranks much higher among your list of priorities than your solicitor's.

In practical terms, much of conveyancing is just a matter of asking the right people for information. Obtaining local searches is fairly straightforward: Simply contact the local council's planning department. It doesn't cost you a penny either, saving you a couple of hundred pounds. Search forms are fairly standard, so once you obtain the ones you need it's not much work adapting them to your particular property purchase. These forms are available from legal stationers. Contact the Land Registry for the forms necessary to register ownership of your property (www.landreg.org.uk).

Take your time and read through the contract and lease thoroughly. If you don't understand something, raise it with the seller's solicitor. There are plenty of good reference books available too, and the Internet is a useful source of information.

Even if you do your own conveyancing, your mortgage lender is likely to insist that you pay its solicitor's fees for preparing the mortgage deeds. Lenders usually allow the buyer's solicitor to do this, saving you the cost of paying for a separate solicitor to act for the lender. But the lender won't allow you to draw up the mortgage deed yourself so you might not save as much money as you think by doing your own conveyancing.

The solicitor does what he does during the conveyancing process for a reason, so make sure you do everything he would. It's foolhardy to assume that the local searches are the most important part of the process so that's what you are going to concentrate your energies on to the detriment of everything else. If you haven't got time to do it all, I recommend you don't attempt any of it – leave the conveyancing to a solicitor who will be more thorough.

It's worth getting a second opinion after you finish your conveyancing. You may be able to persuade a solicitor to go through your paperwork for a fixed fee of around £100.

You are responsible if you get it wrong so you need to be careful. As you are spending so much money on a property, you *must* make sure you get it right – so think seriously about whether you are up to doing your own conveyancing.

Completing the Final Steps

Once your solicitor approves the draft contract, the seller's solicitor draws up a final contract for you and the seller to sign. The contract tends to be full of jargon and can be difficult to understand so you may be tempted not to read it. But you have a lot of money at stake so it's important that you do read it carefully. If anything is not clear, ask. It is your solicitor's job to answer these queries: This is what you pay him for.

Exchanging contracts

Before contracts can be exchanged, several things must have happened. These are

- ✔ The lender has accepted the property valuation and you are happy with the results of your survey.

- ✔ You have received a formal written mortgage offer from your lender and have funds in place to pay the deposit.

> ✔ Both solicitors are satisfied that the conveyancing is complete.
>
> ✔ A completion date has been set and is stated in the final contract.

The final version of the contract is then sent to both parties to sign and contracts are exchanged, usually over the phone. The deal is legally binding on both sides, which means you can't back out. To make sure you don't, you must also pay a non-refundable deposit: This is usually 10 per cent of the purchase price, although you may be able to negotiate a lower figure, such as 5 per cent. The deposit is subtracted from the amount you pay on completion. Solicitors may accept a cheque but some demand electronic transfer by BACS (the Banks Automated Clearing Service), which takes a couple of days, or CHAPS (the Clearing House Automated Payments System), if you need it the same day. This costs around £25.

Your solicitor forwards the deposit to the seller's solicitor, who holds it until completion.

Realising completion

Most buyers and sellers arrange for completion to take place four weeks after contracts are exchanged but this is not set in stone: You can complete the same day if you wish. The date needs to suit both of you and give you time to book the removal van, notify utility companies, and do all that packing.

Avoid completing on a Friday. It may seem sensible to move just before the weekend but if there are problems, such as a leak, you'll have to wait until Monday to call out a plumber – unless you are prepared to pay extortionate call-out fees over the weekend.

Try not to go on holiday at this stage: Your solicitor may need to get hold of you if he has any last-minute questions or documents for you to sign. If you are unobtainable, completion may be delayed.

On completion day, you pay the balance of what you owe (minus the deposit) to your solicitor, who prepares the mortgage documents and arranges for the loan to be available. If you are putting down your own funds, you must transfer these to your solicitor. You also pay your solicitor's fees and VAT, stamp duty, and any other outstanding charges. Your solicitor carries out last-minute searches and enquiries to ensure nothing is registered against the seller at the Land Registry, such as an undisclosed mortgage.

Contracts are now exchanged: The seller moves out, you get the keys and can move in. Your solicitor gets the transfer stamped (and pays your stamp duty) and the title deeds put in your name and sent to your mortgage lender. If the property is leasehold, your solicitor ensures the freeholder is informed that the sale has been completed and your name goes on the lease. You have survived the torturous house-buying process – congratulations!

Restricted parking

When I bought my flat I also bought an off-road parking space for £5,000. I received my contract and struggled through it, trying to make sense of the legal jargon. But while there was a lot that I didn't understand, I did notice that there was no mention of my parking space, even though the cost had been added onto the flat's purchase price.

When I told my solicitor he apologised because he'd 'forgotten' to include it. He was acting for several buyers who were all purchasing flats in the block at the same time and to minimise his workload, he changed the names and flat numbers and sent the same contract to all of us.

If I hadn't noticed that my parking space wasn't included and signed the contract, I would have had a difficult job of proving that I was entitled to a space.

Chapter 11

Buying Property in Scotland

*T*he legal process of buying property in Scotland is very different to the rest of the UK. It is considered to be far superior to the outdated practice in England, Wales, and Northern Ireland because it all happens much quicker. Gazumping (see Chapter 9 for more details) is virtually unheard of as a binding contract is formed when the seller accepts your offer, and the sale is completed within weeks rather than months.

You must be absolutely certain that you want to buy a property because once your offer is accepted you can't pull out. And because you arrange the survey before making an offer (it plays a part in deciding how much you bid), changing your mind means even more cash down the drain. Money is tight enough without throwing it away because you haven't thought things through. In this chapter, I guide you through the process so that you can avoid the major pitfalls.

Becoming an Owner-Occupier

Nearly every Scottish property is sold on an owner-occupier basis. There are no freeholds or leaseholds (see Chapter 10 for more details on these), so you don't have to worry about a complicated lease slowing down your property purchase. However, in Scotland there is a system of *feudal tenure,* which is set to be replaced with outright ownership from the end of November 2004, when the Abolition of Feudal Tenure (Scotland) Act 2000 comes into force.

Under the feudal system, the property owner – the *vassal* – holds the property in a hierarchical structure, so he doesn't own it outright. The original landowner or developer – the *superior* – has a higher interest in the feudal chain. The superior may have set out conditions to the land or property's future use, which the vassal can't remove unless the superior agrees and the vassal pays him a fee. These conditions are restrictive, such as preventing the homeowner from extending their property or running a business from home without the superior's permission.

When the new Act is fully effective, the vassal will own the property outright and superiority interests will disappear. Homeowners may have to pay the superior compensation for their loss, although it is not yet clear how much. For more information, go to the Scottish Executive's Web site (www. scotland.gov.uk).

If you buy a flat, you should know that communal areas – such as the roof, stairs, and hallways – are owned equally by the proprietors of the flats in the block or converted house. If you buy a flat you are jointly responsible for the maintenance of these areas, so during a viewing you should pay close attention to them (your surveyor should also check them out). As well as your joint responsibilities, you own the external walls of your flat and are responsible for their maintenance. The proprietors of the other flats obviously have an interest in this being done. The title deeds should spell out how maintenance and repair costs are split between flats.

Finding a Solicitor

The solicitor's role is much greater in Scotland than it is when buying property elsewhere in the UK – and starts much earlier on. Because an offer is legally binding, you make an offer through your solicitor. Thus, you need to find a solicitor before arranging viewings so that when you find a property you like, you can make an offer quickly.

Although you can do your own *conveyancing* – legally transfer-ring property from seller to buyer – I don't advise it unless you know what you're doing.

Most buyers use a solicitor to do their legal work. You can use an independent qualified conveyancer – who specialises in property transfer, unlike most solicitors who can handle other aspects of the law as well – but these are rare. To find a licensed conveyancer, contact the Scottish Conveyancing and Executory Services Board on 0131 556 1945.

Solicitors don't charge a fixed fee for their services: Prices vary to such an extent that it's difficult to give a general idea as to the likely cost. Therefore, you should obtain two or three quotes for the work and ask how much the outlays (the searches) will be, as these can be substantial. It is also worth asking how much the solicitor charges if the sale falls through: You instruct him at such an early stage in the proceedings there is a strong chance this may happen.

The best way to find a solicitor is through personal recom-mendation, but if you don't have anyone you can ask, contact the Law Society of Scotland, which provides a list of solicitors in its Directory of General Services (0131 476 8137 or www. lawscot.org.uk). Or try the SiteFinder directory, which has lists of experienced solicitors and can be found in your local solicitors' property centre.

You can't use an English solicitor in Scotland because they aren't allowed to practice north of the border. But if you are moving to Scotland from England, your English solicitor may be able to recommend a Scottish one.

Finding the Property of Your Dreams

The process of finding a property in Scotland is similar to that in the rest of the UK, although you are more likely to find a property in a solicitors' property centre than an estate agent's window or in the local paper.

Scanning solicitors' property centres

Solicitors' property centres tend to be located in shopping centres in major towns and cities. Properties are displayed and described in the same way as in an estate agent's window, but the name of the solicitor handling the sale is also included. The centre doesn't sell anything – not even property – it simply provides details of properties for sale. Staff can give only general advice on buying. For further information on a particular property you must contact the solicitor handling the sale.

Solicitors' property centres enable you to view thousands of properties on the books of many solicitors, saving yourself time and effort. For example, the Edinburgh Solicitors Property Centre, which handled 92 per cent of property sales in the city in Autumn 2003, has 265 member solicitor firms, with properties advertised in showrooms in Edinburgh, Dunfermline, Kirkcaldy, Stirling, and Falkirk. It also advertises thousands of properties on its Web site (www.espc.co.uk).

Use of solicitors' property centres is free: Register online for e-mail alerts so you know when a property that might suit you becomes available. For a list of solicitors' property centres, contact the Law Society of Scotland (0131 226 7411) or visit the Scottish Solicitors Property Centres' Web site (www.sspc.co.uk).

Engaging with estate agents

Estate agents work in the same way in Scotland as in England, Wales, and Northern Ireland and you should bear the same things in mind when dealing with them (see Chapter 8 for more tips on using an estate agent). Use an agent who is a member of the National Association of Estate Agents (NAEA) to give you some comeback if you have to make a complaint (www.naea.co.uk or call 01926 496800). If you don't get anywhere with your complaint, contact the Citizens Advice Scotland (www.cas.org.uk or 0131 550 1000).

Estate agents write the description of the property, known as the *property particulars,* which includes the number and type of rooms, their size, and any other little details they feel may be of interest. If you don't understand something, ask. If you like the sound of a property you must go and view it before you contemplate making an offer (see Chapter 8 for details on what to look for during viewings and the questions you should ask). If you still aren't sure, don't be afraid to go back again and again until you are certain either way.

Some of the biggest estate agents in Edinburgh contribute to *Real Homes*, a fortnightly list of properties for sale. You can obtain a copy from the office of any one of these agents.

Reading newspapers

All of the major Scottish papers, such as *The Scotsman* and *The Herald,* carry sizeable weekly property sections and extensive property Web sites, which are updated daily. You can search hundreds of properties by price, size, and region on The Scotsman's and Scotland on Sunday's Web site: `http://property.Scotsman.com`. The sister Web site of the *Sunday Herald* also enables you to take a virtual tour of properties for sale (`www.s1homes.com`).

Don't forget to check the local papers as they often carry a good selection of properties for sale in the area you are interested in.

Getting the Order Right

Because you're committed to a purchase once the seller accepts your offer, it's important not to make one until your finances are arranged and you're certain you want the property. It's worth getting your finances agreed in principle *before* your first viewing; in that way, you won't lose out on your dream home because you couldn't sort out the mortgage in time to make an offer. The best way of finding a good mortgage is to use an independent broker (see Chapter 4 for details).

You don't need a firm offer from the lender at this stage but an *agreement in principle* – a certificate stating that the lender is prepared to lend you a specific amount of cash. You can then start house hunting knowing how much you can afford. You also shouldn't have too much trouble finalising the mortgage once you find a property.

Noting interest

When you find a property you really like, your first phone call shouldn't be to tell your family and friends how excited you are but to your solicitor. Your solicitor contacts the seller's solicitor or estate agent to *note interest*. This gives you the chance to make an offer before the seller accepts one from another buyer.

Completing your mortgage application

Once interest is noted, fill out your mortgage application form (you should already have an agreement in principle). Do this without delay and return it with a cheque for the arrangement fee, if required. If you haven't sorted out a mortgage yet, do so immediately and hope it can be done quickly enough.

The lender arranges for a valuation of the property to ensure it is worth the amount you want to borrow. The valuation covers the lender's back, although you pay for it. It doesn't give any indication of the condition of the property; you need to arrange a survey to discover this.

Don't make an offer before arranging your finances. Doing so may commit you to a purchase you don't have the funds to pay for.

Surveying first, offering after

In Scotland, the seller is not obliged to point out faults in the property, so you need to arrange a survey to unearth these. Unlike in England, Wales, and Northern Ireland though, the survey is arranged *before* you make an offer. Offers are binding so if you discover structural faults after you make one – tough.

It may be tempting to save money by not arranging a survey, particularly as there is no guarantee your offer will be successful. But if the property has serious faults, you'll regret it.

The best way to find a surveyor or valuer is through personal recommendation. But if you don't have one, use a surveyor belonging to a professional body so you have comeback if problems arise. Check for membership of the Royal Institution of Chartered Surveyors (RICS) – the letters ARICS (associate) or FRICS (fellow) after his name. For a list of RICS-registered surveyors, contact RICS Scotland on 0131 225 7078.

 RICS Scotland publishes a free leaflet explaining the different types of survey: *Buying property? Then you need a survey.* For a copy, contact RICS Scotland (see above) or access it via the Web site (www.rics-scotland.org.uk).

The surveys available are similar to those in the rest of the UK:

- ✔ **Valuation report:** This is compulsory and carried out on behalf of the lender to ensure the property is worth what you want to borrow. Expect to pay around £150 for this. It provides no other information regarding the condition of the property.

- ✔ **Homebuyer survey and Valuation:** Most buyers opt for one of these surveys, which cost between £250 and £400. The Homebuyer report is cost-effective, standardised, and compact, telling you what condition the property is in and how much it is worth. It's similar to the home-buyer's report that you can have done in the rest of the UK (see Chapter 9 for more on surveys).

- ✔ **Building survey:** This is the most extensive and expensive survey, costing anything between £500 and £1,000. A valuation isn't included, unless you ask for it. Buyers rarely commission a building survey but if you are buying a very old or unusual property, you should consider doing so. (For more on structural surveys, see Chapter 9.)

If the survey reveals problems, it may be worth the extra expense of instructing a surveyor to investigate further.

Negotiating an offer

If the survey doesn't uncover major problems and your lender is happy with the valuation, you're ready to make an offer. Even if the survey raised problems you may still want to make a – lower – offer.

After you decide how much you want to offer (see the following sections for advice), your solicitor informs the seller's solicitor in writing. Aside from the amount, the offer includes a number of clauses to address such issues as when you wish to move in – the *date of entry* – and the fixtures and fittings you want included in the sale. Your solicitor should also include *qualifications* or conditions with the offer that allow you to withdraw from the purchase if the property turns out to be adversely affected by local authority proposals or notices, such as whether there are any planning proposals that might affect the property (see the 'Beginning the conveyancing process' section later on for more information on local authority issues).

The seller may give a qualified acceptance to your offer – accepting some terms and rejecting others. Letters – or *missives* – continue to go backwards and forwards until an agreement is reached that is satisfactory to both sides.

Once everything is agreed, a *bargain* is made – the equivalent of exchanging contracts. The bargain is binding so if you back out you will have to pay compensation, unless the conveyancing process reveals complications, such as a problem with the title deeds so that your solicitor isn't happy with the title you are offered. No deposits are required in Scotland, unless you are buying a brand-new property, when the builder may insist upon it.

This is why it is vital that your mortgage application is completed before you make an offer as conclusion of missives can happen quickly, leaving you little time to arrange your finances. Don't forget that you will need extra cash to cover solicitor's fees, charges for searches, stamp duty, and the deposit, if you are putting one down.

Offering more than the asking price

In England, Wales, and Northern Ireland, sellers usually expect buyers to offer less than the asking price so they often set the price higher than the amount they're happy to accept to allow for this. But in Scotland bids are invited *above* the asking price or *upset price* – the minimum which will be considered. Very rarely, the price is *fixed*, usually when a builder or developer is selling a property. There is no negotiation if the price is fixed – the first buyer offering that amount is the one who gets the property.

When the seller invites bids above the asking price, it's worth bearing in mind that he may have set the price low in order to encourage interest, and the actual purchase price may be as much as 20 or 30 per cent higher. If the housing market is strong, or the property is highly sought after, expect to pay more than the upset to secure it.

When more than one buyer notes interest in a property, sealed bids are used to determine which buyer succeeds. The seller's solicitor fixes a closing date and time by which you must make a written offer. If you miss the deadline, you miss out. The seller's solicitor or estate agent informs your solicitor shortly after the deadline as to whether your offer has been successful or not.

You get only one shot at a bid, so get it right. You don't want to pay over the odds as you are relying on a mortgage and the lender won't let you borrow more than the property is worth. But you must also ensure that you bid high enough to have a good chance of winning. The trouble is you won't know what the other buyers are bidding.

Instead of bidding a round number, go just above this to see off competitors who bid around this mark. For example, instead of bidding £180,000, try £180,101.

Do some research before you make your bid. Use the survey results to determine what the property is worth. Take into account the upset price. Find out from your solicitor what other properties in the area are fetching and how many buyers are after this one. If there is a lot of interest, your bid should be higher than if there is only one other buyer.

Ask your solicitor's opinion. You don't have to follow his advice – the final decision is yours – but it is worth listening to him as he has done this before.

The highest offer is usually successful but not always. Other factors such as the date of entry, which may be more convenient for the seller than the one suggested by the highest bidder, may swing a lower offer.

Offering below the asking price

Although money is tight and you don't want to pay over the odds, if you offer below the upset, or asking price, you've little chance of success – unless the property has been on the market for some time. Find out whether this is the case (your solicitor should know) before making a lower offer.

You may also be justified in making a lower offer if the survey unearths that the property has many problems. If significant building work is required, get a couple of quotes from builders. Once you know the extent of the problem, you can decide how much you are prepared to pay for the property.

Avoid paying more than the property is worth, particularly if you'll have to spend a lot on repairs later on.

Beginning the conveyancing process

The next step for your solicitor is to check certain documents to ensure that the property can be legally sold to you and that the local authority doesn't have any plans adversely affecting it. The areas to investigate include:

- **Title deeds:** The solicitor checks whether he is happy with the title you are being offered. If the deeds reveal that the seller doesn't actually own the property, or owns it jointly with someone else, she may not be in a position to sell it to you, and the solicitor will query this.

- **Search:** This document is provided by the seller and details the history of the property. It states when each sale occurred and whether there are any outstanding charges on any loans taken out to purchase the property.

- **Property Enquiry Certificates:** Like local authority searches, these are provided by the seller and confirm whether there are any planning proposals that could affect the property.

- **Building warrants or certificates of completion:** Your solicitor will check whether there are any relating to the property.

If your solicitor is happy with the findings, he drafts a *disposition* transferring ownership of the property to you. He will also act for your lender, passing on details of the property title and preparing the *standard security* – the lender's mortgage deed. He will also arrange for the mortgage to be ready at date of entry and get you to sign the mortgage documents.

You are responsible for insuring the property after a bargain has been made. Make sure you have buildings insurance for the property from this point to cover the cost of rebuilding it if disaster strikes (see Chapter 9 for details of this insurance).

Preparing for the date of entry

A fortnight before the date of entry your solicitor will tell you how much money is needed to complete the purchase. You must pay:

- ✔ **The deposit:** How much depends on your savings and the lender's requirements. Some demand 5 or 10 per cent.

- ✔ **Solicitor's fees:** Don't forget that you will also have to pay Value Added Tax (17.5 per cent) on top.

- ✔ **Stamp duty:** This is payable on properties costing more than £60,000. (See Chapter 9 for rates.)

- ✔ **Search and registration charges:** To reimburse your solicitor for drawing up the disposition and registering the title in your name.

The *date of entry* is the day you've been waiting for! You get the keys for the property and can move in. The date of entry tends to be the same as the *date of settlement*, or the date the sale is completed.

The day before the date of settlement, you must pay your solicitor the deposit, his fees, and the cost of the local searches.

Your solicitor will transfer funds equivalent to the full purchase price to the seller's solicitor. In return, he will receive the title deeds – these are sent to your mortgage lender – the disposition, which proves the property has been transferred to you, and the keys.

The property is then yours! All your solicitor has to do is register the disposition and standard security in the General Register of Sasines or the Land Registry of Scotland and pay your stamp duty to the Inland Revenue.

Chapter 12

Buying a Wreck or Building Yourself

In This Chapter

▶ Deciding how much renovation work you are happy to take on

▶ Finding a wreck to do up and sticking to budget

▶ Working out whether you can cope with a listed property

▶ Saving money by building your own home from scratch

*P*roperties in pristine condition tend to come with hefty price tags. But if you opt for one requiring a bit of tender loving care, you should be able to get it for a knockdown price. And if you do the renovations right, you can increase its value by thousands of pounds. As if that wasn't challenge enough, an increasing number of first-time buyers are even building their own home from scratch in order to save costs.

But with the undoubted hassle factor, is it really worthwhile? TV home makeover shows may be fuelling interest in property renovation but not everyone is cut out for it. It's time and labour intensive, and mistakes can be costly. In this chapter, I help you figure out whether renovating or self-building is for you – or not.

Weighing the Options

Renovating can save you money. A property in need of a lot of work is bound to be cheaper than one that has been renovated recently. The lower price reflects the fact that you will have to spend perhaps a considerable sum of money modernising the property and making it habitable.

But if you carefully calculate how much the project will cost (calling on the advice of a builder or surveyor) before you start and stick to budget, the total cost should be less than it would have been if you'd bought the property in pristine condition.

While you may save thousands of pounds on the asking price, you must expect to spend some serious money doing the place up. You also need to anticipate dedicating equally serious time and effort to the project. Depending on how big a task you set yourself, renovations may take weeks or even months, and you need somewhere to live while the work is carried out.

It may be tempting to cut corners to get it all done as quickly as possible, particularly if you are kipping on a mate's sofa in the meantime. But it will only cost you more in the long run if you have to pay someone to put shoddy workmanship right at a later date.

Making sure you can stomach renovation

Before you buy a property in less than perfect condition, assess whether renovation is something you are comfortable with. Many of the people who make a killing on doing up dilapidated properties are experienced developers who know what they are doing. And even those who aren't trained architects, surveyors, or builders know good people they can call upon to do the work for them. Such contacts are vital to a renovation project's success. And if you haven't got good contacts, you need to make some – and quickly (see 'Handling the hands-on workers' later in this chapter).

No two renovations are the same so when buying a property you must assess whether the amount of work it needs is within your range or out of your league. Even something that appears straightforward at first may be revealed as something you don't want any part of – for example, finding that the cracks in the living room are due to subsidence and the foundations need extensive underpinning. Subsidence is a big problem for properties built on clay soil because during dry weather the lack of moisture in the ground makes the soil crumble, causing the foundations to move and weaken.

Take a critical look at your skills and the amount of time you can devote to the project. This can make the difference between a successful renovation and a costly disaster. If you have no building expertise, planning to do an extensive renovation on your own is madness. And if you have a busy, stressful job with long hours and are planning to leave the renovation to weekends and evenings, it will take forever. If your heart is still set on renovation, call in the experts rather than get your hands dirty, get in the way, and make more of a mess than there was to start with.

If you like to dabble in DIY and are planning on doing the bulk of the work yourself, look for something suited to your skills. Completely gutting a house may be a bigger job than you feel happy attempting. Try a less extensive project such as interior refurbishment or replacing kitchen units, perhaps. Leave knocking down walls or replacing the roof to the experts.

 Even if you plan to hire contractors for most of the work, if you have some building experience or DIY expertise and time on your hands, you can save a lot of money by doing some of the 'easier' work yourself, such as chipping old plaster off walls or grouting. Just make sure you don't get in the way!

Finding Your Wreck

Estate agents are your first port of call when looking for a property in need of renovation. Register with several and tell them exactly what you are looking for. The Internet is another good source: Register with as many property sites as you can. And don't forget to keep an eye on the local paper as well.

Auction is another good source of dilapidated properties – sellers know they will get a quick sale in exchange for a knock-down price. But if you buy at auction, take care. Ask yourself why the seller wants to get rid of the property in a hurry: Perhaps there is some problem he's hoping won't be spotted. View the property with a builder or surveyor before bidding so you know what work is needed, how much it will cost – and whether it's worth it.

You can literally stumble across the perfect renovation project while you are going about your daily business. If you come across an old wreck with an estate agent's board outside, you're in luck: All you have to do is contact the agent and arrange a viewing. If there isn't a board, ask the neighbours who owns it and whether they know what the owner's plans are for the property. It may be that the owner would be delighted for someone to take it off his hands, especially as he won't have to pay commission to an agent for arranging the sale.

Matching Valuation to Asking Price

Sometimes the lender's valuation concludes that the property is overpriced and worth less than the amount you have applied to borrow. This is bad news. If you can drum up the shortfall from your savings or by taking out a personal loan, you can still buy the property even if the surveyor thinks you are paying over the odds. But ask yourself whether it's worth it – do you want to get yourself further into debt? If you're struggling now, how will you cope if you go over budget and the debts start racking up?

If you haven't got enough cash to cover the shortfall and don't fancy taking on more credit, ask the seller whether he'll reduce the price. You have a good case as you have the lender's valuation and chances are other buyers won't be able to get a mortgage for that amount either. But if he won't reduce the price, you may have to pull out and look for a property you can afford.

Tapping the Talents of the Right People

In order to ensure that your renovation project is a success, you need to find the right experts to help you carry out the necessary work.

Making use of a surveyor

The best way of calculating how much work is needed is to ask a surveyor to assess the job. She'll know what is causing cracks in the walls, for example, and what remedial work is needed. Not employing a surveyor may save you a few quid in the short term but is a risky strategy and strongly inadvisable in the long run because you might miss out on something that only a professional would spot.

Personal recommendation is the best way of choosing a surveyor. Estate agents and mortgage lenders should also be able to recommend one. Ensure the surveyor is a member of the Royal Institution of Chartered Surveyors (RICS), the main professional trade association. Members have the letters MRICS, FRICS, or TechRICS after their name. For extra peace of mind, check with the RICS whether their qualifications are genuine (0870 333 1600). As with builders, not all surveyors are used to working with all types of property. Try to find one who has experience of properties similar to yours, especially if it is of unusual construction, such as thatched or timber. Follow up references and check previous projects to ensure employers were satisfied with the surveyor's work.

Spending now to save later

Even though money is tight, you'd be mad to buy a property that needs a lot of work without a full structural survey. Although such a survey can set you back several hundred pounds, if it uncovers serious faults that cost a fortune to put right – money you just don't have – it's better to find out sooner rather than later. And it's certainly better to find out before you commit yourself to a project you can't afford to complete. Building surveys are expensive, though, costing anything between £400 and £1,000 – depending on your requirements – which is a lot for someone on a budget. It may be tempting not to bother but I assure you that it is money well spent if you are buying a dilapidated property in need of much work.

The structural survey uncovers hidden problems, giving you the fullest picture of what you are committing yourself to. With a full picture, you can establish whether you can afford all the necessary work: If you don't have the full structural survey, you may take on more than you can afford to put right. And given that you are spending thousands of pounds buying the property in the first place, the survey cost is relatively small fry.

A survey that reveals that serious work you hadn't bargained on is required can be a useful negotiating tool for haggling with the seller over the purchase price.

Coping with structural problems

If the survey reveals subsidence or a condemned boiler, all is not necessarily lost. Your lender might still let you have a mortgage but may hold back some of the funds until you have rectified the problem to the surveyor's satisfaction. The trouble is you'll have to pay for the repairs out of your own pocket: You get the money back from the lender only after they're completed. If you can't afford to pay for the repairs out of your savings, you'll have to extend your overdraft, take out a loan, or use a credit card. If you are happy taking on more debt, make sure you shop around for the cheapest rate: To compare deals on loans, credit cards, and overdrafts, go to www.moneysupermarket.com.

If you pay for a building survey, the surveyor will indicate how much the work will cost: You have to decide if you can afford it. If you can't, and even if you can, try haggling with the seller over the price. He might be persuaded to reduce it accordingly. If not, and you really can't afford it, you might have to pull out.

Going deeper with additional surveys

The survey won't tell you whether you should buy a dilapidated property or not but it will indicate whether it's a good idea. The surveyor will be able to indicate the cost involved in putting any problems right. If a lot more work is needed than you anticipated, you may want to reconsider taking on the project.

Sometimes the survey indicates a potential problem that needs further investigation. Before you panic, this is not uncommon and is often just the surveyor covering her back. Wait until the findings of these further investigations are available before making a decision. If the specialist survey reveals a significant problem, this may put you off the purchase.

If the surveyor calls for further reports, the lender will insist upon these so you will have to pay for them if you are still interested in the property.

Handling the hands-on workers

Building up your own experience and knowledge is essential even if you hire experts to do the work. You must ensure that the workers you hire don't pull the wool over your eyes and that they do a good job. There are many reputable contractors who won't con you but there are plenty of cowboys as well – spotting when someone is trying to take you for a ride is crucial to the success of your renovation.

Get at least three quotes for your project and try to resist the temptation of opting for the cheapest one: The contractor may cut corners in order to offer such an attractive price. Check out previous jobs for each candidate and ask previous employers whether they are happy with the work the firm did.

Realising the importance of the project manager

Overseeing an extensive renovation is a full-time job, and you need a project manager to make sure that everything runs as it should. The project manager is responsible for hiring contractors, ordering materials, and ensuring the project finishes on time and to budget. Project managers work long hours and don't come cheap: Expect to pay anything up to 10 per cent of your total budget, depending on the work involved.

Because your budget is limited, consider being your own project manager. Even if you are inexperienced, you may be able to cope if you are organised and can spare the time to be on site at least several hours each day. But if you don't have the time or an eye for it, leave it to the experts. It's false economy if the job isn't done properly.

Personal recommendation is the best way to find a project manager. Ask friends, relatives, neighbours, and builders or other contractors you trust, whether they can suggest someone suitable.

Finding good contractors

If you've never done any renovation before, you probably don't have a contacts book of reliable builders, plumbers, and electricians. If you're serving as the project manager, you need to build one up quickly. A hired project manager will have her own contacts.

To find good contractors, ask around. Family, friends, and neighbours, who have had similar work done, may be able to recommend a builder or plumber. Inspect their work and take up other references. Make sure builders belong to the Federation of Master Builders (FMB) or Guild of Master Craftsmen, as they are vetted before joining and follow a code of practice. And if you are unhappy with their work, there is a complaints procedure. To find a member, look out for the FMB or Guild logo on builders' vans, stationery, and advertising.

If you are stuck, check out www.improveline.com, which enables you to search for contractors in your area. These contractors are recommended by the public and screened for their credit and legal history and number of years in the business. The *Yellow Pages* lists contractors but use it as a last resort as you have no idea how good they are. If you do pick a contractor out of the *Yellow Pages*, ask to see samples of previous work and follow up references.

Don't take on a contractor simply because he is a friend of a friend. Treat it as a business relationship. If anything goes wrong, it can be hard to seek redress and plus you risk falling out with your friend. Make it a rule only to work with qualified contractors who are unrelated to you, or your friends.

Good builders are in great demand and will struggle to fit your project into their schedule, so start looking well in advance.

Using an architect

If the property requires extensive changes, consider hiring an architect. Architects have completed a course of study in buildings and design so will be able to direct the renovation of the property, such as advising you how to knock down walls and ensure that the property remains safe. This bumps up the price – a consultation costs between £55 and £95 an hour – so only hire one if absolutely necessary: if the project is specialised or complex, for example.

Architects should belong to the Royal Institute of British Architects (Riba). You can find one on Riba's Web site (www.riba.org). Members are subject to a code of professional conduct and Riba offers practical assistance if you encounter a problem.

Considering where to live during renovation

If your property is going to be without a roof during the renovation, you'll have to live elsewhere during this time. And even if the roof stays on, do you really want to live in a property full of dust, noise, rubbish, and strangers coming and going?

If you have to stay in a hotel, costs will rocket so try to find a sofa to kip on. This will save you money, which is handy as the renovation is likely to swallow up all your spare cash and may take many weeks, if not months, to complete. If the project looks as if it will take weeks, you may need to call on the goodwill of several friends rather than risk outstaying your welcome with one.

Budgeting for the Renovation

One of the biggest mistakes people make when renovating property is to go wildly over budget. You simply can't afford to do this because you don't have the spare cash to bail yourself out. Blowing your limited budget can have a catastrophic effect and put the project months behind schedule. Don't forget the hidden costs: Not only do you have to purchase the property in the first instance you must budget for contractors' wages, materials, fixtures, and fittings.

Try to maintain a contingency fund – 10 per cent of your total budget – to cover unexpected expenses. Don't regard this as an optional extra: it is as integral to your budget as the money earmarked for materials. If an unexpected expense crops up, these reserves ensure your project is not delayed – or abandoned – while you find the shortfall.

Estimating costs

You can't set a budget until you know how much work is needed. And if you are new to property development, you must rely on experts to guide you. Talk through your aims with the builder and try gauging how helpful and cooperative he is. If he is dismissive or patronising he may prove difficult to work with and you may be better off finding someone else to do the work.

Submit clear instructions in writing before the builder starts and agree on a written quote. Be sure to keep copies of everything. Your quote should specify whether materials are included and what, if any, you are expected to supply.

The costs of renovations vary according to the property and work needed but as a general rule, for the full refurbishment of a three-bedroom semi-detached house, expect to pay:

- ✔ **New roof:** around £45 per square metre for a tiled roof
- ✔ **Underpinning the foundations:** £3,000
- ✔ **Rewiring:** £3,000
- ✔ **Plumbing**: £3,000 to £5,000
- ✔ **New kitchen:** £3,000
- ✔ **New bathroom:** £1,500
- ✔ **Loft conversion:** £8,000

The above estimates include labour costs as well as materials. To estimate the cost of any work that isn't included in the above list, ask a builder for advice.

Sticking to your budget

The budget is there to ensure you don't overspend. Stick to it ruthlessly. Don't get carried away. If your budget doesn't cover marble flooring in the bathroom but you decide as the work is being done to go for it regardless, you will run out of money before the renovation is finished. And, if you run out of cash, you'll have to live in an unfinished property until you can raise enough money to complete the job.

The other problem with running over budget is that if you're using tradespeople to complete the work, they are likely to have other jobs lined up, which they need to get on with. You may have to wait months before they can come back and complete your renovation.

Being Wary of Listed Property

When you are looking for a property to renovate, there's a chance that you'll come across one that is listed. A *listed property* is one that is protected because it is considered to be of historic or special architectural interest.

Listed buildings often fall into disrepair because they tend to be old (most properties built before 1840 are listed) and more expensive to maintain and repair than a modern property. If you own a listed building, you need permission to make any changes to it. Listed properties are often charming but they can also present all kinds of problems, which you must be aware of before buying one.

For further information, contact: English Heritage (www.english-heritage.org); Cadw in Wales (www.cadw.co.uk); Scottish Heritage (www.historic-scotland.gov.uk); or the Environment and Heritage Service in Northern Ireland (www.ehsni.gov.uk). For listed properties for sale, try the Society for the Protection of Ancient Buildings (www.spab.org.uk) or Pavillions of Splendour, an estate agent specialising in listed properties (www.heritage.co.uk).

Listing grades and what they mean

There are around 500,000 listed buildings in the UK and several different types. In England and Wales, these are Graded I, II*, and II. In Scotland, grades A, B, and C are used, while in Northern Ireland, where just 2 per cent of properties are listed, it's A, B+, B1, and B2, all of which roughly signify the same thing. In England, 90 per cent of listed buildings are Grade II and in Scotland, Grade B is the most popular (60 per cent of properties). These grades roughly translate as:

✔ **Grade I/A:** buildings of exceptional interest

✔ **Grade II*/B:** particularly important buildings of more than special interest

✔ **Grade II/C:** buildings of special interest that warrant every effort to preserve them

Dealing with building regulations

While you can't install modern double-glazing into a Grade I listed seventeenth-century cottage, you don't necessarily have to live with something you don't like. As long as you get listed building consent from your local planning authority beforehand, renovations and extensions are not always out of the question if your request is reasonable.

Demolishing, altering, or extending a listed building without consent is a serious offence: The penalty can be an unlimited fine or up to 12 months' imprisonment.

Familiarise yourself with what is allowed before you start any work and if in doubt, contact your local planning office. In addition to extensions, alterations needing consent include:

✔ Painting over brickwork

✔ Replacing doors and windows or changing roofing materials

✔ Removing external surfaces, and moving or removing interior walls

✔ Installing a satellite dish, TV aerial, or burglar alarm

✔ Building new doorways

✔ Removing or altering fireplaces, panelling, and staircases

Budgeting for maintenance costs and insurance

Renovating a listed building costs more than a standard renovation because you need specialist materials in keeping with the original style, such as reclaimed bricks or tiles.

A number of grants are available to assist with urgent major repairs on Grade I, Grade II*, or Grade A or B listed buildings but you're unlikely to get a grant for a Grade II or C listed building. Apply for a grant by contacting your Conservation Officer via your local council. VAT is not payable on alterations – as long as a VAT-registered builder carries out the work and you have listed building consent. Remember that

VAT remains payable on repairs and other work not requiring consent: the builder adds this cost onto his final bill.

If you don't look after your listed building properly, you'll get into trouble with the local authority. It can serve a *repairs notice* specifying work it considers necessary for the building's preservation. If you do not comply within two months, the authority may make a compulsory purchase order on the property.

When arranging insurance, a specialist insurer is your best bet. Buildings insurance is essential and covers the cost of rebuilding the property should it be destroyed in a fire, so take professional advice from a surveyor on the cost of rebuilding. Specialist insurers will also be able to advise you on reducing risks, such as fire precautions, so pay heed.

Building Your Own Home

Many buyers on a budget who despair of ever being able to afford their first home are taking the desperate measure of building their own. This sounds like a great deal of hassle – and it is – but self-build can be cheaper than buying a ready-built property. By the time the property is built, the average self-build house is worth 25 to 30 per cent more than its cost due to saving in several areas, including:

- **Stamp duty:** You pay stamp duty only on the purchase of the plot, and then only if it costs more than £60,000. You pay no stamp duty on the structure, no matter how much it is worth when completed. If the land costs you £100,000 and the final value of the property is £600,000, for example, you pay stamp duty of £1,000 (1 per cent of £100,000). If you bought the finished property, however, you'd pay £24,000 in stamp duty (4 per cent of £600,000) – £23,000 more! (See Chapter 2 for more details on stamp duty rates.)

- **VAT:** You don't pay value added tax on new housing so you can claim back VAT on construction materials. This is charged at 17.5 per cent of the purchase price, so not paying it represents a big saving.

Self-build is a bit of a misnomer as only 5 per cent of self-builders do the work themselves – the vast majority hire builders to do it. But the principle is the same: You buy a plot of land, ideally with outline planning permission (see 'Finding the right plot' later in this chapter), and commission an architect or surveyor to draw up the plans for your home. These are submitted to the local planning authority (your local council) and once they are approved, construction can begin.

If you're tempted by the thought of self-build, do your research carefully to get an accurate idea of the costs involved. The average self-build costs £150,000, so it may be cheaper than a ready-built property but it still isn't cheap. However, if you are prepared to do a lot of the donkeywork yourself and aren't afraid to get your hands dirty you will be able to keep costs down.

Deciding whether you've got what it takes

Even though 20,000 people build their own homes every year, it doesn't suit everyone. Although many self-builders don't do any of the building work themselves you will need to oversee the project (because a project manager will stretch your budget further still). And, if your idea of hell after a hard day in the office is to spend the evening digging foundations or grouting a bathroom, avoid any hands-on involvement whatsoever. Self-build best suits

- ✓ **Those in the building trade.** The more work you do yourself, the cheaper the project. You should at least be prepared to fetch and carry, dig foundations, pile up bricks, paint, and decorate. But if you can also do the wiring or plastering (don't attempt these if you aren't experienced) you'll save significant amounts of cash.

- ✓ **Those with great contacts.** You don't have to be a builder or electrician but it helps if you know reliable tradespeople. If you don't, your job will be much harder.

- ✓ **Those with great organisational skills.** Planning your project to the smallest detail before you begin can reduce the likelihood of something going wrong.

- ✓ **Enthusiastic people who are willing to roll up their sleeves and get stuck in.** Don't interfere with things you don't understand but simply offer your services where they are required.

✔ **Those with enough time and energy to manage a large project such as this.** Building works can be very time consuming and stressful – be sure you know what you're getting yourself into.

✔ **The financially astute.** Working to a budget is crucial, so if you generally have tight control of your finances you'll be at a great advantage. You must know roughly what each stage will cost: Ask a surveyor or builder to help you calculate this.

A number of excellent Web sites can help you decide whether self-build is for you and also guide you through the project if you decide it is. Check out Self Build ABC (www.selfbuild abc.co.uk) or Buildstore (www.buildstore.co.uk) for details.

Apportioning time and hassle

Set a timetable before work begins to ensure you have the finances ready for each stage (see 'Financing the project' below). But be warned that when builders are involved it's easy to run over schedule. Even the best-laid plans can go awry but if you do your planning carefully, you can minimise the likelihood of problems cropping up.

Self-build can be a hassle so if you like a quiet life so think twice before taking on a project. Even if you aren't hands-on with the building work, you'll have to make the financial arrangements and manage the build, making sure the various steps of the project are completed satisfactorily and on time. Unless you have a project manager, you'll spend a lot of time chasing tradespeople, deliveries of materials, surveyors, and council inspectors.

Financing the project

Before building work begins, set a budget divided into stages to avoid running out of cash before it's finished. Allow for:

✔ The cost of the plot. This can be as much as a third of your budget if it already has planning permission.

✔ Architect or quantity surveyor fees. An architect is responsible for the design of your new home and provides the drawings that the quantity surveyor uses to work out the necessary labour, materials, and machinery hire required to complete the project.

✔ Application fees to the local planning authority for permission to build the property. Outline planning permission (see 'Finding the right plot' later in this chapter) costs £220 per 0.1 hectare up to a maximum of £5,500. Your local authority will be able to give you an exact figure.

✔ Connection to water drainage, electricity, and gas. Together, these can cost a fortune if the plot is particularly remote. Expect to pay upwards of £2,000.

✔ Valuation fees for surveys required by your lender.

✔ Labour costs and materials.

There are two main types of self-build mortgages:

✔ **Payment in arrears:** Funds are released in stages after building work is completed to the lender's satisfaction. The disadvantage is that you need cash in the first place to pay for the work (the lender is, in effect, reimbursing you for work already completed). If you don't have savings to call upon, you'll have to take out a loan. It isn't ideal to be saddling yourself with more debt, so shop around for a cheap deal to minimise costs. You may even have to pay for the plot out of your own pocket, although some lenders will agree to a loan for this if the land has outline planning permission (OPP).

✔ **Advance stage payments:** The lender lets you have the cash *before* the work is done. You can borrow up to 95 per cent of the cost of the plot and each stage of the build, but you'll still have to raise the remaining 5 per cent. Ideally, you should do this before building work starts to avoid hold ups while you raise the funds.

Finding the right plot

There is a shortage of land for self-build in the south-east of England. To find a plot, contact estate agents, auction houses, local and national newspapers, and look on the Internet. For a fee, you can also register with PlotSearch, which has details of nearly 6,000 plots for sale (www.buildstore.co.uk) and a one-off subscription fee of £44: This gets you details of self-build plots for sale in three counties of your choice. An extra £15 gets you e-mail alerts when new plots become available.

To make life as easy as possible for yourself, buy a plot that already has outline planning permission (OPP). This means the local planning authority has already agreed in principle to the building of a house on the land. There may be restrictions and conditions attached relating to access, boundaries, style of property, and types of material used in the construction, however. Examine the documents carefully so you know what these restrictions are: You can obtain these from the seller of the plot or the local planning authority.

Some plots have detailed planning permission (DPP) rather than OPP, meaning that detailed plans of a specific type and size of house have been agreed by the local planning authority. This may not be the type of property you had in mind so examine the documents carefully before purchasing a plot with DPP. Making changes is difficult: You must reapply for planning permission – which isn't guaranteed.

If your plot has OPP, the next step is to progress to DPP. You submit plans to the planning authority for approval and once these are accepted, building work can start. OPP is valid for five years from when it's granted and you must apply for DPP within three years. Building work must commence within two years of DPP being granted; otherwise, planning permission will lapse and you must apply for it all over again.

Ask a surveyor to value the plot to ensure you are paying a fair price for it. When you buy a house you can get a good idea of how much it's worth by the price similar properties in the area are fetching, but this isn't as easy with land. The surveyor can also give you an idea of the cost of building the property and its final value. Mortgage lenders will need this information before agreeing to finance the project.

Getting planning permission

A plot without planning permission tends to be much cheaper than one where permission has been granted because obtaining permission isn't straightforward and there's no guarantee you'll get it. If you buy a plot without permission, you must apply to the local planning authority for permission to build on it. In Northern Ireland you must apply to the Building Control Department of your district council.

Obtaining planning permission can take a long time so it may be worth calling in the experts – architects, surveyors, or designers, although it will cost you – to make sure you have a good stab at your application. You must be patient and be prepared to cooperate with the local planning authority. Planning Consultants UK offer hints on making a successful application (www.planning-consultants-uk.com).

Complying with building regulations

Once you've got planning permission and building work has started, you aren't off the hook. The building control surveyor makes at least nine visits to the property during construction to ensure you're meeting building regulations. You'll be told at what stage an inspection is compulsory and how much notice is needed. The stages are:

- Commencement of work
- Foundations dug
- Concrete foundations
- Damp proof course: The layer of material put at the bottom of the property's walls to stop water rising through the bricks
- Hardcore laid over the site: Used in the foundations and comprises broken bricks, masonry and concrete
- Drain connection with sewer
- Drains inspection
- Drain backfilled and ready for test: Drains must be surrounded with shingle and tested in the presence of the building control surveyor to ensure that water doesn't leak out of the drain
- Final completion or occupation

If you don't comply with building regulations, the building control surveyor can force you to amend the work. If you refuse, you can be prosecuted and will have to pay costs. You can't move onto the next stage until the building control surveyor has given the previous one the okay. And only after the local authority is convinced that the work meets all the building regulations will you receive a certificate of completion.

Part IV
Alternative Ways of Home Buying

"I knew that taking on a lodger would cause problems."

In this part . . .

*I*f you need a more creative solution to your lack of cash, this part contains the answer. You can call upon family, friends, lodgers, or tenants to realise your goal of purchasing your own property – these chapters show you how. Or you can contact a housing association or the council for help. And if you're a key worker, you may get a sizeable loan to put towards the purchase price. If you're struggling to raise the necessary cash, you can't afford not to read this part.

Chapter 13

Reducing Your Repayments via an Offset Mortgage

*M*ost children expect to be able to cut the apron strings and gain some much-needed independence from their parents once they're ready to buy their own place. But if you're seriously thinking about buying your first home you've probably already realised that it may not be that easy. Most properties are beyond the wildest dreams of first-time buyers on low salaries with minimal savings. There's a strong possibility that you won't be able to afford much more than a broom-cupboard.

If affordability is a problem, I suggest you don't rule out your parents and other relatives just yet. They can be rather useful when it comes to buying your first home – even if they aren't extremely wealthy or prepared to hand over thousands of pounds that they may never see again. Family offset mortgages enable your mum, dad, grandma, or any other number of relatives, to hang onto their savings while letting you enjoy the benefit of them. The upshot is that you pay less interest in the long run – and you might even be able to pay your mortgage off early.

In this chapter, I explain how family offset mortgages work, how much money they can save you in the long run, and how your relatives retain full control over their savings.

Reducing the Interest You Pay with an Offset Mortgage

Offset mortgages are gaining a reputation as one of the most flexible options available to homebuyers. These mortgages enable you to use your savings to reduce the amount of interest you pay on your mortgage – costing you less money in the long term. But rather than paying off a chunk of your mortgage debt with your savings – money you won't ever see again – your nest egg remains in a separate account. This means you can still withdraw your cash, if required, while at the same time benefiting from paying less interest on your mortgage.

With an offset deal your bank or building society accounts (savings and/or current accounts) are linked to your mortgage. You have several different accounts with the same lender – otherwise known as 'jars' or 'pots' – so you pay interest only on the difference between the amount in your bank account and the amount of your mortgage debt. This reduces the total interest you pay over the term of your mortgage, which you can take as either lower monthly repayments or repay your mortgage faster. Potentially, you could save thousands of pounds.

For example, if you have a £150,000 mortgage and have a nest egg of £10,000 in your savings account, with an offset mortgage you only pay interest on £140,000. But as your repayments are calculated on the £150,000 loan, you will be overpaying each month (if you don't ask your lender to reduce the payments accordingly) so you pay off your mortgage quicker.

You earn no interest on the money in your savings account; instead it is counted against your mortgage debt. And as the interest you are charged on your debts is higher than the interest you earn on your savings, you are quids in.

If your mortgage doesn't have an offset feature, you could end up paying a lot more interest over the long term. In Table 13-1, I demonstrate the effect of offsetting savings of £5,000, £15,000, and £25,000 against a £100,000 mortgage. The example assumes that you carry on making repayments calculated against your original loan, reducing the total interest in the long run and enabling you to pay off your mortgage years ahead of schedule.

Table 13-1	Potential Savings on a £100,000 Offset Mortgage	
Savings Offset Against Mortgage	*Amount Saved*	*Reduction in Mortgage Term*
£5,000	£9,563.80	2 years, 2 months
£15,000	£24,996.51	6 years
£25,000	£36,701.04	9 years, 3 months

Figures based on a repayment mortgage of £100,000 on a property worth £120,000, taken out over 25 years. Assumes interest charged at 3.9 per cent for the first six months, followed by 4.5 per cent for the remainder of the term. Source: Newcastle Building Society

The greater the savings you have, the less interest you pay during the lifetime of the mortgage. But while adding to your savings account reduces the interest you incur on your mortgage, likewise, if you withdraw cash the interest you're charged on your mortgage rises accordingly.

Offset accounts don't require you to keep a minimum amount in your savings account: You can withdraw all your cash at any time if you need to get your hands on it. Ultimately, you lose out if you haven't got any savings because they aren't working to reduce the interest on your mortgage.

Offsetting the Family's Savings Against Your Mortgage Debt

What if you haven't got any savings of your own to offset against your mortgage? Family offset mortgages work in a similar way to standard offset deals only they enable you to use your relatives' or friends' money as an offset against your mortgage for interest charging purposes. As with standard offset mortgages, this reduces the amount of interest you are charged, while your relatives retain control of their savings.

If one (or several) of your relatives or friends has a few thousand pounds in savings, they are unlikely to be earning more than a paltry rate of interest in a bank or building society account. And if they don't need this income and want to help you buy a property – without losing control of their cash – offsetting could be the solution.

To make the most of your relatives' or friends' savings, they must open savings accounts with a lender offering a family offset mortgage. The money remains in their name(s); they retain total control and can access it at any time. You can't get your hands on their cash: You simply get the benefit of it. However, instead of your relatives receiving interest on their savings, the interest on your mortgage is reduced accordingly.

Table 13-2 demonstrates how your family's savings could be offset against your mortgage to reduce the interest you pay. In this example, three savings accounts worth a total of £32,000 are offset against a £125,000 mortgage. This means the borrower only pays interest on £93,000.

Table 13-2	How Family Offset Pays
Saving Pot	*Amount*
Mum and Dad	£12,000
Grandma	£15,000
Auntie Ethel	£5,000
Total Savings	**£32,000**
Your mortgage	£125,000
Total savings offset	– £32,000
You pay interest on	**£93,000**

Figure 13-1 illustrates how these accounts are offset against your mortgage.

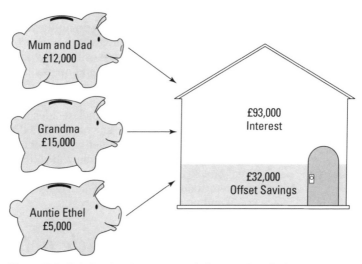

Figure 13-1: Relatives' savings pots can help towards reducing your mortgage in the long run.

 The main advantage of family offset mortgages from your relatives' standpoint is that they don't have to hand over control of their savings. If your parents lend you £20,000 to put down as a deposit on a flat, on the other hand, there's a strong chance they won't ever see that cash again. This causes problems if there is a chance that they may need that cash at some point in the future – to live off in retirement, for example. This may prevent them letting you have it in the first place, even if they would like to help you out. But if they offset it against your mortgage, everyone is happy as they retain control of their cash while you still benefit from it.

 It's worth making sure that your family understands that they won't personally earn any interest on their savings if they offset them against your mortgage. Instead, you get the benefit by paying less interest on your mortgage. Make sure they are happy with this arrangement before you apply for an offset mortgage.

If anyone offsetting their savings in the example shown in Table 13-2 wants to use their money, they can simply withdraw it. There is no penalty to pay, they don't have to give any notice, and there is no restriction to the amount they can withdraw. They don't have to consult you or get your permission.

However, it's helpful if your relatives do notify you before withdrawing some, or all, of their cash from their offset savings account. This is because there will be less money offset against your mortgage debt, so you end up paying more interest on your mortgage. Say, for example, that your family's savings are offset against your mortgage so you pay interest only on the difference: £75,000. Auntie Ethel decides she wants to go on that Mediterranean cruise she has always dreamed about and withdraws £5,000 from her savings account, which is offset against your mortgage, leaving you with having to pay interest on £80,000, rather than just £75,000, because you have less savings offset against your mortgage. In this scenario, you'll end up paying more interest.

Getting by with a little help from your friends

Terms and conditions on family offset mortgages differ between lenders, so check the small print carefully before applying. Out of the two lenders currently offering family offset mortgages, one allows only family members – those related to you by birth or adoption – to offset their savings against your mortgage. The other lender allows friends to offset their savings as well.

If you've got a wealthy friend or two prepared to help out, it's worth opting for an offset deal that allows you to offset friends' savings as well as those of family members. Remember, though to spell out to them that they won't personally benefit as they won't make any interest on their savings.

Staying within the restrictions

Some lenders place restrictions on the number of savings accounts that can be offset against a mortgage while others have no such limitations. But even those with restrictions are fairly generous: One lender limits the number of accounts that can be offset against any one mortgage to 11 – more than enough for the majority of people.

While the number of pots might be restricted, there is no limit to the amount that can be invested in an account.

Weighing up the Pros and Cons of Family Offsetting

As with most types of mortgage there are advantages and disadvantages to a family offset deal. Be sure to consider the risks as well as the benefits before asking for – and accepting – an offset deal with your family or friends. Money issues make a lot of people nervous and sometimes they're difficult to talk about, but it's important for everyone involved to have a clear idea of what they're getting out of the deal.

Reaping the offsetting benefits as a borrower

As long as you can call on substantial savings to offset against your mortgage, the benefits of offsetting far outweigh the disadvantages. Some of the benefits are listed here:

✔ **You end up paying considerably less interest on your mortgage, which could mean clearing it several years early.** The savings you make depend on how much cash your relatives and friends are willing, or able, to offset against your mortgage.

✔ **Interest on offset mortgages is calculated on the balance of your account at the end of each day.** This means the money starts working for you almost as soon as it hits one of the savings accounts linked to your mortgage. So if your sister has relatively modest savings but comes into a windfall of several thousand pounds that she adds to her account, you will benefit immediately. Alternatively, if you have a standard mortgage with interest calculated monthly, or, even worse, annually, it could take several months before such a deposit reduces the interest you pay on your mortgage.

✔ **There are no penalties for early repayment so you can pay the whole mortgage off, without incurring a fee, at any time.** The majority of standard mortgages have a limit as to the amount you can overpay without penalty each year – usually 10 per cent of the outstanding loan. But with an offset or family offset mortgage there are no such restrictions.

✔ **There is no limit on the amount of money that can be offset against your mortgage.** If you are lucky enough to have lots of relatives with thousands of pounds in savings who are willing to offset this money against your mortgage, you could pay a lot less in the long run. Bliss.

Advantages for friends and family

The beauty of offsetting is that it's not just the homeowner who benefits. If your parents or other relatives or friends want to help you while retaining control of their cash, an offset account enables them to do exactly that. The main benefits are:

✔ **Friends and family retain control of the money they put up through offsetting.** This is particularly important given the growing emphasis on individuals providing for their own financial future and retirement. Your parents simply might not be in the position to hand over their life savings to help you onto the property ladder because there's a strong chance you might never be able to pay them back. If they are relying on these savings for their retirement, they could find themselves short. But with a family offset mortgage they can do their bit to help you out and still have access to their cash.

✔ **Offset accounts have no restrictions on cash withdrawals or deposits.** Your family and friends won't incur penalties for accessing their money. You won't pay a penalty either, though the interest payments on your mortgage will increase in the long run.

✔ **Family offset mortgages are highly tax efficient.** Your family and friends can pay less tax – completely legally of course! – by offsetting their savings against your mortgage. If they usually pay tax on their savings, they'll no longer have to because their money is being used to reduce the interest debited on your mortgage account. As they are not making a profit on their savings, there is no tax to pay. And if they are higher rate taxpayers, this could save them a considerable sum.

Considering the downside: where family offsetting loses its sheen

Overall, there are many excellent benefits associated with family offset mortgages. But there are disadvantages you should also consider before taking the plunge. These are

- ✔ **You pay for flexibility.** Interest rates on offset deals are higher than on standard loans as they usually track a few points above the Bank of England base rate. This means your repayments will move up and down in line with changes in the base rate. As cheap fixed or discounted rates don't apply to offset deals – one lender offers a 0.1 per cent discount for an introductory period of six months only – you are likely to end up paying 2 or 3 per cent more interest than on a standard mortgage. You only pay less interest in the long run if your family and friends have a substantial amount of money to use in offsetting your mortgage. Offset deals with the best rates of interest tend to be less flexible than those with higher rates, so decide what matters most to you (see 'Finding a Family Offset Mortgage' below).

- ✔ **Repayments on offset mortgages can fluctuate from month to month as they follow movements in the base rate.** Many first-time buyers prefer the certainty of a fixed monthly mortgage repayment – at least until they've got the hang of budgeting each month. If you agree, the only way you can know for certain what your repayments will be for the next two, three, or five years – or even longer – is to opt for a fixed-rate deal, rather than an offset mortgage. (See Chapter 6 for more details on the different types of mortgages available.)

- ✔ **Friends and family helping to offset your mortgage lose out on income.** The downside for relatives and friends is that they won't personally benefit from their savings. This means they should calculate whether they need an income from their savings and only offset them if they don't. If they rely on income from their savings to cover everyday outgoings or they're looking to increase the amount of their savings with interest, they'd be better off not offsetting against your mortgage at all.

Finding a Family Offset Mortgage

Although offset mortgages are growing in popularity and are now offered by several lenders, family offset deals are a newer concept and therefore harder to find. However, as they grow in popularity, more lenders will likely launch their own family offset mortgage in future.

Offset mortgages differ considerably between lenders and family offset deals are no exception. Pay particular attention to the rate of interest you would be charged and the features on offer. It might be important for you to offset your current account as well as your family's savings against your mortgage, for example, or you might want to include friends' savings too. Not all offset deals enable you to do this.

As with standard mortgages, you have to do your homework to find the best deal. An independent mortgage broker is a good place to start: She can help you decide whether offsetting is right for you, and find the right mortgage for your circumstances. She can also help you through the application process, reducing your effort and stress levels. Not all brokers charge a fee, which is great news as you are on a budget. (For more details on finding a broker, see Chapter 6.)

Whether you use a broker or approach lenders directly, the questions you should ask remain the same:

- ✔ Can friends' savings be linked to my mortgage as well as those of my immediate family?
- ✔ Is there a limit on the number of pots that can be linked to my mortgage?
- ✔ Is there a competitive rate of interest on offer? If it's a base rate tracker, is there a discount at least for an introductory period? Ask yourself whether you can cope without a fixed rate.

As well as asking questions of the broker or lender, there are a couple of points you need to consider yourself:

✔ Are you opting for an interest-only, repayment or part-interest-only, part-repayment deal? (See Chapter 6 for more details on the difference between these.) Do you understand the risks associated with interest-only mortgages – that you'll still owe the capital you borrowed in the first instance at the end of the mortgage term because you've only been paying back the interest? And if you did opt for an interest-only deal, have you got another investment product in place to pay off the capital at the end of the mortgage term?

✔ Can you afford your mortgage repayments if your relatives or friends need their savings? You may have calculated that offsetting will enable you to pay off your mortgage several years early, but if your family withdraws a significant amount – or all – of their cash, you might not benefit as much in the long term. Or if you opted for lower repayments each month, you are likely to find that your monthly repayments rise accordingly: Would you be able to afford the increased payments? Lenders offering offset mortgages have calculators on their Web sites enabling you to work out what impact a sudden withdrawal of funds would have on your loan; check out the Woolwich's (www.woolwich.co.uk) or Newcastle Building Society's (www.newcastle.co.uk) Web sites.

Calculating How Much You Can Afford to Borrow

If you are offsetting your mortgage against family savings, this doesn't normally influence the amount you can borrow. If you hope to buy a £100,000 flat, for example, with a £5,000 deposit, this may be deemed too little and your mortgage application rejected if you also want to borrow more than three and a half times your income – even if your parents are prepared to offset £20,000. But if you added this £20,000 to your £5,000 deposit you wouldn't need to borrow as much so the lender might agree to the mortgage. The downside, of course, is that your parents' savings will be swallowed up rather than offset so they won't be able to access their money if they need it.

One lender will take your family's savings into account when calculating the *income multiple* – how many times your salary it will lend to you. But these savings must be offset against your mortgage for a minimum of five years. This reduces the flexibility of the deal and you need to check whether your relatives are happy to do this before committing their funds.

Coping When Your Relatives Need Their Money

It's worth bearing in mind what happens if family and friends need to withdraw their savings – no matter how unlikely this may be. If they withdraw their cash, your monthly mortgage repayments might increase (if you were paying a reduced amount to your lender as a result of the offsetting).

But if you haven't been making lower repayments than you would have done without an offset mortgage – just shortening the length of your loan by, in effect, making overpayments each month – you won't see a change in your monthly outgoings. However, you will have to make payments for longer, so may need to budget for this accordingly.

Chapter 14

Taking in a Lodger

· ·

· ·

Rigsby, the miserly, mean-spirited, and cynical landlord of a rundown boarding house in the 1970s sitcom *Rising Damp*, was everything you wouldn't want your landlord to be. Not only was he prejudiced, he had a total disregard for his tenants' privacy and the condition of the accommodation left a lot to be desired: It wasn't called *Rising Damp* for nothing.

But while Rigsby is a prime example of how *not* to go about it, taking in a lodger and becoming a landlord is one way of getting on the first rung of the property ladder. An increasing number of first-time buyers rent out a spare room to help them pay their mortgage. Part of the attraction is that you don't have to pay income tax on the rental income – as long as it's less than £4,250 a year. And this extra cash could well make life that little bit easier.

A small number of lenders take this rental income into account when calculating how much you can borrow in the first place. With a rent-a-room mortgage (also known as buy-to-lodge), the lender figures that the rental income enables you to afford bigger mortgage repayments. This can make the difference between being able to buy the property you want or not.

There are potential pitfalls to consider when taking in a lodger, such as whether you can cope with the loss of privacy and can handle sharing your home with a complete stranger.

You also have to decide what sort of lodger you want – you may have to advertise and vet them carefully *before* you consider letting them move into your home. In this chapter I look at these issues, along with how you cope if you can't find a lodger.

Deciding Whether You're Willing to Live with a Lodger

If you've got a spare room, taking someone in to help you pay the mortgage sounds like the perfect solution to coping on a tight income. But don't let visions of extra cash blind you to the serious issues you need to consider.

Renting out a room in your home has a number of advantages and disadvantages. I list the main ones you need to consider when weighing up whether it's worth your while.

Some of the advantages follow:

- ✔ **You'll have more money:** Your lodger's rent will undoubtedly make life easier. And you don't even have to pay tax on it if the rent is less than £4,250 in one tax year (see 'Qualifying for the rent-a-room exemption scheme' later in this chapter for more details).

- ✔ **You can buy a bigger property if the lender is prepared to take the rental income into account when calculating what you can borrow:** The rental income enables you to cope with a bigger mortgage. A larger house means you won't outgrow it as quickly as you may otherwise have done, so won't have to move so soon.

- ✔ **You won't get lonely:** Not everyone is happy living by themselves and having a lodger means that you've usually got someone around to chat to.

- ✔ **Your security will be enhanced**: When you're away on holiday there's someone still at the property, keeping an eye on it and reducing the risk of burglary.

Don't forget these disadvantages you should consider before deciding to take in a tenant:

✔ **Losing your privacy:** Are you prepared to share your home with someone else? As it's your first home, you may well be looking forward to living on your own and doing exactly what you want. Sharing with someone else from the beginning may prove to be quite a wrench.

✔ **Living with a stranger:** Most people would rather live with someone they know but there's a strong chance that this isn't possible and you end up living with a stranger. Consider how you feel about this.

✔ **Paying more council tax:** Council tax is calculated on the basis of two people living in a property, so if there are two of you at the moment (before the lodger comes along) you won't end up with a bigger council tax bill if you take on a lodger. But if you live on your own you qualify for a single person's 25 per cent discount, and you lose this once a lodger moves in. It's fair enough to ask your lodger to pay the difference but remember that if this pushes his rent above £4,250 a year, you'll be taxed on the surplus (see 'Qualifying for the rent-a-room exemption scheme' later in this chapter).

Renting out the spare room can help you meet your mortgage payments until you're in a position where you can afford to cover the whole mortgage comfortably by yourself – perhaps once you've had a pay rise or two. At that point, you can give the lodger notice to leave – the amount of notice depends on what you agree between yourselves when the lodger moved in (see 'Getting it in writing' later in this chapter) – and live in the property on your own.

Figuring Out the Financial Aspects

While there may be several reasons why you'd quite like to take in a lodger – perhaps to ward off loneliness, for example – the main reason most people rent out their spare room is to boost their income.

Reaping the benefits of a rent-a-room mortgage

Although most lenders don't take into account rental income from letting your spare room when calculating how big a mortgage you can have, some lenders do. A rent-a-room mortgage enables you to borrow more than you can otherwise.

With a *rent-a-room mortgage,* the maximum rental income you can receive before you have to pay tax (£4,250) is added onto your salary when the lender calculates the income multiple. So if the lender lets you borrow 3.25 times income, you can borrow £13,812.50 more than before (£4,250 × 3.25).

In a practical example, if you earn £25,000 and can add £4,250 to that, you can borrow £95,062.50 (£25,000 + £4,250 × 3.25). Without the rental income, you can borrow only £81,250 (£25,000 × 3.25). This can easily be the difference between buying a one- or two-bedroom place.

Finding a rent-a-room mortgage

Rent-a-room mortgages are few and far between so the best place to start your search for one is via a mortgage broker (see Chapter 4 for more details on finding and using a broker). The broker can find a lender who offers what you need.

A rent-a-room mortgage can be more expensive than a standard deal, so shop around to ensure you get a good rate.

Lenders offering rent-a-room mortgages tend to have a range of rates for you to choose from – a two-year fixed rate deal or discount tracker, for example – so pick what suits your circumstances best, bearing in mind that a fixed rate may be higher but gives you more certainty. See Chapter 4 for more on choosing the right type of mortgage for your circumstances.

The best rent-a-room mortgage is flexible so that you can make over- or underpayments or even take a payment holiday if you need to (as long as you have overpaid enough beforehand). Being able to vary your payments accommodates fluctuations in your income. For example, if your spare room is empty for a month (or several), you may struggle to pay the mortgage on your own. With a flexible deal you can overpay when you can afford to (when you have a lodger), building up a reserve of cash for when the room is empty. Then you can make lower payments until you find another lodger and go back to overpaying again.

Qualifying for the rent-a-room exemption scheme

Broadly, a *lodger* is someone who pays to live in your home and shares the family rooms, such as the living room, kitchen, and bathroom. So if you rent out your spare room to someone, she qualifies as a lodger.

Regular landlords must pay income tax on the profit they make from renting out property. (See Chapter 15 for more details on being a landlord.) But if you take in a lodger, you may not have to pay tax.

If you rent a furnished room in your home – and the rent is less than £4,250 in any one tax year (from 6 April one year to 5 April the next) – you don't have to pay any tax. The £4,250 allowance has been set at this amount for nearly a decade.

You don't have to fill out a tax return; in fact, you don't even have to tell the Inland Revenue that you have a lodger. If you do get a tax return from the Revenue because other portions of your income are not taxed at source, simply tick the box that says that your rental income is less than £4,250 per annum.

If your rental income is higher than £4,250 per year, you have to pay tax on the surplus. If this is the case, you must choose between:

> ✔ **Paying tax on the profit:** With this option you don't take advantage of the rent-a-room exemption but pay tax on your profit from renting the room as you would if you were a regular landlord and renting out the entire property. You can offset certain expenses against the rent, such as gas and electricity; buildings and contents insurance; and

maintenance and repairs (although not improvements). Your profit is whatever is left over. If your gross annual rent is much more than £4,250, this is the better option for you.

You can also claim a 10 per cent wear-and-tear allowance on furnishings if you choose this option. See Chapter 15 for more details on this.

✔ **Paying tax on anything above £4,250:** With this option, you qualify for the rent-a-room exemption and pay tax on any rent you receive above this amount. If your gross rent is not much more than £4,250, this method of calculating tax is likely to be the best option for you.

If you choose to be in the rent-a-room scheme, you must tell your tax office by 31 January, 22 months after the end of the tax year that you wish to be taxed on the letting income you receive over £4,250. So if you have income from the room during the tax year ended 5 April 2004, you must declare by 31 January 2006 that you want to be taxed using this method.

You can switch between the two methods of calculating tax so don't worry too much if you choose the wrong option at first and end up paying more tax than you really need to. Ask an accountant for advice if you are confused.

Even if you think you should be charging more than £4,250 a year in rent, think twice before doing so. You may have to do some complicated calculations and generate a whole load of extra hassle for not much reward once you have deducted tax (at your highest rate) from the surplus.

Keep a careful note of the rents you receive and expenses as they arise. You have to retain these records for six years after the tax year in question in case the Inland Revenue wishes to investigate at a later date.

For more details on renting out a room, get hold of a copy of leaflet IR87 from the Inland Revenue, available on the Revenue's Web site (www.inlandrevenue.org.uk). Your local Tax Office or any Inland Revenue Enquiry Centre can also give you more information (see *Yellow Pages* for your nearest office or centre).

Telling the Right People about Your Lodger

You may think that what you do is your own business, particularly in your own home, and to a certain extent you're right. But when it comes to taking in a lodger you need to tell certain people if you want to avoid problems later on. These people include:

- ✔ **The freeholder:** If you're buying a leasehold property, check the lease to see whether you need permission from the freeholder before taking in a lodger. (See Chapter 10 for more on the difference between freehold and leasehold properties.)

- ✔ **The mortgage lender:** When you have a rent-a-room mortgage, you don't need to request permission to take in a lodger. But if you take out a standard mortgage and decide at a later date to rent out your spare room, you must inform your lender.

  Most lenders are unlikely to have a problem with you renting out your spare room to a lodger, particularly as this increases your ability to pay the mortgage. But there may be something in the small print of your mortgage documents saying you can't do this so it's better to be safe than sorry. To strengthen your case, make it clear that the lodger is paying rent and you are not giving them a tenancy.

- ✔ **The insurers:** Inform your contents insurer that you are taking in a lodger because they may view a lodger as an increased risk and this will be reflected in your premium. If you don't inform your insurer and then later make a claim, it can be rejected. (See 'Insuring your home for lodgers' later in this chapter.

Insuring Your Home for Lodgers

Insurance is an important consideration when you rent out your spare room. First, you must notify both your buildings and home contents insurers that you plan to take in a lodger.

If you don't, and you have to make a claim on your policy, you may find that your insurer rejects it, leaving you with having to stump up to replace your belongings out of your own pocket – which can prove to be a huge financial strain. (See Chapter 4 for more details on the type of insurance you need and how to find the best cover.)

Once your lodger has moved in, continue to pay your buildings insurance as normal: Your lodger isn't expected to contribute to this. As for home contents insurance, continue to pay your own premiums. Your policy doesn't cover the lodger's possessions, however, so tell her to arrange her own cover. She is not obliged to, but point out that if you are burgled, she won't be covered under your policy.

If your lodger steals from you, replacing the items isn't covered under your home contents policy: Only theft by forcible entry is covered. Therefore, it's very important to vet prospective lodgers carefully before allowing them to live in your home.

Finding a Lodger

As you'll be sharing your home with someone you may not know beforehand, you must screen your prospective lodger very carefully before agreeing to let her move in. You don't want to end up with a nightmare scenario – someone who moves their boyfriend in as well, even though that wasn't part of the deal; doesn't clean up after herself; and refuses to pay the rent for months on end. Don't be taken advantage of: Screen applicants carefully and get the deal in writing before letting anyone move in (see 'Getting it in writing' later in this chapter).

Think carefully about what sort of person you want as a lodger before starting your search. Do you want a male or female, someone your age or younger/older, someone who does the same job as you or who is going to be out at work while you are at home? Can you cope with a smoker or pet-owner? Once you've got a general idea of who you are looking for you can actually start searching.

Lodgers from Hell

A friend overstretched herself on her mortgage but wasn't too concerned about this as she planned to rent out her spare room to help cover it. At first all went according to plan as her ex-flat mate was happy to become her lodger. She carried on paying the rent she'd paid before – only this time it was to my friend, not their previous landlord.

However, after six months, the lodger bought her own place and moved out. My friend asked around but nobody knew anyone looking for a room. She advertised in the local paper but it took six months to find someone – during which time she struggled to pay the mortgage on her own (she had to take out an overdraft, stopped going out, and ate cereal every night). She finally got a response to her ad. She didn't like the guy when he came round but she was desperate so she agreed to let him move in.

It was a disaster from the start. While he wasn't an axe murderer or anything like that, he just wasn't her kind of person. He was untidy and didn't make any effort to help clean the communal areas. He ran up the phone bill and was evasive when it came to paying. And within a couple of weeks of him moving in, he'd been signed off work with stress, which meant he was at home 24 hours a day. She felt like the place just wasn't her own and couldn't wait for him to move out. But they'd both agreed he would stay for six months so she had to stick to this. However, at the end of six, very trying, months, even though he indicated that he would like to stay and his money was useful, she had no hesitation in giving him his marching orders.

Remember. Living with a lodger can work but make sure you screen them very carefully beforehand and set out the ground rules *before* they move in.

There are several ways of finding a lodger:

- ✔ **Ask friends, relatives, or neighbours.** Most people prefer to live with someone they know, or a friend of a friend or relative. This isn't a foolproof way of finding a reliable lodger – they could still miss a rent payment – but you reduce the chances of things going belly up if someone you trust can vouch for them. Even if someone has been recommended, check references from a previous landlord or current employer, so at least you know that she can afford to pay the rent.

✔ **Advertise at work.** Put an advert on the staff notice board or on the Intranet. The advantage of finding someone through your workplace is that there's more of a chance that they're similar to you, which may make living with that person easier.

In contrast, if you advertise in the paper you take pot luck on the type of person you get: You may work night shifts so need peace and quiet to sleep during the day while your lodger may run their carpentry business from home, involving a lot of noise during the day. Compatibility is important.

✔ **Advertise in the local paper.** If all else fails, you may have to put an advert in the paper. This is a good way of reaching potential lodgers but bear in mind that you may well get calls from unsuitable people and be extra careful in wading through the applicants to find the right person.

It's especially important to check references when dealing with strangers. Don't forget your gut feeling: Can you really imagine yourself living with this person? If you don't get good vibes, continue looking for someone else. Don't take the first person who comes along out of desperation (see the nearby 'Lodgers from Hell' sidebar).

Getting it in Writing

Although you don't need a full-blown tenancy agreement, as you would if you were renting out your home to a tenant (see Chapter 15 for more on this), you must get something in writing. The agreement needs to include:

✔ **How much rent the lodger has to pay, how often, and how it will be increased, if necessary.** Check what other landlords in the area are charging before setting the rent.

✔ **What services are provided, such as a cleaner.** You may employ a cleaner a couple of days a week and be happy for the lodger's room to be cleaned as well.

✔ **How much notice either of you have to give to end the arrangement.** This is up to you but one or two months is usually ample on both sides. Notice should be given in writing by either party.

> ✔ **Terms for sharing common areas and bills.** Talk about use of the telephone, how you'll share bills, and so on. Get this in writing at the beginning to avoid falling out later on.

You don't need a rent book as your lodger isn't a tenant in legal terms. But it may be handy to have one anyway so you can keep a record of payments. You can buy a rent book at any high-street stationery shop.

Don't forget to ask for a deposit. A month's rent in advance is reasonable and should be payable before the lodger moves in. A deposit comes in handy if she tries to abscond owing you rent or does any damage. It provides you with an extra layer of protection.

Coping Without a Lodger

The problem with a rent-a-room mortgage is that you end up borrowing more than your salary justifies because the income from the room is brought into the equation. So if your spare room lies empty, despite your best efforts to find a lodger, you may find paying the mortgage a real struggle. However, if you plan ahead you can reduce the chances of this happening.

You don't have to inform your lender if the room is vacant. Once the mortgage has been agreed, your lender won't care what you do (within reason) as long as you manage to make your monthly repayments, on time. You only have to notify the lender of your change in circumstances if you can no longer cope with the repayments.

Your aim must be to have enough money put away to cover the mortgage on your own for three months or so, which gives you ample time to find another lodger if yours moves out. Of course, the longer you can manage the mortgage on your own, the less likely you are to panic and take in someone who isn't suitable simply because you are desperate.

If you have a flexible mortgage (see 'Finding a rent-a-room mortgage' earlier in this chapter), you can get into the habit of overpaying each month when you do have a lodger. In this way you can build up a reserve, which you can draw upon if the room is empty for any period of time. If your mortgage isn't flexible, aim to build up three to six months' salary in an instant access savings account using any surplus rent from the lodger (after the mortgage has been paid that month). This account needs to pay the highest rate of interest you can find: check out Web sites www.moneyfacts.co.uk or www.moneysupermarket.com for the best deals. These savings provide you with a cash reserve to tide you over in case of any emergency – not just an empty room.

Chapter 15

Renting Out Your Home to Cover the Mortgage

*O*ne of the reasons you may be keen to buy a home is that you've had enough of renting – you consider paying rent throwing money down the drain. But if the figures just don't add up and you can't see how you can possibly afford the mortgage on a property of your own, one option is to rent your new home out to tenants – while you live somewhere else. The tenants' rent covers your mortgage until you're in a financial position to handle the mortgage payments yourself – you can then move them out and finally move in yourself.

The alternative is to wait months, perhaps years, until you can afford the mortgage on your own. And all the while property prices are likely to be edging upwards, making that first step onto the ladder seem even more unattainable. Renting your property out enables you to get onto the property ladder sooner rather than later – even if you are still renting yourself – so you don't risk being priced further out of the market.

In this chapter, I help you decide whether you've got what it takes to be a landlord and how to hire a managing agent if you haven't. I also give you information about the specialist mortgage you'll need if you want to rent your property out to tenants.

Considering Buy-to-Let

It may sound odd to buy a property in order to rent it out to someone else. But it's a good way of getting on the housing ladder if you aren't really in a financial position to pay a mortgage on your own every month. By renting your property out to tenants, you can cover your mortgage and expenses – anything left over at the end of the month is a bonus. And eventually, you'll be in a position to move in yourself.

As with any property purchase, you need to work out a budget (see Chapter 2 for more on this) and stick to it.

Understanding the risks involved

Becoming a landlord may seem daunting if you don't have any personal experience of managing property and dealing with tenants. But don't let this lack of experience put you off. Every successful landlord with hundreds of properties started out this way.

There are risks involved, of course, not the least of which is that if you can't find tenants you'll have to pay the mortgage yourself, for example. And as money is tight this may prove to be a problem.

Try to build up some savings (if you haven't got any) in an instant access account paying the highest rate of interest you can find. You can use any surplus left over from the rent after you've paid the mortgage and your running expenses to build up your savings for emergencies. Aim to cover several months' worth of mortgage repayments, so that if you have a void period when you don't have a tenant, you won't be in a blind panic about paying the mortgage.

When your property isn't attractive to tenants, or is in an area where tenants are few and far between, you can have problems renting it out. And if dropping the monthly rent and employing an agent to find you tenants still doesn't work, you have a tough decision to make: Do you cut your losses and sell up in order to buy another property that is more attractive to tenants? If the property is *your* idea of a dream home, you may be reluctant to do this and may have to find other ways of keeping it on (perhaps by living in it yourself and renting out the spare room, if you have one, to cover the mortgage).

Allowing for void periods

No matter how carefully you research your property before buying it, how beautifully you furnish it, and how carefully you advertise for tenants in all the right places, you'll have periods when your property lies empty. If the rental market is quiet, it may be that there is simply a dearth of tenants at that particular time. These *void periods*, when your property sits empty, can be very worrying for a fledgling landlord.

To make matters worse, you're unlikely to have cash reserves to pay the mortgage yourself for months on end – you're renting out your property in the first place because you simply can't afford to live in it yourself.

 If you can't find a tenant when you first attempt to rent out your property, perhaps you're doing something wrong. Maybe the property looks shabby and is putting off prospective tenants. Ask a friend to look round the property with you and ask him what he thinks. It's worth getting another opinion because your friend may spot something you've missed.

If the property's presentation is fine, check that the rent isn't too high. Find out from letting agents what other similar-sized properties in the area are fetching. If you're charging over the market rate, you need to reduce the rent to find a tenant. Check also whether you are advertising in the right places: A single advert that appears once a week in the *Sunday Times* property section, for example, may not be reaching prospective tenants. Assess whether you need to change your advertising strategy.

If you have had a tenant in the past but the property has been empty since he moved out, again, check that the property is in good condition, the rent is still competitive (other landlords may have reduced their rent if the rental market is going through a quiet period), and your advert is well-written and appears in the right places. If all of these details are spot on, try contacting a letting agent to see whether he can find you tenants.

Don't panic. If your property has been empty for a few days, you may be worrying unnecessarily about the prospect of it being vacant for months. You should have some savings in reserve to cover a void period of a month or two (professional landlords allow for a void period of two months every year and expect to make a couple of monthly mortgage payments themselves). See 'Understanding the risks involved' earlier in this chapter for more on building up your savings.

But if the property is empty for several months, and an agent has had no joy finding tenants for you either, you need to think carefully about what you do next. It may be that you'll never find tenants for the property because you've bought in an area where tenants are few and far between or you've bought an extremely unusual property, which doesn't suit the majority of prospective tenants. If you can't afford to pay the mortgage yourself, you may have to consider selling up and buying another property that you can rent out. This is expensive: You must pay for surveyor's fees and legal expenses, as well as stamp duty, all over again. But it's better than the lender repossessing your home because you haven't been able to pay the mortgage.

Don't rush into the decision to sell up. There's a real danger that you'll sell up and not buy another property because you got your fingers burnt this time around. And it may be several years before you are in a position to get back on the housing ladder. Do all you can to hang onto the property before you throw in the towel.

Getting a buy-to-let mortgage

Standard residential mortgages aren't suitable if you are planning to rent out your property: You need a specialist buy-to-let mortgage to reflect the extra risks involved. The main differences between the two are that with a buy-to-let loan the interest rate tends to be higher, you need a bigger deposit, and the lender works out how much to let you borrow based on the rental income rather than your income.

Most buy-to-let loans are now offered by mainstream lenders so you won't end up paying a much higher rate than that on a residential mortgage.

You must be aged 25 or over to qualify for a buy-to-let mortgage. The lender insists that the property is ready to rent before it lets you have a buy-to-let mortgage – it will frown upon a dilapidated property and is unlikely to lend on this. When choosing your buy-to-let mortgage, you need to make many of the same decisions as for a residential mortgage. See Chapter 4 for more details on mortgages.

Explaining rental cover

The big advantage of a buy-to-let mortgage is that your income isn't the deciding factor when the lender works out how much you can borrow. Buy-to-let mortgage providers will ask you how much you earn but what they are really interested in is the *rental cover* – the proportion of the mortgage payment that the rent covers. When you're on a low income, a buy-to-let mortgage may allow you to borrow more than a standard residential mortgage.

Most lenders require a minimum rental cover of 130 per cent. So if the monthly mortgage payments on your rental property are £500, you need to generate rent of £650 a month from your tenants. Some lenders require rental cover of 150 per cent, so you may need to shop around for another loan if the rent won't cover this.

Some lenders take your income into account as well as the rental cover. The amount you have to earn from a source other than your rental income varies from lender to lender, so shop around if it is too restrictive.

Calculate your rental income carefully. Most lenders want some written evidence of how much money the rental property is likely to generate. You can get an estimate of the likely rent from a letting or estate agent who has some knowledge of the local rental market. If agents estimate that the rent you can reasonably expect is much less than what you need to cover 130 per cent of the mortgage repayments, stop wasting your time and look for another property.

Looking at deposit requirements

You need a bigger deposit on a buy-to-let mortgage than on a traditional mortgage because the risks are thought to be greater. Most lenders require a 20 per cent deposit but some ask for as much as 30 per cent and others no more than 15 per cent. If you don't have a big deposit, shop around for a lender requesting a low deposit, or try raising a bigger one. But think twice before taking out a loan to raise a deposit. You are already taking on a lot of debt: Work out whether you can afford to take on more.

Evaluating Your Property-Management Abilities

One of the first things you need to decide is whether to completely self-manage your property or to delegate some or all of the duties to other people. This decision is a personal one, but you can make it more easily by thinking about some of the specifics of managing property. The best way of doing this is by analysing your own skills and experience.

Deciding whether you have a landlord's personality

Being a landlord is a labour of love: You must love people, you must love working with your hands, and you must love solving problems. If you're impatient or easily manipulated, you won't make a great property manager.

Conveying a professional demeanour to your tenants is important. You want them to see you as someone who takes responsibility for the condition of the property. You must also insist that tenants live up to their part of the deal, pay their rent regularly, and refrain from damaging your property.

Take stock of your abilities by answering the following questions, which directly relate to personality traits and abilities that a good hands-on property manager needs. Interview yourself as though you are a job applicant and answer honestly:

✔ Are you a people person who enjoys working with others?

✔ Are you able to keep your emotions in check and out of your business decisions?

✔ Are you a patient and reasonably tolerant person?

✔ Do you have the temperament to handle problems, respond to complaints, and service requests in a positive and rational manner?

✔ Are you well organised?

✔ Do you have strong time-management skills?

✔ Are you meticulous with your paperwork?

✔ Do you have basic accounting skills?

✔ Do you have maintenance and repair abilities?

✔ Are you willing to work and take phone calls on evenings and weekends?

✔ Do you have sales skills?

✔ Are you a good negotiator?

✔ Are you willing to commit the time and effort required to determine the right rent for your property?

✔ Are you familiar with or willing to find out about the laws affecting property management?

✔ Are you willing to consistently and fairly enforce all property rules and rental policies?

✔ Are you interested in finding out more about property management?

Ideally, you answered yes to all of these questions. But even if you didn't, you may still make a good property manager if you're prepared to be flexible. If you answered mainly no, it could be time to call in a managing agent (see 'Finding an agent' later in this chapter).

Evaluating affordability

If you have the right traits for managing property, and if you have the time and live close to your property, consider managing the property yourself.

The big advantage is that you save money because you don't have to pay a monthly fee to a letting agent.

The letting fee can be as much as 15 per cent of the rent for a full management service. And if you're purchasing a small flat you may not be able to generate enough money to pay for a letting agent and make a profit.

By managing the property yourself, you may also save on maintenance costs because you decide who does the repair work or mows the lawn. And if you can do these tasks yourself, you can save even more cash. If you can't, develop a list of reliable handymen and gardeners who do good work and charge low rates.

If your property is in another part of the country from where you are living, it may prove impossible to manage it yourself. You need to be in the vicinity to routinely inspect and maintain a buy-to-let property, especially when a leaky roof or broken pipe demands immediate attention.

Finding the Right Property

You may be wondering how finding a property to rent out differs from finding one to live in. But because you'll be renting out your property – for a few months, if not longer – you also need to consider where tenants want to live, not just your own preferences.

The perfect rental property is located in an area with a rich source of suitable tenants to fill it. The best landlords are dispassionate and ruthless about their purchase because they realise that the type of property they may want to live in may not appeal to tenants. This is where you may encounter difficulty because you *will* be living in the property at some point so it's hard to remain completely disinterested.

Ask dedicated letting agents – not estate agents – for advice on renting property. Estate agents want to earn their commission and get the sale, so they're unlikely to be completely unbiased. The letting agent can provide more useful opinions on location and a particular property.

In your favour is the fact that the easiest properties to let are small one- or two-bedroom flats because more people are living on their own than ever before. Because your budget isn't likely to stretch to a property bigger than this, you're at an advantage already. You may well discover that your property is perfect for people who would be buying their first home if they could afford it.

Flats near local amenities, such as shops and public transport links, always go down well with tenants. Many tenants don't have the resources to run a car, or if they live in a major city such as London, it may not be necessary anyway. If the train or bus station is more than 10 minutes' walk from the property, it's likely to put prospective tenants off. If the property is near a college, university, or hospital, you may have plenty of prospective tenants on your doorstep.

Do your research carefully before making an offer for a property. The sale process is the same as for any property purchase (see Chapters 9 and 10 for more on making an offer and the conveyancing process).

Setting the Rent

Once you get the keys to your new property, you'll be keen to start advertising it and showing prospective tenants round. But first you need to set the rent. Understandably, you want to get as much rent as you can but you must be reasonable. If you set the rent way too high, you aren't going to get any interest from tenants – and if the property is empty, you lose money because you must pay the mortgage out of your own pocket. Set the rent too low and you may not be able to cover the mortgage payments – or you may just about break even. Setting the rent just right is a delicate balancing act.

Knowing how much money you need to break even (once your mortgage payments, insurance, and maintenance costs are taken into account) is important for evaluating the potential return on your property. But the reality is that the amount you need or want to collect in rent is subject to market conditions. Although you may have calculated that you need £750 a month in rent if you're going to break even, if comparable properties are going for £700 a month, you have to accept that you may not make the profit you want.

Beware of overestimating the potential income from your property by using an above-market rent and anticipating virtually no void periods or bad debt. When reality strikes, you can be faced with negative cash flow, and ultimately may even lose your property. Don't fall into this trap: stay realistic. Be conservative in setting your rent, anticipating rental income at 95 per cent of the market rent for a comparable rental property and allow for a void period of one to two full months each year. Anything you make over and above this is a bonus.

Finding Suitable Tenants

The key to success is keeping a tenant in your property for as long as you need one to cover the mortgage. When your property is empty, you have no rental income and must pay the mortgage yourself. Making sure you get a steady stream of tenants who pay the rent on time is central to your success.

Having someone live in your property isn't enough. Your tenant must also pay the rent on time every month and treat your property and the neighbours with respect.

Finding the right tenants also involves working out what your target market is: Who is most likely to find that your property meets their needs? The target market can be relatively broad or fairly narrow, depending on the location, size, and features of your property:

- **Location:** What are some of the benefits of your property's location? Is it near transport links, factories or offices, shops, or other important facilities? Paying attention to your property's location may provide you with a target market that includes employees of certain companies or people who have a need to live in close proximity to certain facilities, such as a mainline train station.

- **Size:** Studios and one-bedroom flats suit single tenants or couples on a budget, while a larger property may appeal to friends sharing or even a family.

- **Amenities:** If you allow pets and have a large garden, you widen your pool of prospective tenants. If your property has storage space and a garage, advertise this.

Looking at methods of attraction

The best advertisement for your property is its exterior appearance. The *kerb appeal* is the impression created when the building is first seen from the road. Properties with well-kept gardens are much more appealing to tenants than those with peeling paint and a broken fence.

You also have a number of options for getting the word out that you have a place to let. I cover them in the next sections.

Using word-of-mouth referral

The most effective and cheapest way of finding tenants is by word-of-mouth referral. Ask around: Work colleagues or friends may know someone who is looking to rent and the added advantage is that you aren't letting your property to a total stranger. Put a notice on the message board at work or send round an email.

Even if you find a tenant through word-of-mouth, you need to check their references as thoroughly as if they answered your advert in the local paper. Don't take anything for granted.

Posting a 'To Let' sign

Erect a 'To Let' sign outside your property. This won't cost you anything – apart from the board itself. You don't need a professional to make a sign – have a go yourself. Just make sure that the board

- ✔ Is in perfect condition, with large, crisp lettering that is easy to read.

- ✔ Is clearly visible from the street.

- ✔ Is not cluttered. You don't need any details other than 'To Let' and a contact number. Don't be tempted to put the monthly rent on the board as you'll inform your competitors how much you are charging and may put off prospective tenants if they think it's too high.

Advertising in newspapers

Most landlords insert a classified ad in the local paper, which is much cheaper than advertising in one of the big property sections in a national newspaper – and more likely to reach your target audience. Many newspapers also have Internet sites and advertise your property here too.

While you need to keep advertising costs under control, don't overlook the fact that each day your property sits empty is another day of lost income that you'll never see.

The key to effective advertising is not the overall number of calls you receive but the number of suitable prospective tenants per pound you spend on advertising. Typically, advertising that costs £10 to £30 per suitable prospective tenant is an effective ad in most regional newspapers. So if your ad in the *Evening Standard* costs £55, expect to receive two or three calls from suitable prospective tenants every time the ad runs. Of course, you'll receive additional inquiries from people who aren't suitable, but you can also measure the effectiveness of your ad by noting how few unsuitable prospective tenants call in response to your ad. Forgive the shameless plug for another of my books, but you can find more information on what to include in your advert in *Renting Out Your Property For Dummies,* also published by Wiley.

Showing tenants round your property

Showing your property to prospective tenants is time-consuming but a vital part of finding the right people to rent to. You need to be organised so that prospective tenants aren't simply wandering round on their own: Act as tour guide, showing them from room to room. But try not to be too controlling – instead, let prospective tenants view the property in the manner that suits them. Encourage them to look at the entire property, including the garden. Avoid making obvious statements such as 'This is the living room' or 'Here's the bathroom' and instead point out the real benefits of particular rooms.

The best way of saving time and effort is to hold an open house, whereby you show the property to several interested tenants within a couple of hours. The alternative is to schedule a separate appointment with every interested potential tenant, which involves constantly making trips back and forth to the property. The only problem with an open house is that it's harder to devote attention to everyone. Try to courteously greet and speak with each potential tenant individually; cover the basic information and get them started on the property tour before beginning work with the next interested party.

Checking references

Even if you hit it off straight away with a prospective tenant, check his rental history and satisfy yourself that he earns as much as he says he does. This vetting reduces the chances of ending up with a duff tenant who takes you for a ride and you have to evict at great expense at a later date.

Ask each prospective tenant to complete an application form. This form needs to include:

- ✔ The tenant's full name and current address.

- ✔ Name and contact details of current and previous land-lords. Check with the landlords whether the tenant has a history of paying his rent on time and looking after the rental property.

- ✔ Employer's name and address, and tenant's salary. Contact the employer to check the tenant's income – it's central to whether he can afford to pay the rent. If he relies on commission or bonuses, make sure you review at least six consecutive months of his most recent pay slips.

- ✔ A character reference. This can be a friend of the family who can vouch for the tenant.

- ✔ Details of a guarantor. If the prospective tenant is currently living with his parents, he won't have a history of paying rent and can't call upon a landlord for a reference. Instead, you can ask for a guarantor, such as a parent, who agrees to pay the rent if the tenant defaults on a payment. Make sure you screen the guarantor as you would a tenant to ensure they are financially qualified, or the guarantee is worthless.

If a prospective tenant provides you with a letter of reference from his landlord or what he says is a copy of his credit file be careful to evaluate the authenticity of such documents. It's not unheard of for a tenant to provide a glowing reference actually written by her boyfriend. Double-check all references.

If the information you receive about your applicant from his current landlord is mostly negative, you may decide you've heard enough and not bother to check with any other former landlords before turning the applicant down. However, be wary that the current landlord may have an agenda: he may be upset that the tenant is moving out. Or you may come across a landlord who doesn't want to say anything bad about a problem tenant so that he can get the tenant out of his property and into yours.

Be particularly careful of prospective tenants who seem to have plenty of cash to pay the deposit and first month's rent, but no verifiable sources of income. The applicant may be involved in an illegal activity, and you may need to evict her later at considerable expense and loss of income.

Taking Care of Your Tenant

It's not enough to find the right tenant, move her in and then simply leave her to it. As landlord you have several ongoing tasks to complete to ensure the rent is paid on time, your tenants are happy and your property is properly maintained.

Collecting the rent

Once a prospective tenant has passed your screening process, you can discuss a suitable move-in date. You must also confirm that you require a banker's draft or building society cheque for a month's rent in advance and the deposit – equal to at least a month's rent – *before* the tenant gets the keys and can move in. Don't accept a personal cheque as you have no way of knowing whether it will clear.

The easiest way for the rent to be paid is by monthly direct debit straight to your bank account. You don't want to mess about with cheques or cash each month or have to chase the tenant when the rent is late – particularly as you are relying on the money to pay your mortgage. Give the tenant your bank details and insist that the rent is paid direct to your bank account on a set date each month. And if the tenant persists in paying his rent late, ensure you crack down on this as soon as possible (see 'Dealing with Tenant Problems' later in this chapter).

Dealing with the deposit

The deposit covers any damage or cleaning needed at the end of the tenancy if the tenant doesn't leave the property as he found it. If he does clean the property thoroughly, the only damage is normal wear and tear, and all his rent is paid up to date, you must return the deposit in full at the end of the tenancy. But if this is not the case, you can make reasonable deductions to cover the repairs, cleaning, or shortfall in the rent.

Don't lower or waive the deposit. If you don't collect the deposit in full you lose your bargaining tool. The tenant may abscond further down the line without paying the rent he owes you if he doesn't have the incentive of the return of his deposit. Or he might think nothing of making cigarette burns on the sofa or wine stains on the carpet if he knows he won't be penalised for it by losing some, or all, of his deposit.

Signing agreements and doing inventories

Legal documents are part and parcel of being a landlord. And while these may appear to be full of complicated jargon, they protect you and your property so you must pay close attention to them.

Each tenant must sign a tenancy agreement, for example, specifying the terms and conditions of the agreement binding you and them. This agreement is a contract between yourself and the tenant for the possession and use of the property in exchange for the payment of rent. Most landlords use the Assured Shorthold Tenancy agreement, which grants you a series of guarantees that make it easier to rent out property and recover possession of it, if needed. You don't have to pay a solicitor to draw one up: A standard tenancy agreement can be bought off-the-shelf from most stationers for about £20.

The tenant has no security of tenure after the end of the term agreed between yourselves; you are certain to obtain possession of the property and don't have to give a reason why. So you can move into the property yourself, when you are ready, so long as you give your tenant two months' written notice.

Assured Shorthold Tenancies tend to start with an initial fixed period. No upper limit is specified but six months to a year is normal. If you opt for six months you can't repossess your property during this time unless the tenant breaks the terms of the agreement. You can't increase the rent or change the terms of the agreement either. After the fixed term, you can renew the agreement for another fixed period or allow it to continue indefinitely on a periodic basis, such as month to month.

Ensure that both you and the tenant sign the tenancy agreement in the presence of witnesses – it then becomes legally binding.

Don't forget to do an *inventory* when the tenant moves in, which is a list of the contents of the property. You need to go through this inventory with the tenant before he moves in so that you can agree on the condition of the fixtures and fittings. Ask the tenant to sign the inventory. If anything is damaged, broken, or missing at the end of the tenancy, you then have proof and can deduct the necessary charge from the tenant's deposit.

Maintaining your property

If you're managing your property rather than hiring an agent, you have to pay attention to routine maintenance, such as washing exterior windows; cutting the grass and weeding the garden; and trimming hedges. If you allow the paint to peel, the gate to remain broken, and the garden to get overgrown, not only will you upset your tenants, you may also adversely affect the value of your property. Make sure you stay on top of the maintenance.

If you don't want to mow the lawn or fix broken doors yourself, you have to find a good gardener or handyman to do these for you. You can save money by doing these jobs yourself however, so think about learning some DIY if this isn't your forte.

You are required by law to properly maintain and repair your rental property to meet all building, housing, and health and safety standards. From the day the tenant moves in until the day he moves out, you must keep the property in a safe and habitable condition (see the nearby sidebar 'Safety and security').

Safety and security

Landlords are legally obliged to install smoke detectors on every floor in all rental properties built after June 1992. Even if your property was built before this date, I strongly recommend that you install smoke alarms in all hallways and just inside sleeping areas, in compliance with the manufacturer's specifications. Don't forget to inspect and test them when a new tenant moves in and ask the tenant to test them on the first day of every month (this date is easy to remember).

Gas appliances come with very strict legal requirements. The Gas Safety (Installation and Use) Regulations Act 1994 requires all landlords to maintain the gas appliances in their rental properties through annual inspections and safety checks. You can't do these checks yourself: You must have a CORGI-registered engineer carry them out and you must give your tenant a copy of the gas safety certificate each year. Failure to ensure that these annual checks are carried out can result in a fine or imprisonment.

If your property is furnished, remember that it's an offence to have furniture that doesn't comply with the 1988 Fire and Safety Regulations. Beware of old sofas because those manufactured before 1988 are considered a fire hazard and must not be used. If in doubt, throw the furniture out – if you break these regulations you can be fined up to £5,000 or, worse still, imprisoned for up to six months.

Deal with maintenance requests from your tenants quickly and professionally. This is the only way to keep tenants happy. You also enhance your investment by looking after your property so if the tenant tells you a damp patch has appeared on the bedroom ceiling, you'd be mad not to deal with it as soon as possible.

Emergency maintenance requests at all hours of the day and night are part and parcel of being a landlord. When you get a call like this from your tenant, you first need to determine whether the urgent maintenance request really is an emergency – one that needs doing immediately in order to prevent further property damage or minimise the chance of endangering people. Most common are plumbing or electrical problems. If a genuine emergency occurs, advise the tenant of the steps to take to limit further damage. If a pipe is leaking, tell the tenant to turn the water off at the stopcock, for example.

It's a good idea to develop a preventative maintenance plan. This plan can involve an annual check of the property, for example, and enables you to address problems while they are still minor, saving you money – and night-time call outs – in the long run.

Dealing with Tenant Problems

Although checking references thoroughly greatly enhances your success in picking good tenants, there are no guarantees. Some tenants don't pay their rent, some disturb the neighbours, damage the property, or keep a growing collection of old bangers on the front lawn. In extreme cases, you need to take immediate steps to remove a tenant from your property and replace them with someone else.

Other tenants – like the one who pays his rent a few days late every single month, or the one who sneaks in a dog even though pets aren't allowed – are more subtle in the problems they present, and their behaviour may not warrant eviction.

Whenever you have a problem with a tenant, make a note of it, even if it is only a minor concern, because over time problems may add up or increase in severity. If you need to evict a tenant later on, having written proof of how long the problem has dragged on is essential, especially if the matter comes to court.

View eviction as a last resort because this is emotionally draining and costly in terms of lost rent and legal fees. Try communicating with your tenant instead, and make a note of conversations you have or agreements you reach (see the 'Serving legal notices' sidebar nearby).

Late payment of rent

One of the toughest issues you may encounter is how to deal with a tenant who is consistently late paying his rent. The tenant may not create any other problems, but he just can't seem to get the rent in on time. In my experience, this nagging problem won't go away unless you put a stop to it. Inform the tenant in writing that he has breached his tenancy agreement – and be sure to do so each and every time he pays late. It's worth including a clause in the tenancy agreement whereby a charge is incurred for late rent payments – and make sure you enforce this. Let the tenant know in writing that late payments are grounds for eviction – even if you're not necessarily ready to go that route just yet.

Additional occupants

If you suspect your tenant has moved an additional occupant into the property, such as his girlfriend, you must first talk to the tenant to find out what's going on. If it's clear that the additional occupant is not a guest but living in the property full-time, write to the tenant telling him he's violating his tenancy agreement. Insist that the additional occupant leaves as soon as possible or is formally added to the tenancy agreement. If that person is an adult, they also have to go through your screening process and have their references checked.

Too much noise

You usually hear about a noisy tenant from one of the tenant's neighbours. If you receive a complaint, go round yourself and investigate. You can witness at first-hand the extent of the problem – information which can be useful when speaking to the noisy tenant. Knock on the door while the music is blaring because the tenant will then find it hard to deny that the noise is excessive. If the problem continues, issue a written warning.

Broken tenancy agreements

Unfortunately, some tenants do a moonlight flit and scarper before their tenancy agreement has come to an end – usually owing you rent. First, check that the tenant has indeed vacated the property (and hasn't just gone on a long holiday). Then, get the property ready to rent again as soon as you can. You may have to write off the lost rent if you can't get hold of the tenant – but the deposit may cover what you are owed.

Serving legal notices

Non-paying or unsatisfactory tenants can be evicted after eight weeks of behaviour that directly defies their tenancy agreement. In order to evict a tenant you have to instruct a solicitor to serve an eviction notice, which must be handed to the tenant in person. You have to pay for this; be aware that you may not recover your money. If your tenant doesn't pay up, the next step is to take him to court.

Taking a tenant to court is a quick and simple process. Nobody wants a county court judgement (CCJ) against them because it blots their credit file and makes renting another property hard. Right-minded tenants will want to avoid that scenario at all costs and may well pay the money they owe before it comes to court. If they don't, you must fill out a form, available from your local county court, detailing the amount you are owed in arrears, plus any damage to the property or goods stolen. You'll be charged a court fee, calculated on a sliding scale and depending on the amount you are owed. If you win your case, you get this money back from the tenant.

The court sends the completed form to the tenant. The tenant can pay up there and then, counterclaim, or let the judge decide the outcome of the matter at a court hearing. If the tenant simply can't afford to pay, you'll be advised that there's no point taking legal action.

If the case does go to court and a CCJ is made against the tenant for non-payment of rent, the judge decides how much the tenant needs to pay you. If the tenant doesn't pay up, he may receive a visit from a bailiff with the legal authority to remove goods to sell to pay off the debt he owes you. Alternatively, the judge may decide that the debt is deducted in instalments from the tenant's wages or benefit.

Departing housemates

If one housemate is leaving in the middle of the tenancy, he may request his portion of the deposit be returned to him. Retain the entire deposit until all occupants on the tenancy agreement have vacated the property. If one of the tenants moves out early, he must resolve deposit issues with the remaining tenants.

If a new housemate is replacing the departing tenant, check their references as normal. And if the remaining tenants can't find someone else to move in, remind them that they are responsible for paying the full amount of the rent, as agreed on the tenancy agreement – it's in their interests to find a replacement quickly.

Finding an Agent

If you've heard lots of horror stories about how things can go wrong with property management, or simply don't have time to do it yourself, you may decide to use a managing agent to do it all for you.

There are several advantages to using a management firm:

- ✔ They have the expertise and experience to manage rental property, plus knowledge about relevant legislation and safety regulations.
- ✔ They're able to remain fair, firm, and friendly with tenants.
- ✔ They have screening procedures and can typically screen tenants more objectively than you can yourself.
- ✔ They handle property management issues throughout the day and have staffing for after-hour emergencies.
- ✔ They have contacts and preferential pricing with many suppliers and contractors who can quickly and efficiently get work done.
- ✔ They handle all bookkeeping, including rent collection.
- ✔ They have well-established rent collection policies and procedures to follow when tenants' rental payments are late.

Of course, there are some disadvantages to using a letting agent as well:

- ✔ Management fees eat into your profits.
- ✔ They often won't have the same care, consideration, and concern that you have for your property.
- ✔ They may take longer to find tenants if they have several other vacancies they are trying to let at the same time.
- ✔ They may not be as diligent in collecting late rent as you would be.

Make sure you consider the pros and cons to determine whether working with a letting agent is right for you.

Screening through affiliation and insurance

Letting agents don't have to be affiliated to a national body but it makes sense for you to opt for one that is so that you know that they are of a certain standard. In addition, if a dispute arises, you can appeal to the body the agent is affiliated to, to intervene on your behalf.

Examine the letting agent's credentials. Are they a member of the Association of Residential Letting Agents (ARLA), the professional and regulatory body solely concerned with residential lettings? Members are kept up to date with changes in legislation and are governed by ARLA's Principles of Professional Conduct, providing a framework of professional and ethical standards. To gain membership, agents must, among other things, demonstrate that their client accounts are professionally managed. They must also offer a full management service to landlords on top of basic letting and rent collection. Other accreditation to look out for is membership of the government-backed National Approved Letting Scheme (NALS), membership of the Royal Institute of Chartered Surveyors (RICS), or membership of the National Association of Estate Agents (NAEA).

Check that the letting agent is properly insured. The company should be a member of the Client Money Protection scheme, which provides professional indemnity insurance. This scheme safeguards both your rent and the tenants' deposits if the management company runs into difficulties or even goes bust. The management company is your agent and collects your rents and deposits, so they also need to have fidelity insurance to protect you in case an employee embezzles or mishandles your money. Controls on client accounts are very strict for ARLA members.

Examining the management contract

Some property management companies request long-term management contracts that can only be cancelled with good reason. Avoid signing a property management contract if it can't be cancelled by giving 30 days' written notice. A property management company that knows it's only as good as its most recent month's performance stays motivated to treat your property with the time and attention needed to get top results.

Make sure all your concerns are addressed in the management agreement. You need to know exactly what weekly or monthly reporting the agent provides, when your property expenses will be paid, and who is responsible for payment of critical items such as the mortgage, insurance, and property taxes. Leave nothing to chance.

If the letting agent can't clarify the language used in the contract or provide a complete list of services you can expect for your fee, he's unlikely to go out of his way to help you later. Treat this vagueness as a warning sign, and find a letting agent who acts more reasonably.

Ask your solicitor to look over the contract to ensure nothing is included which is detrimental to your interests. Agreements are usually written strictly in the best interests of the property management company and not the owner of the property.

Deciding what type of agent you want

Don't assume that a big letting agent can do the best job for your property or that the small company has the credentials, experience, and knowledge that you need. Try to find a letting agent familiar with your kind of property – with a little research, you can find the right fit.

Professional letting agents can handle a wide range of duties. If you opt for full management, you'll typically get the following services:

- Preparing, advertising, and showing the property.
- Introducing, vetting, and selecting the tenants.
- Preparing the tenancy agreement.
- Advising on inventories for furnished property, changes in legislation, and Council Tax.
- Collecting the rent and paying the balance to your account.
- Providing regular accounts.
- Regularly inspecting the property and overseeing repairs.
- Enforcing your rules and regulations.
- Dealing with tenants' complaints.

More limited management services are also available. Maybe you just need help finding tenants in the first place and are willing to pay a basic fee for this. Or you may want help finding tenants and collecting the rent as well. Each letting agent has his own scale of charges and terms and conditions.

Looking at the costs involved

Make sure you understand how much the letting agent's services cost: Charges can vary considerably in different parts of the country. But don't be swayed by price alone because more often than not, you get what you pay for. Don't be afraid to negotiate the fee, either – you never know your luck.

Agents generally charge 15 per cent of the monthly rent for a full management service, 12.5 per cent for rental collection, and 10 per cent for simply finding tenants. But there are no hard-and-fast rules and charges may vary between agencies. In addition, comparing fees charged by different firms can be difficult because they are calculated in various ways. Some charge a set-up fee for preparing the initial contract; others charge for preparing the inventory. You can also be charged a fee if the tenant renews the tenancy. The best way to compare prices is to ask several agents for a written quotation of exactly what is covered.

Letting agents essentially charge for services based on the amount of time that is required of different staff members to manage your property. A letting agent has an idea of the average number of hours the company has to spend each month on managing your property – he then calculates a management charge that generates the fee necessary to provide the proper resources to effectively do so.

Most management companies operate on a no let, no fee basis, receiving a percentage of the collected income for managing a rental property. However, a few companies also charge a flat fee per month. Go with a company whose management fee is a percentage of the collected income; this kind of fee is a strong motivator to the agent to ensure that rents are kept at market rate and actually collected on time. Never pay a management fee that is based solely on the potential income of a property.

Chapter 16

Buying with the Help of a Housing Association

. . . .

. . . .

*I*f you've done the sums and still can't work out how you can possibly afford to buy a property, it's worth thinking about social housing in the form of the Homebuy or shared ownership scheme. You can get help purchasing your first home, and with developers working closely with housing associations there are plenty of properties to choose from.

Affordable housing isn't all cramped bed-sits and poky flats. Most new developments, even the swankiest ones in glamorous locations, must include a proportion of affordable housing. Affordable apartments can now be found in exclusive riverside developments in London, for example, boasting gorgeous views. Living space can also be extremely generous: Apartments in the region of 30 to 35 square metres are not unheard of.

Sound tempting? Well, if you want to find out whether you can get a piece of the action, read on. In this chapter I look at the two main schemes offered by housing associations: shared ownership (part buy/part rent) and Homebuy, which enables you to buy a home on the open market with a loan from the association.

Investigating Housing Associations

A housing association is just one type of *registered social landlord (RSL),* which is a non-profit-making organisation that provides and manages homes for rent and sale for people who need housing but can't afford to rent or buy privately. Other types are housing societies or non-profit-making housing companies.

Most RSLs in England use money from the Housing Corporation (www.housingcorp.gov.uk) or local authority. The Housing Corporation is a non-departmental public body sponsored by the Office of the Deputy Prime Minister to fund and regulate housing associations in England. It visits social landlords intermittently to make sure they are managing their property and finances well.

Northern Ireland, Scotland and Wales have their own organisations, which provide a similar role. In Northern Ireland, contact the Northern Ireland Housing Executive (www.nihe.gov.uk); in Scotland, Communities Scotland (www.communities scotland.gov.uk) and in Wales, the Welsh Assembly (www.housingwales.gov.uk).

RSLs offer two main schemes to help you step on the housing ladder (availability depends on where you live). These are:

✔ Shared ownership (known as Co-ownership in Northern Ireland)

✔ Homebuy (available only in England and Wales)

I explain both schemes in more detail in the following sections.

Seeing What's Involved in Shared Ownership

Shared ownership provides financial assistance to people who can't afford to buy a property on their own. In a *shared ownership* scheme, you buy a percentage of a property and pay rent on the remainder to the housing association. Gradually, you buy further shares until you own the property outright. I look at how shared ownership works, who can apply, and how you do so in the following subsections.

Shared ownership isn't offered only by government-funded associations. Private developers sometimes offer shared ownership schemes that work on the same principles, though the details may vary and a wide range of conditions apply.

Contact the Housing Corporation (www.housingcorp.gov.uk) for more details on all the shared ownership schemes in the area in which you wish to buy.

How the system works

Under shared ownership, you buy a share in a property – usually 50 per cent, though you can buy anything from 25 to 75 per cent, depending on your income and savings – from the housing association. You pay for your share by taking on a mortgage, which you arrange with a bank or building society: The percentage of the property you buy initially depends on how much the lender is prepared to let you borrow (see 'How the mortgage works' later in this chapter for more details). You rent the remaining share of the property from the housing association. So, each month you pay the mortgage to your lender and also pay rent to the housing association.

To make this affordable, the rent is kept artificially low. The greater the share of the property you purchase, the less rent you have to pay. The rent is usually reviewed on an annual basis. If you are buying a flat, you must also pay a service charge to the housing association to cover the building's maintenance.

The housing association grants you a 99-year lease, which details your rights and responsibilities and entitles you to live in your home as an owner-occupier. The lease also spells out how you go about buying further shares in the property. If there are any terms you don't understand in the lease, ask the housing association or your solicitor to explain these to you.

Even though you don't buy the property outright initially, you have the usual rights and responsibilities of a full owner-occupier and are responsible for all repairs and bills.

The lease also includes restrictions. If you want to make improvements or alterations to the property you must ask the housing association for permission first. There are also certain restrictions that come into play when you sell the property (see 'How to go about selling up' later in this chapter).

To help you decide how big a share of the property to buy, first calculate how much your mortgage repayments will be and then how much rent you'll have to pay to the housing association. Don't forget to budget for service charges and remember that you'll pay the usual survey and valuation costs and legal fees. (See 'What it costs' later in this chapter for more details on cost.)

Who qualifies

Priority for shared ownership is normally given to existing public sector tenants or those on local authority or social landlords' waiting lists. In order to register your interest and join the waiting list (which is usually rather long, depending on how popular the area is), you must usually have been living in the borough for two years. If this applies to you, put your name down straightaway. The housing association can give you an idea of how long you are likely to have to wait.

Up to four people can become joint owners under shared ownership as long as every applicant individually and jointly meets the eligibility criteria. Your solicitor can advise you on this.

As a rule, you need a minimum income of £17,000 a year: The maximum household income usually allowed is £42,000 for an individual, or £50,000 for a couple.

Many housing associations only accept first-time buyers although some will also consider homeowners.

What it costs

Consider whether you can afford to buy a shared ownership home in the same way as with any other property. (See Chapter 2 for more on budgeting and working out how big a mortgage you can afford.) The same rules apply – you must pay your mortgage every month or your home will be repossessed by your lender and sold to clear your debts. You must also pay the same fees for the valuation or survey, stamp duty, and so on. (See Chapter 2 for full details of these.)

You must also pay for all repairs and redecoration – internal and external. The housing association does help by paying for the upkeep of the building and buildings insurance, though you pay a service charge to cover these expenses. As with any leasehold property, the landlord must tell you how your service charge is spent and consult you before any major repair or maintenance works are undertaken.

As well as paying the mortgage and rent each month, allow for a few other ongoing costs. Council tax must be paid to the local authority: Contact your local council (you will find the contact details in the local phone book) to find out how much you will have to budget for this. You're also responsible for your own utility bills, of course, furnishing the property, and ensuring its contents are insured (Chapter 4 has more on insurance).

What the steps are

To successfully purchase a home under shared ownership, follow these steps:

1. **Get the terms of shared ownership and an application form from the housing association in your area.**

   To find one, check out Housing Net's Web site (www. housingnet.co.uk), which has a database of all housing associations in the UK. You can also try the Housing Corporation if you live in England, as this funds English housing associations (www.housing corp.gov.uk) or Scottish Homes' Web site, which has details of housing associations in Scotland (www. communitiesscotland.gov.uk).

2. **Complete and return the application form.**

   If the housing association is satisfied that you're a suitable applicant they ask you to come in to chat through your application.

If successful, you can start looking for a property to buy.

3. **Find a property that suits you.** (See 'Where to find a property' below.)

   Discuss with the housing association how big a share of it you can afford.

4. **Apply to a lender for a mortgage to cover your share.**

   (See 'How the mortgage works' later in this chapter.)

5. **Pass on your solicitor's details to your housing association.**

   (Chapter 9 has details on how to find a solicitor.) The housing association sends your solicitor a copy of the draft lease. He goes through this, advises you on what it says, conducts local authority searches, and investigates the title to the property (see Chapter 10 (England, Wales, and Northern Ireland) and Chapter 11 (Scotland) for the solicitor's role during conveyancing).

6. **Complete the sale.**

   If all is fine, you own part of the property.

Avoiding stamp duty

One benefit of shared ownership is that you can avoid paying stamp duty – completely legitimately, of course. Stamp duty is a tiered tax, payable on properties that cost over £60,000 (see Chapter 2 for more details).

So, if your property costs less than £120,000, and you buy a 50 per cent share initially, your share will be below the level at which stamp duty is charged. If you buy more shares of the house in small chunks – 10 or 25 per cent each time – you stay below the stamp duty threshold – unless the property has shot up in value during that time.

So you can eventually purchase the full 100 per cent without paying any stamp duty. On a £120,000 property, this will save you £1,200 so while the Chancellor of the Exchequer might not be pleased I imagine you'll be thrilled.

Where to find a property

If your housing association decides that you qualify for shared ownership, you can start looking at the properties owned by the housing association to find one to suit you. Housing associations own many properties, including new and renovated flats and houses, so you should be able to find one you like.

Prices vary according to location but expect to pay less than the going rate – this is supposed to be affordable housing after all.

 View properties in the same way as if you weren't buying through a housing association: Ask similar questions (see Chapter 8 for more details on what to look for when viewing a property).

For details of shared ownership properties for sale, contact HOMES (Housing Mobility and Exchange Services) at (www. homes.org.uk) or call 020 7963 0200.

You don't always *have* to buy a housing association property: In some areas you can find a property on the open market. This is known as *do-it-yourself shared ownership* and otherwise works in the same way as conventional shared ownership, only the housing association buys the property first – and then you buy a share from them. As long as the housing association is satisfied with the condition of the property and its location, it can arrange for you to purchase it on a shared ownership basis. Contact your local housing association for more details of this scheme.

How the mortgage works

Once you find a property you want to buy, you need a shared ownership mortgage. Not all lenders offer these because they are considered more risky than conventional lending, as a third party – the housing association – is involved, and you're more likely to be someone who may otherwise struggle to buy a property. However, this attitude is changing: As house prices skyrocket, the type of person buying through shared ownership is likely to be someone who simply doesn't earn enough to buy a property in the area they live or work in.

Interest rates can vary dramatically so shop around for the best deal. Start with your bank or building society and compare what they offer you (if anything) with what else is available. The housing association can suggest sympathetic lenders.

The lender may require a copy of the lease to help it make a decision about your application: You can get a copy of this from the housing association.

If you have a bad credit history you may still be able to get a mortgage, although your options are more limited. Check first to be sure the housing association is happy with your credit history – if they are, shop around for a lender who feels the same way. A mortgage broker can point you in the right direction (see Chapter 4 for more details on using a broker).

If your housing association doesn't allow you to buy 100 per cent of the property over time, you may find it difficult to get a mortgage. Check before you commit yourself to anything.

How to buy further shares

Once you have bought a share, you have the option to *staircase* up to full ownership – by buying the remaining shares in the property – as, and when, you can afford to. You don't have to purchase further shares at a later date, although if you don't intend to do so you may find it difficult to get a mortgage (see 'How the mortgage works' earlier in this chapter).

Your first opportunity to buy more shares usually comes up after a year. Check your lease and contact the housing association when you're ready to purchase further shares in your home. The landlord then has the property valued (you have to pay for the valuation) and tells you how much a further share will cost you. You have three months to arrange a mortgage to buy the further share. Time to go back to your lender and ask for the extra funds.

How to go about selling up

You can sell your property whenever you like, but you must inform the housing association in writing that you intend to do so. Because housing associations exist to service the community and provide affordable housing, you can't simply stick your housing association property on the market and sell it to the highest bidder when you are ready to move.

If you don't own the property outright it may affect what happens when you sell it. Clauses in the lease may enable the housing association to nominate potential buyers and restrict the asking price to what an independent valuer says the property is worth. This ensures that the property remains available to people for whom shared ownership is intended. Ask the housing association whether you have such a clause in your lease.

Even if there's a price cap on what you can sell the property for, it doesn't mean you can't make a profit, as your property is valued according to its market value. But remember that prices can go down as well as up so you may end up losing money.

You don't have to own 100 per cent of the property in order to sell up: If you own 50 per cent, for example, you get half of the sale price and the housing association keeps the rest.

Homing in on Homebuy

A handful of housing associations and other registered social landlords (RSLs) in England offer the Homebuy scheme, which helps you buy a property on the open market using a loan from the RSL. Key Homebuy is aimed at key workers in London (see Chapter 17 for more information on this).

Wales has a very limited provision. Find out from your local council if it operates such a scheme.

Checking your eligibility

Eligibility for Homebuy is very strict. You must be at least one of the following:

- ✔ A council or housing association tenant.
- ✔ On a housing waiting list and nominated by your local council as being in housing need.

✔ Able to obtain a mortgage to cover 75 per cent of the purchase price of a property (see 'Paying attention to the process' later in the chapter).

You also need money to cover the other costs of buying a home such as legal fees and stamp duty (if applicable).

The money available under Homebuy is extremely limited so even if you are accepted, you may spend a significant amount of time on a waiting list. The length of the list depends on where you live.

Up to four people can jointly buy a property under the Homebuy scheme as long as the total of everyone's savings and income does not qualify the group to buy a home outright. At least one of you must be a tenant of a local council or RSL. If any of the people you are buying with already has a home, it has to be sold before you can proceed.

Paying attention to the process

Under the Homebuy scheme in England, you pay 75 per cent of the property's purchase price using a mortgage and savings (if you have them). The more savings you have, the less you'll be allowed to borrow. You apply for a mortgage in the normal way (see 'Getting a suitable mortgage' later in this chapter) and the housing association lends you the rest of the money. (In Wales, you pay 70 per cent of the purchase price; the housing association purchases the remaining 30 per cent.)

You don't pay interest on the loan from the housing association and you don't pay it back in monthly instalments. You don't repay the loan until you sell your home. You repay 25 per cent of the current market value of the property when you sell (an amount that may be more or less than you borrowed depending on how property prices have fared). For example, if you buy a £100,000 home with £25,000 from the Homebuy scheme, and decide to sell after seven years when the property is worth £150,363, you repay £37,591 – the equivalent to paying an annual percentage rate (APR) of approximately 6 per cent on the loan.

You can repay the loan early if you like. The amount you repay depends on the value of the property at the time. But the important thing is that the loan is repaid.

For more information on the Homebuy scheme in England, contact the Housing Corporation on 020 7393 2000 or your local housing association. In Wales, contact the Welsh Federation of Housing Associations on 020 2930 3150.

Filling out an application

The first step toward qualifying for the Homebuy scheme is to fill out an application form. You can obtain a form from a housing association operating the scheme in your area. Once the form is completed and signed, send it back. Keep a copy for your own records.

The housing association checks the information you supply and may ask for evidence of income and savings. If the housing association is satisfied with your answers, you'll receive a letter informing you that you qualify for the scheme. Once funds become available, you receive approval to look for a home up to a certain price limit. This amount reflects property prices in the area in which you are buying.

Once you find a property (see 'Finding a property' later in this chapter) and agree a price with the seller, you can apply for a mortgage and commission a survey (see Chapter 4 for mortgages and Chapter 9 for more on surveys). You also need to appoint a solicitor to act on your behalf. The housing association provides you with guidance notes to pass on to your lender as to how the Homebuy scheme operates.

Don't enter any legal agreement to buy a property until your application is approved by the housing association. Once you receive mortgage approval, pass on details of the property to the housing association. If the property is approved, the sale goes through in the same way as any other, apart from the fact that 25 per cent of the funds are coming from a source other than you.

As well as the cost of the property itself, you must pay for a number of other items, including legal fees, a survey, and possibly stamp duty. Chapter 2 has information on these costs.

Finding a property

Unlike shared ownership, with the Homebuy scheme you can buy any property in England (or Wales, if you are buying via the Welsh scheme) for sale on the open market and fit to live in – meaning it doesn't need extensive renovations to make it habitable. But there are some restrictions:

- ✔ There is an upper limit on the price of a property considered for the scheme, depending on the area. Key Homebuy, which covers London (www.keyhomebuy.com), lends buyers a maximum of £50,000 and the maximum value of any home bought through the scheme is £160,000.

- ✔ The property should be close to your place of work. For example, Key Homebuy insists that the journey to your usual place of work by car or public transport not take longer than 90 minutes.

- ✔ The property should have vacant possession (meaning no sitting tenants).

- ✔ You can't buy at auction.

- ✔ You can't buy the home you are currently renting.

- ✔ You must have a valuation *and* a homebuyer's report. The housing association requires evidence of this. You don't have to pay for a full structural survey, however.

- ✔ If the property is leasehold, there should be at least 55 years left to run on the lease.

Getting a suitable mortgage

To get a mortgage to pay for your 75 per cent of the purchase price you must deal with a lender approved by the housing association. Such lenders include building societies, banks, friendly societies, or insurance companies. Your housing association can give you more details about this when you are accepted onto the Homebuy scheme.

For information on which type of mortgage and what sort of rate suits you best, go to Chapter 4 for more details.

Owning up to your responsibilities

When you purchase through the Homebuy scheme, you're considered to own the property outright. Thus, you're responsible for all property repairs and maintenance, as well as paying your mortgage.

If you buy a house, take out buildings insurance to cover the property in case disaster strikes. Your lender will insist upon you doing this (see Chapter 4 for details). If you own a flat, the landlord is responsible for the buildings insurance: You pay for this via the service charge.

If you want to build an extension on your property or carry out other improvements, you must get permission from the housing association first. And if you need to take out a further loan from your bank or building society to cover the work, you need the housing association's consent before you do so.

Selling your home or repaying the loan

As soon as you want to sell your home or repay the loan, contact the housing association who gave you the Homebuy loan in the first place. They'll obtain a valuation, which you pay for in addition to 25 per cent of the market value of the property.

Chapter 17

Getting Assistance Because You're a Key Worker

· ·

In This Chapter

▶ Understanding what makes a key worker

▶ Buying property through the key worker living scheme

· ·

*R*ising property prices, particularly in the south of England, are causing real problems for businesses trying to recruit and retain staff. Many workers in the public sector, such as nurses, teachers, and fire-fighters, simply can't afford to buy property close to where they work and as a result are quitting their professions in droves for more lucrative employment.

According to research from mortgage lender The Halifax, the average house price is now almost six times the average salary for nurses and fire-fighters. Other research shows that teachers are finding it difficult to buy property close to where they work. In a sample of seven London Local Education Authorities the Institute of Policy Studies in Education found that teachers said that the overwhelming reason to leave London was the cost of housing. And 60 per cent of nurses who responded to the *Keep London Working* survey said cheaper accommodation was a reason for looking for work outside London.

To make life easier for workers key to keeping the community functioning and to encourage them to stay in their chosen professions, the Government has introduced a number of schemes aimed at helping them get onto the first rung of the property ladder.

In this chapter I look at the various schemes targeted at key workers, who qualify for these schemes, and what the application process involves. I also help you assess which scheme is the best one for your circumstances.

Defining Key Workers

The definition of a *key worker* is constantly expanding, but the term generally means someone who provides a public service – including teachers, nurses, police officers, health and social workers, train and bus drivers, paramedics, fire-fighters, and local authority planners. Whether you qualify for a particular key worker scheme or not depends on the aims of that scheme, the priorities of the local authority and the money available.

Key workers tend to earn a low wage, making it nearly impossible for most of them to buy a home in city centres close to their place of work. Yet key workers may well have to work unsociable shifts and so benefit from living near their workplace. The various schemes designed to help key workers aim to address this problem by offering financial assistance to enable them to purchase a property close to their place of work.

Qualifying as a key worker

To qualify for the key worker living scheme, you must have a frontline role in delivering an essential service in the public sector. The sector you work in must have serious recruitment and retention problems and your maximum household income needs to be no more than £60,000. Key workers who are eligible for assistance include:

- ✔ Nurses and other National Health Service (NHS) staff
- ✔ Teachers in primary or secondary schools, further education colleges (teaching A-Levels and NVQs to those aged 16 and over), and sixth form colleges
- ✔ Police officers and civilian staff in some police forces
- ✔ Prison service and probation staff

> ✔ Social workers, educational psychologists, local authority planners (on a pilot basis, in London only), and occupational therapists employed by local authorities
>
> ✔ Fire-fighters (all grades) in some fire and rescue services (currently Hertfordshire)

Eligibility criteria vary across regions depending on local recruitment and retention policies. To find out whether you qualify for assistance, see 'Applying for key worker assistance' below.

Applying for key worker assistance

To find out whether you qualify for key worker living and to apply if you do, you must contact the zone agent that covers the area you work in, rather than the area in which you currently live.

The zone agent is a registered social landlord, usually a housing association, who markets housing schemes for key workers across the area. They deal with applications and arrange the help you need. To find the relevant zone agent for you, go to the Office of the Deputy Prime Minister's Web site (www.odpm.gov.uk) where they're listed.

Understanding the Key Worker Living Scheme

On 1 April 2004, the Government launched a new scheme to help key workers get on the property ladder – *key worker living*. This replaced the starter home initiative.

Key worker living is a £690-million scheme that operates in London, the South-East, and the East of England – areas where it is proving particularly difficult to recruit and retain public sector workers. It offers key workers four options:

- ✔ To buy a first home using an interest-free equity (Homebuy) loan from a registered social landlord or housing association.

- ✔ To upgrade to a family home. You may already own a property but need somewhere bigger to accommodate your family. Upgrading wasn't allowed under the starter home initiative and the scheme came in for much criticism because of this.

- ✔ To purchase a newly-built property through the shared ownership scheme (see 'Sharing ownership of newly-built properties' later in this chapter).

- ✔ To rent a home at an affordable price. *Intermediate renting* can help you rent a home for 75 to 80 per cent of the local market rent for that type of property. Because this book focuses on buying a property rather then renting, it doesn't include information on intermediate renting. You can get information from the Housing Corporation (020 7393 2000) or go to www.housingcorp.gov.uk.

All of the schemes are administered by the Housing Corporation, which aims to help 6,000 key workers a year realise their property ambitions.

The property you buy under key worker living must suit your household's needs and be within a reasonable travelling distance of your workplace. The particular scheme you opt for affects the property you can buy: Under key worker Homebuy, you can purchase a home on the open market but with key worker shared ownership, you must buy a newly-built home already owned by the housing association. Check with your zone agent to find out what properties are available.

For details of shared ownership properties for sale, contact HOMES (Housing Mobility and Exchange Services). There is a £30 fee for registering (www.homes.org.uk) or call 020 7963 0200.

Key worker Homebuy is very popular and most areas regularly exhaust their annual funding each year, so put your name down as soon as possible if you are interested. For more details on the scheme, go to the Office of the Deputy Prime Minister's Web site at www.odpm.gov.uk/keyworkerliving.

There is also a small scheme for key workers in the South-West. For more details, contact the Housing Corporation local office on 01392 428200.

Joining a Homebuy scheme

Key worker Homebuy works in the same way as the nationwide Homebuy scheme, in which low-income workers can buy a home on the open market with the help of a loan from the housing association of up to £50,000. The remainder of the property purchase price is covered by a mortgage, applied for in the normal way.

Chapter 16 explains all the ins and outs of Homebuy, and the same rules and benefits apply with just a few exceptions:

- ✔ The property must be within 90 minutes travelling time from your workplace.

- ✔ The property must cost no more than £210,000.

- ✔ In a regular Homebuy scheme, you don't have to pay off the interest-free loan from the housing association until you sell the property. However, if you're involved in a Homebuy scheme as a key worker and then leave your profession so you are no longer a key worker, you have two years to repay the assistance you received. However, if you are forced to retire due to ill health, this rule may not apply. Contact your zone agent for more information.

- ✔ If you already own property, it doesn't necessarily mean you can't buy a property under the key worker living scheme, but it may affect your eligibility. Check with the zone agent, usually a housing association, running the scheme in your area. (See 'Applying for key worker assistance' elsewhere in this chapter.)

Loans of up to £100,000 are available for small groups of schoolteachers with the 'potential to become leaders of London's education system in the future', under the London challenge teacher key Homebuy scheme. Teachers likely to qualify are those in their thirties and forties who would otherwise be forced to move out of London because they can't afford a family home.

Sharing ownership of a new-built property

Another alternative for key workers trying to get on the property ladder is shared ownership of newly-built properties. Under this scheme, you buy a share (say, 50 per cent) of a newly-built property within reasonable travelling distance of your workplace. You pay a reduced rent on the portion of the house you don't buy to the registered social landlord, usually a housing association, who owns the rest of the property. Turn to Chapter 16 for the details of the shared ownership scheme, although it's worth remembering that under general shared ownership the property you buy doesn't have to be newly-built, as it does under key worker shared ownership.

When considering buying under shared ownership, you need to bear the following restrictions in mind:

- ✔ **You can't buy a property on the open market.** Under key worker shared ownership you must buy a share in a property owned by a housing association (contact your local association for a list of these in your area).

- ✔ **You must purchase a newly-built property so if you really want a period home, you'll be disappointed.** The Government insists that developers provide a certain amount of affordable housing on new developments for those on low incomes to purchase under shared ownership.

- ✔ **You don't own the property outright initially.** The housing association owns a share of your home and you must pay rent on this every month. Thus, your monthly outgoings aren't as low as they might have been if you'd opted for an equity loan under the key worker Homebuy scheme.

If you stop being a key worker you're no longer eligible for help under the key worker shared ownership scheme. Your zone agent will be able to explain what happens next.

Even if you already own a home you may be eligible for shared ownership, as long as you meet the eligibility criteria. Shared ownership can enable you to move to a larger home for your family's needs. And if you need to move from your shared ownership home because your family has expanded so you need a bigger place, this may also be possible. You can simply sell your first home and carry forward the help you received. You can use the proceeds of the sale, plus the help you initially received and any further help you are entitled to (a maximum of £50,000 or higher in the case of some London schoolteachers), to buy a bigger home.

Chapter 18

Purchasing Your Council Home

*R*ight to Buy is one of the most popular low-cost home ownership schemes, helping 50,000 people become homeowners every year. Under the Right to Buy scheme, if you rent a council property, you have an opportunity to purchase your home for significantly less than the market value, which may well be the difference between being able to afford to buy and not.

How big a discount you get is calculated according to how long you've been a tenant and where the property is situated.

In this chapter, I look at how the Right to Buy scheme works and how to apply. Right to Buy operates slightly differently in Scotland and Northern Ireland to England and Wales, so I also highlight the main differences between the countries.

Looking at Qualifications and Discounts

Before you buy, make sure you can cope financially. Tenants can get housing benefit to help with the rent but there's no housing benefit to help pay the mortgage.

If you wish to exercise your right to buy, seek independent legal advice before you sign anything.

For more information on Right to Buy get hold of a couple of free booklets: 'Long leaseholders – your rights and responsibilities' and 'Thinking of buying a council flat'. These booklets are available from your landlord, Citizens Advice Bureau, or the Office of the Deputy Prime Minister.

Discovering who can and can't buy

The Right to Buy scheme is aimed at secure tenants of local authorities. A *secure tenant* is one whose tenancy can be ended only through a court order – most local authority tenants are in this position. If you're a secure tenant of a district council, London Borough Council, non-charitable housing association or other registered social landlord, or a Housing Action Trust, you should also qualify for the scheme.

Aside from being a secure tenant, you must have lived in the property for at least two years to be eligible to buy your home in the first place. These two years can include time spent in different properties and with different landlords.

You may be able to exercise right to buy jointly with other family members who have lived with you during the past 12 months or with someone who is a joint tenant with you.

If your council home was transferred to a housing association (so you were previously a secure tenant), you may have a preserved right to buy. The *Preserved Right to Buy* scheme is similar to right to buy but the discount is reduced to take account of the cost of any work the landlord has done to the property.

You are also restricted in that you can't buy your property through the Rent to Mortgage scheme (see 'Figuring Out Whether Rent to Mortgage is For You' later in this chapter).

You do not have a right to buy if

- ✔ You're an *assured tenant* of a registered social landlord (RSLs), such as a housing association. As an assured tenant, your rights are much more restricted than a secure tenant. For example, you aren't able to pass your home on to someone in your family living with you when you die and you can't take on lodgers.

- ✔ You're an undischarged bankrupt or have a bankruptcy order pending against you.

- ✔ You've made an arrangement with creditors and still owe money to them.

Watch out for companies offering to help you buy your property under the Right to Buy scheme. Such companies tend to charge a fee for services that are normally free – for example, they might try to charge you for a right to buy application form, even though these are available free from your landlord. Be on your guard and don't part with any cash unnecessarily.

Dealing with discounts and qualifying periods

To qualify for right to buy, you must be a secure tenant, have spent at least two years as a public sector tenant and your house or flat must be a separate home and your only home. If you purchase your home via right to buy, you can get a sizeable discount off the market value. The discount varies in different regions. The following maximum discounts apply to England and Wales:

- ✔ East Midlands and Yorkshire and the Humber: £24,000.

- ✔ Eastern Region: £34,000, unless your home is in Watford, where the maximum discount is £16,000.

- ✔ London: £16,000, unless your home is in Barking and Dagenham or Havering, where the maximum discount is £38,000.

✔ North East: £22,000.

✔ North West and West Midlands: £26,000.

✔ South East: £38,000, unless your home is in the local authority areas of Chiltern, Epsom & Ewell, Hart, Oxford, Reading, Reigate & Banstead, Tonbridge & Malling, Vale of the White Horse, or West Berkshire. In these areas, the maximum discount is £16,000.

✔ South West: £30,000.

✔ Wales: £16,000.

You must be a tenant for at least two years to be eligible to buy your home. After you meet this standard, you can buy your home at a discount of 32 per cent off the price of a house and 44 per cent off the price of a flat.

If your home was recently purchased by your landlord or if she's spent money doing it up, your discount may be reduced. Under the *cost floor rule,* your discount cannot reduce the price you pay below what the landlord has spent building, buying, repairing, or maintaining the property. If the cost of works is greater than the market value of your home, you won't receive any discount.

The discount you are eligible for increases according to the length of time you've been a public sector tenant. If you've lived in council property for longer than two years, you can get a further discount:

✔ **For a house,** you are eligible for another 1 per cent per each additional year up to a maximum of 60 per cent.

✔ **For a flat,** you are eligible for 2 per cent more discount for each extra full year, up to a maximum of 70 per cent.

So if you are buying a £85,000 house that you've lived in for five years, you can qualify for an initial discount of £27,200 (32 per cent of £85,000) plus an additional discount of £2,550 (a further 1 per cent for each of the three extra years), giving you a total discount of £29,750.

Your discount cannot be greater than the maximum for your area (see the list earlier in the chapter). So in the preceding example, in which your discount works out at £29,750, you get the full amount off the purchase price if you buy in Barking and Dagenham because the maximum discount is £38,000. But if you buy your home in another part of London, your discount may be no greater than £16,000.

If you are buying jointly with someone who has a longer qualifying period than yours, you get the higher rate of discount, subject to the maximum discount for your area.

The same discount scheme applies in Northern Ireland (contact the Northern Ireland Housing Executive for further details at www.nihe.gov.uk).

However, under Scottish law, the residency qualifying period is five years. The discount is 20 per cent after five years, rising by 1 per cent for each additional year up to a maximum of 35 per cent of the value or £15,000, whichever is lower. For more information, contact the Scottish Executive for its free leaflet, 'Your Right to Buy your Home' (www.scottishexecutive.gov.uk).

The government plans to lengthen the qualification period and the discount repayment period to five years in England and Wales, as has happened in Scotland. However, these changes must be approved by Parliament and at the time of writing, there were no immediate plans to do so.

Going through the Process

You must go through several stages when applying for right to buy. The following steps apply primarily to England and Wales, but are broadly similar to Scotland and Northern Ireland (you need to get hold of different forms in these countries). I outline the stages below:

1. **Ask your landlord for a right to buy claim form (Form RTB1) or application to buy form in Scotland (Form APP1).**

   There is no charge for this form, although some companies may try to get you to pay: If they do, refuse. If you have trouble obtaining a form, apply to the Office of the Deputy Prime Minister on 020 7944 4400 or contact the Scottish Executive Development Department on 0131 244 2105.

2. **Fill out the form.**

   The information you provide is used to determine whether you have the right to buy and how much discount you get. Return the completed form to your landlord. Because it's an important legal document, it's worth paying for recorded delivery or going to the trouble of delivering the form by hand (make sure you get a receipt). Keep a copy of the completed form for your own records.

   Upon receiving the form, your landlord is required to send you a notice (Form RTB2) informing you as to whether you have the right to buy. You should receive Form RTB2 within four weeks from the date on which your landlord received your RTB1 (or eight weeks if you have been a tenant of your landlord for less than two years).

3. **Receive an offer notice from your landlord.**

   Within eight weeks of receiving notice that you have a right to buy your freehold or house (12 weeks if you're buying a flat or maisonette) your landlord sends you an offer notice (Section 125 Notice). This notice gives you the valuation of the property – the price you have to pay – estimates the service charge; gives details of any structural defects the landlord knows about; and the terms and conditions of the sale.

4. **Decide whether the price seems reasonable.**

   You may feel that the price on the Section 125 notice is too high. If so, you can obtain an independent valuation from the District Valuer: Contact your local authority for more details. Before doing so, you must tell the landlord – within three months of receiving the Section 125 notice – that you want a 'determination of value' under Section 128 of the Housing Act 1985. You have four weeks to put your case to the District Valuer, who inspects your home. Be warned that the District Valuer's valuation may be higher than the landlord's and if it is, you still have to accept it. The alternative is to withdraw your application to buy your home.

5. **Commission a survey.** The survey gives you more information about the condition of the property, such

as whether there is any damp or subsidence you need to worry about, for example. There are two types of survey: the homebuyer's report or a full structural survey. The former is suitable for most properties; the latter for very old properties or those in poor condition.

See Chapter 9 for more details on surveys.

6. **Make a decision about whether and how to buy or not.**

   At this stage, you have several options. You can

   A. Buy the property outright for the full right to buy price less any discount for which you are eligible.

   B. Apply to buy on rent to mortgage terms (see 'Figuring Out Whether Rent to Mortgage is For You' later in this chapter).

   C. Forget all about it, withdraw your application, and carry on paying rent.

   Whatever you decide, inform your landlord in writing within 12 weeks of getting the valuation. If you don't respond during this time, your landlord will send you a reminder. If you don't respond within 28 days of receiving the reminder, the landlord will assume you don't want to continue with right to buy.

7. **Apply for a mortgage if you decide to buy and need one.**

   (See 'Arranging a mortgage and allowing for other costs' later in this chapter.)

8. **Finalise the terms.**

   Once the mortgage is finalised and you are happy with your landlord's terms for selling your home to you, you are ready to buy. Tell your landlord you are ready and ask your solicitor for advice on the legal documents and making your payment. It may take a couple of months before you finally own your home.

   Before you sign anything, get legal advice. For more details on finding a solicitor, go to Chapter 9.

Sometimes the procedure isn't straightforward and you encounter hold-ups, such as:

- ✔ Your landlord does not send you Form RTB2 or Section 125 notice within the timeframe mentioned in Step 3. If this happens, you may qualify for a reduction in the purchase price. To apply for this reduction, fill in an initial notice of delay (Form RTB6) and send it to your landlord. If your landlord has since submitted these forms to you, she may issue a counter notice.

- ✔ You may be told you don't have the right to buy and disagree with the explanation your landlord gives.

Try first to resolve issues with your landlord, and if that doesn't work, contact your solicitor or the Citizens Advice Bureau (www.nacab.org.uk) for advice. If you're still not satisfied, write to the Office of the Deputy Prime Minister (26 Whitehall, London, SW1A 2WH) or the Welsh Assembly Government (Cardiff Bay, Cardiff, CF99 1NA) or you can e-mail the Housing Corporation (enquiries@housingcorp.gsx.gov.uk) for details of your local office).

If an issue can't be resolved, you can go to the county court for a ruling. But this can be expensive, so get legal advice before you take such action.

Paying Attention to the Money Matters

When buying your home under the Right to Buy scheme, there are several things you need to consider when it comes to your finances.

Arranging a mortgage and allowing for other costs

Most people need a mortgage to cover the cost of purchasing their property. The amount of the mortgage is the purchase price of your home, less the discount you receive, and any savings you can put down as a deposit. Your local authority can tell you how much your home is worth when you apply to buy it so you know how big a mortgage you need.

See Chapter 4 for more information on mortgages.

If you lose your home because you can't afford the mortgage repayments and your lender has to sell it to cover your debts, the council is under no obligation to let you have another council home to rent. So make sure you can afford the mortgage repayments before exercising your right under the Right to Buy scheme. See Chapter 2 for more details on budgeting for the mortgage and for the extra costs associated with home ownership, such as the following:

- **Council tax and water charges:** You may pay council tax and water charges as part of your rent but once you purchase your home, you're responsible for paying these straight to the water services company and the council. When comparing the cost of buying with renting, don't forget to allow for these bills in your calculations.

- **Buildings insurance:** If you are buying a freehold property, you're responsible for arranging buildings insurance (and your mortgage lender will insist upon this). If the property is leasehold, your landlord will arrange buildings insurance and you pay for it out of your service charge. Your service charge also covers the cost incurred by the landlord of maintaining the communal areas of the property, such as the entrance, corridors, stairs, and lift (if the building has one).

   You also need to think about taking out contents insurance, if you don't have it already, in case you're burgled. And some form of payment protection may also be a good idea to ensure your mortgage is paid off if you die or lose your job. See Chapter 4 for more details on the different types of insurance available to work out what you need.

See Chapter 2 or the Cheat Sheet at the front of the book for a complete list of the extra charges you need to be prepared for.

Repaying the discount

You can sell your home whenever you want to. However, if you sell within three years of buying it, you have to repay some or all of the discount you received. Table 18-1 shows the costs.

Table 18-1	Costs of Selling Early
Sell Period	*Amount of Discount to Repay*
Within the first year	The entire amount
During the second year	Two-thirds
During the third year	One-third

Paying more for leasehold property

If you buy a flat or maisonette under the Right to Buy scheme, it will be a leasehold property. If you buy a leasehold property you have the right to live in it for a fixed period of time, usually 125 years. The landlord retains ownership of the property itself and is responsible for the upkeep of the building and communal areas, and for providing building insurance. But you have to pay for this via an annual service charge, which can cost you hundreds of pounds a year (or more, if a lot of work is needed, such as repairs to the roof). So be careful before you commit yourself to a leasehold property. Work out the cost of the mortgage plus the service charge when comparing it with the rent to find the true cost of owning a leasehold property.

To find out what the service charge is in your block of flats, ask someone who has already bought their flat. Or contact your local residents' association for more information. If you decide to buy your home, the landlord should give you an estimate of the service charge you have to pay during the first five years of the lease. Once she has given you this estimate, the landlord cannot change the service charge during the first five years, except to allow for inflation.

Don't forget that as a leaseholder you also have to pay ground rent of £10 a year to the landlord.

Being a leaseholder doesn't affect your right to sell your home: The person who buys it simply takes on the remainder of the lease. So if you sell a property with a 120-year lease after six years, the buyer gets a 114-year lease.

There are exemptions in certain circumstances, such as if the property has to be sold because of the breakdown of a relationship or a death. Check with your landlord for details of exemptions.

If you live in the country you may have to sell your property to someone who lives or works locally, or to the council, because of the shortage of affordable housing in some rural areas – ask your landlord for more details.

Weighing up the pros and cons

To help you decide whether you are ready to buy your council property, it's worth weighing up the pros and cons, some of which I list in Table 18-2.

Table 18-2	Pros and Cons of Buying
Advantages	**Disadvantages**
Security: You can't get kicked out of your home by a landlord.	Responsibility: You no longer have a landlord you can call upon to do all the maintenance and repair work to the property.
Buying at a substantial discount: As a result of the discount, when you finally sell your home you may find that you make a serious profit on it (as long as you sell after three years so that you don't have to pay any of the discount back).	Cost: Although you are receiving a discount on the purchase price, you may find that your monthly mortgage repayments are higher than your rent was. And if you buy a leasehold property, you also have to pay a service charge and nominal ground rent (see the nearby sidebar 'Paying more for leasehold property' for further information).
No more rent: Paying rent can feel like throwing money down the drain. Instead, you have an investment, which should grow in value over time.	Three-year selling restriction: You must stay in the property for at least three years if you don't want to repay any of the discount. If you need to move for whatever reason during this time, you must repay some (or all) of the discount.

Figuring out Whether Rent to Mortgage is For You

If you want to buy your council home but can't afford to – even with the discount – rent to mortgage may be the answer. With the *Rent to Mortgage scheme,* you pay off part of the landlord's share of your property by making an *interim* payment or pay off the whole amount via a *final* payment. A final payment can be made at any time but must be made if you sell your home or die.

With Rent to Mortgage, you make an initial payment: There is a minimum you must pay and an upper limit on how much you're allowed to pay. If you're buying a house, your landlord calculates the minimum initial payment based on the rent you are paying at the time. This should reflect what lenders are willing to lend you on a standard 25-year repayment mortgage and what you can afford based on the rent you currently pay. If you're buying a flat or maisonette, there is a 20 per cent discount on the minimum payment to reflect the fact that you may have to pay service charges in the future.

You can pay more than this minimum initial payment but the maximum you can pay is four-fifths (80 per cent) of the Right to Buy price. If you want to pay more than this, you should consider buying the property outright under the Right to Buy scheme.

You also get a discount on the initial payment, depending on the Right to Buy discount rate (see 'Dealing with discounts and qualifying periods' earlier in this chapter). If you pay two-thirds of the Right to Buy price, you get two-thirds of the Right to Buy discount, and so on.

After you've made your initial payment, you can decide at any time to buy further shares in the property from your landlord. If you decide to make an interim or final payment, you must inform your landlord and the two of you must agree how much your home is worth – if you can't agree, you'll have to commission an independent valuer, which you have to pay for. After the valuation has been done, you must make your interim or final payment within three months, otherwise the landlord assumes you have withdrawn notice and you'll have to start again.

Interim payments must be at least 10 per cent of the value of your home at that time. You get a discount of 20 per cent when you make the payment as long as this doesn't take your discount above the maximum available for the area in which your home is located.

If you sell your home within three years of buying under Rent to Mortgage, you must pay back some or all of your discount.

If you're interested in Rent to Mortgage, ask your landlord for a Rent to Buy claim form (RTB1), which you need to fill in and return.

Part V
The Part of Tens

"Well, I hope you can enjoy living here in Scotland &
I understand your neighbours are preparing a
typical Scottish welcome for you."

In this part . . .

This wouldn't be a *For Dummies* book without the Part of Tens. Here you can find short bursts of information on everything from what you need to know as a first-time homeowner, to dealing with estate agents, to useful contacts every homebuyer needs.

Chapter 19

Ten Things a First-Time Buyer Needs to Know

*B*uying your first property can be an extremely daunting prospect. While it's very exciting – I can guarantee that you can't beat walking into your new home for the first time after taking possession of the keys – it's also a huge responsibility. In this chapter, I give you ten tips to bear in mind when you buy your first property to make sure you enjoy it while at the same time meeting your financial obligations.

Budget to Ensure You Can Pay the Mortgage

Many first-time buyers fall into the trap of thinking that once they've managed to persuade a lender to give them a mortgage, they don't have to worry about the financial side of things any longer. But you are still on a tight budget and a mortgage is a big financial commitment. You must make sure you meet your monthly payments, on time, every month. If you fall behind with your repayments, your home is in danger of being repossessed. (If you do fall behind, notify your lender rather than sticking your head in the sand and trying to forget all about your mortgage arrears.)

By drawing up a budget – and sticking to it – you can afford to pay your mortgage every month (see Chapter 2 for more on this). It may sound boring but I can't stress enough how important budgeting is. And if you aren't very sensible with money you'll have to teach yourself good habits.

You managed to persuade your lender to let you have the funds to buy your home in the first place so you should be able to repay your debt. Meeting the mortgage payments may just require a few sacrifices.

Introduce Yourself to the Neighbours

Even as you're moving your stuff into your new home, be on the lookout for the neighbours. The newspapers are full of stories about neighbours from hell: One way of minimising the chances of ending up with one or two of these is to get off on the right foot. Pop round and introduce yourself within a day or two of moving in. Pick a good time for your visit: Early evening is probably the best time – or at least better than first thing in the morning when they are trying to get ready for work or late at night as they are going to bed. Be polite, friendly, and not too pushy: You don't want to come across as a right pain because they'll pretend to be out every time you ring the door bell.

If you're planning a housewarming party (see the 'You're Expected to Throw a Housewarming Party' section later on in this chapter) – you must invite the neighbours. You may find that you don't particularly like them once you've met them or they may not be your kind of people. Odds are they won't even come. But if you don't invite them, you risk alienating them for good, particularly if your music is blaring all night so they can't get to sleep. It's not worth the hassle: Keep your neighbours on side in case you ever have to borrow that cup of sugar.

Insurance is a Necessity, Not an Option

Money may be too tight to mention now you've bought your new home, paid the stamp duty, and your solicitor's fees. You may also be planning a trip to your local furniture store. The last thing on your mind is likely to be insurance. Indeed, you may even think you can cut costs by taking out cover at a later date when you're flush. But skimping on insurance is false economy. Lenders insist you take out buildings insurance before they let you have a mortgage (see Chapter 4 for more on this) so you can't avoid this cover. But consider contents insurance: Can you afford to replace all your belongings if you have a fire or are burgled? Probably not, if you're trying to skimp on cover in the first instance. What if you have an accident and can no longer do your job: Could you afford to pay your mortgage? If the answer is no, you need some form of mortgage payment protection or critical illness cover (see Chapter 4). You may think you are saving money by not taking out insurance but it covers the unknown – so you never know when you may need it.

Buy Everything but the Kitchen Sink

The most exciting element of buying a home is that it's the perfect excuse for spending lots of cash on new stuff: sofas, chairs, television, curtains, and carpets – the list is endless. While shopping for your new home can be great fun, I advise a modicum of caution: Don't spend money that you don't have. Yes, it's easy to get credit but you'll have to pay it back at some stage. By all means have fun and buy that impractical cream sofa your mother will disapprove of because it isn't a sensible colour. But don't spend so much on furnishings that you can't afford to go out for the next year while you pay it all back.

You're Expected to Throw a Housewarming Party

Everyone who moves into a new place – whether they are renting or buying – is expected to throw a party, so you may as well accept that this is what your friends and family want, bite the bullet, and set a date.

Although it's understandable if you want to get your new place perfect and decorated to your taste before you ask anyone round, it makes more sense to have the housewarming *before* you do the place up. How are you going to relax if your guests are swigging red wine while standing on your new pristine white rugs? The 1970s-style swirly floral carpet with the brown background that the previous owners left behind may not be to your tastes, but if you leave it in the sitting room for the party you'll have as good a time as your guests. The carpet is likely to create a talking point and you can have a good laugh about it. And if it makes you feel better, you can always tell your guests that your new carpet is on order.

Switch Utility Providers to Slash Your Bills

Fuel bills can be expensive but short of wearing chunky knitted jumpers around your home and going to the pub instead of heating your sitting room, you have to put up with them. Well, to a certain extent. Deregulation of the gas and electricity industries means you can shop around for a cheaper deal – there's no need to stick with the provider you inherit when you move in.

Take gas, electricity, and water meter readings as soon as you move in and contact the relevant suppliers to inform them of these. (You may not have a water meter so this reading may not be possible.) Next, find out whether you can get a cheaper gas, electricity, or telephone deal from a different supplier.

A number of Web sites allow you to compare costs and if you find a cheaper provider, the process of changing is straightforward – your new supplier will do all the work for you. Try Energywatch, the gas and electricity watchdog (www. energywatch.org.uk) or www.saveonyourbills.co.uk (or 0870 005 2095). If you wish to compare phone and digital TV costs as well, try www.uswitch.com (or 0845 601 2856).

Learn to Operate the Washing Machine

This is it – no more trips down the launderette sitting for hours watching your smalls whizz round the drier. You can do your own laundry now, in your own machine. Read the operating instructions very carefully before shrinking your best knitwear or dyeing your favourite white shirt a delicate shade of pink.

 Don't just get to grips with the washing machine: Read the manuals for the cooker, fridge, freezer, and boiler as well if you want everything to function smoothly.

You Can Go as Mad as You Like When Decorating

When you live in rented accommodation, the amount of decorating you can do is usually very limited: if the landlord has any sense, he won't allow you to do any at all. Or you may think it's not worth spending the time or money doing it because you'll be moving out in six months and someone else will benefit from your hard work.

But your own place is different. You don't have to ask anyone for permission before you start work. You don't have to temper your tastes or opt for neutral colours: you can paint or wallpaper your walls exactly how you want. So if pink walls with green spots have always been your dream, you can have them. And it's not money down the drain because you are – hopefully – improving your property. If your tastes are highly unusual at best, you can always paint over your artwork when you come to sell your home.

Accept that Dinner Party Conversation Will Never Be the Same Again

Before you got your foot on the property ladder, you probably never understood those conversations about house prices that people with their own homes seem to find endlessly fascinating. But as soon as you've bought your own home you instantly get it. Dinner parties will never be the same again as you boast about how your flat in an edgy part of town has doubled in value since you bought it. Or you may take an unhealthy interest in what the Bank of England plans to do with interest rates. These topics, which were previously as dull as ditch water, you'll now find riveting. Give your non-property owning friends a break and don't invite them to dinner parties in future.

Property Prices Go Up and Down: There's No Point Worrying about It

Once you've invested a large chunk of your hard-earned cash in property you're bound to start obsessing about how much it's worth. Was it a good investment and has it gone up in value? Or have you made a big mistake because it's now worth less than you paid for it and you've fallen into negative equity? (See Chapter 2 for more on avoiding negative equity by buying during a property slump rather than a boom.)

Property prices move up and down, it's a fact of life. However, over the long term prices are more likely to go up – and that's all you need be bothered about. Remember that your home is the place where you live rather than a way of making a quick buck. See any appreciation in the price as a welcome extra, not the motivation for buying the property in the first place. And if you plan to live there for several years at least, the inevitable short-term fluctuations in price needn't bother you one bit. The housing market is certainly not worth losing any sleep over.

Chapter 20

Ten Tips for Dealing with Estate Agents

In This Chapter
▶ Remaining sceptical when dealing with estate agents
▶ Knowing how to get the best out of agents

*O*ne of the things most people hate about flat or house hunting is dealing with estate agents. Many estate agents have a bad – albeit fully justified – reputation, yet this is not the case with all of them. And estate agents remain the most common channel for buying or selling property in England, Wales, and Northern Ireland. In Scotland, solicitors are used more commonly than estate agents to sell property (see Chapter 11 for more details).

As there's a strong chance you are buying your property through an estate agent, in this chapter I suggest ten tips to make this as painless an experience as possible.

Ignore the Codswallop!

Estate agents are salespeople and exaggeration is the name of the game. As long as you remember this, and take most of what they tell you with a hefty pinch of salt, you won't go far wrong. Also bear in mind that the agent receives commission from the seller for finding her a buyer so the agent works for her rather than you.

Even though you aren't footing the bill, the agent is legally obliged not to mislead you. However, a fine line exists between being economical with the truth and being deliberately misleading: Be on your guard and read between the lines. A flat described as cosy in agent-speak may be more accurately described as poky, for example.

Check out all property details for yourself: Don't believe anything you're told without making sure it really is the case. And if you find discrepancies between the property particulars (drawn up by the agent) and what you actually see when you view the property, bring this up with the agent.

Check Out an Agent's Credentials

No professional qualifications are necessary to set yourself up as an estate agent, which is why there are so many people selling property who aren't up to the job. But you can protect yourself by making sure you only use an estate agent who belongs to one of two professional bodies:

- ✔ **The National Association of Estate Agents:** This association is the main professional body for estate agents. Membership is voluntary and agents follow a professional code of practice and rules of conduct – if they breach these they can receive a formal warning, a fine, or be suspended or expelled.

- ✔ **The Ombudsman for Estate Agents:** Again, membership is voluntary but members can be forced to pay you compensation if they breach the rules.

Alternatively, look for an agent who is registered with the Royal Institution of Chartered Surveyors. (See Chapter 8 for more details of these schemes and how to check whether agents are registered). Choosing a registered agent can reassure you that certain standards will be met and you reduce the possibility of something going wrong.

Register with as Many Agents as Possible

Being loyal and registering your interest in purchasing a property with just one estate agent gets you nowhere fast. The best way of finding the right property for you in the shortest possible time is to register with as many agents as possible offering the type of property you're interested in – and can afford – in the area you're keen on.

You don't have to pay for the agent's services – this is the seller's responsibility – so there are no costs involved in registering with several agents. And the more you widen the net, the better your chances of finding what you want.

Make the Estate Agent Your New Best Friend

Before you accuse me of being desperately sad, I'm not suggesting you go down the pub every night with the agent or invite her round for dinner. But if you want to find a property you can afford on your budget, it's vital that you get the agent on your side. There's a lot of competition for the type of property you're after. Your aim is to ensure you are the first person that pops into the agent's mind when a property fitting your criteria comes onto her books – so you get the first call, are the first to see it, and the first to make an offer (if you're interested). Being first to view a property can give you a crucial head start.

Keep in regular touch with the agent and demonstrate that you are actively looking for a property: You are a serious buyer. Make frequent calls and visit the agent regularly to check what's available. Ensure you're easily contactable by phone at home, work, or on your mobile, and by email. Return the agent's calls as soon as you can if you can't answer when she calls. Build up a friendly rapport rather than just being another anonymous buyer. A sure-fire way of getting an agent onside is to prove how serious you are. Agents have a sixth sense for rooting out timewasters so make sure you aren't one of them. Produce an agreement in principle from your lender stating that it's prepared to let you borrow a certain amount of money.

Be Honest about Your Budget

Because money is tight, many properties will be well out of your price range. Although it's tempting to pretend to the agent that you can afford more than you can – in an effort to be taken more seriously – be honest. Being economical with the truth wastes your time, and the agent's (to say nothing of putting her back up once she finds out). If your budget only stretches to a small studio flat, there's no point saying you're interested in four-bedroom family homes.

 Money may be tight but that doesn't mean you're not a serious purchaser. Ensure you get this message across to the agent. Organise your finances (see Chapter 2) before you even step foot inside an estate agent's.

Be Flexible over Your Demands

First-time buyers often have unrealistic expectations about what sort of property they can get for their money. The estate agent can help you set a realistic goal – if you are honest with her about how much you can afford to spend.

There's no point asking the agent for advice if you're not prepared to listen to it – even if you don't like what you hear. The agent may recommend that you revise your expectations: For example, if you want a two-bedroom house with a garden in central London and have a maximum of £150,000 to spend, she may tell you that you aren't going to get this. If you don't want to live anywhere else, she's likely to recommend that you downsize your ambitions and look for one-bedroom flats instead. Or if the size of the property is more important than where it is, you may have to look at less desirable locations to get the bigger flat you want.

If you ignore the advice and hold out for that centrally located two-bedroom flat you're unlikely to find what you want, no matter how long you look. You'll have to downscale your ambitions eventually – and can have wasted many months before you do so.

Drop Everything When an Agent Calls

Be prepared for house hunting to take over your life. If you're going to find a decent property on a budget, you need to dedicate a lot of time and effort to it. Don't delay when an agent calls with details of a property that sounds as if it may be what you're looking for. Make an appointment to view it as soon as possible – or risk missing out. You can guarantee that if you don't get yourself round to look at a property, there will be another first-time buyer who is prepared to do just that. And if she likes what she sees, she may put in an offer before you've even had a chance to look round.

Warn friends that you're going to be busy for a few weeks and arrange to view properties instead of going down the pub. After you find a property, you can resume your social life.

Listen to the Agent's Advice

As well as helping you work out what sort of property you can get on your budget, an agent can offer advice on other aspects of the purchase. An agent can advise you on whether it's worth making an offer below the asking price, for example, if she knows that the seller is desperate for a sale (see Chapter 9 for more on this). Even though the agent is working for the seller – and wants to make as much commission as she can – she also has to be realistic about securing a sale. Thus, she may suggest you offer less rather than miss out on finding a buyer.

Listen to the agent's advice: You don't have to take it but you may hear something that proves useful to you.

Refuse the Agent's Offer of Finance

As well as selling property, many agents have a financing arm offering buyers mortgages. But you don't have to take advantage of one of these and my advice is that you don't.

If you haven't yet arranged a mortgage you may be tempted to take the agent up on her offer of finance rather than go to the trouble of arranging an appointment with an independent broker (see Chapter 4). But, at best, you'll be offered the most competitive deal out of a limited sample so it won't be the best mortgage on the market. If you do secure a really good deal, it will be down to luck more than anything else.

The other problem is that as you're on a tight budget, you may need a specialist mortgage – such as a guarantor deal (see Chapter 5) or family offset plan (see Chapter 13) – which the agent is unlikely to be able to offer. By all means listen to what the agent's financing arm can do for you (this consultation is free) and then compare this with other deals on the market.

Consider the Agent's Solicitor or Surveyor Recommendations

Most agents can recommend solicitors or surveyors who can offer you a cheaper price for handling your legal work or surveying the property than you would get from a solicitor or surveyor you find in *Yellow Pages*. Unlike with mortgages, where there's so much competition and a strong chance that you'll need a specialist lender, you may get a cheaper deal by opting for the agent's recommended solicitor and surveyor.

The agent is likely to put a lot of work their way, so prices can be lower than if you shop around and find your own solicitor or surveyor. You must still ensure that the solicitor belongs to the relevant Law Society (see the Cheat Sheet at the front of the book for contact information) just as you would if you found the solicitor by other means. Check the surveyor belongs to the Royal Institution of Chartered Surveyors (see Chapter 12 for more details) to make sure you have some comeback in case anything goes wrong.

To ensure you are getting a good price for your legal work or the survey, get a quote from the solicitor or surveyor recommended by your agent. Compare this quote with prices charged by other solicitors or surveyors because you may find a cheaper deal elsewhere. If you do find a cheaper solicitor or surveyor, go for it – you are not obliged to use those recommended by the estate agent.

Chapter 21

Ten Contacts Every Homebuyer Needs

*B*uying your first home can feel a bit like venturing into the great unknown. There are so many unfamiliar things to get your head around – from organising your finances and trying to get enough cash together in the first place to buy the property to the legal process and surveys.

Thankfully, there are plenty of experts you can call upon to guide you through the process. But finding the right one for your needs – who isn't going to charge an extortionate amount for his services and won't forget to tell you something necessary for a smooth sale – can be a bit hit and miss. In this chapter, I suggest ten contacts you need to ensure you have access to all the information you need – and where to find them.

Estate Agent

Although we love to hate them, most people buy their home through an estate agent. An agent has hundreds of properties for sale on his books and is a useful one-stop shop for a buyer.

A seller has to choose an agent carefully because he pays commission if the agent manages to sell his home – choosing the right agent can make the difference between selling his home quickly, for a good price, or not at all. As a buyer you don't have such concerns: Register your requirements with as many estate agents as there are selling property of the kind you're interested in, in the area in which you wish to buy. The more agents you use, the better, as you are widening your net and may find the property of your dreams more quickly.

You don't have to pay a fee to the agent for helping you find a property. See Chapter 8 for more information on dealing with estate agents.

Mortgage Lender

Unless you've won the Lottery, come into a sizeable inheritance, or recently married a sugar daddy – and have enough cash to buy your first home outright – you need a mortgage. A mortgage lender lets you borrow a certain amount of cash, based on your income, as long as it's happy with your credit rating. If you have a county court judgement (CCJ) against you or have been declared bankrupt in recent months, for example, you are likely to struggle to find a mortgage (although it may not be impossible).

There are scores of mortgage lenders out there, which is good news for you because deals are competitively priced and you should find one that suits you. But the huge choice of lenders also means that sourcing the best deal can be a daunting task: The easiest way of doing this is to use an independent mortgage broker (see the following section).

Independent Mortgage Broker

Selecting a mortgage can be challenging for first-time buyers. You're entering uncharted waters so there's a good chance you won't know where to start. You may well not know anything about the different mortgages available (until you read Chapter 4, that is) and need someone to guide you through the process. Also, on a tight budget you may not be able to borrow enough on a standard mortgage. A guarantor mortgage (see Chapter 5 for more details) may be your only chance of getting on the property ladder, for example, but if you don't know it exists, you can't take advantage of it.

A mortgage broker examines your circumstances and suggests deals that may suit you. Use a broker who is truly independent – one who has access to all the loans on the market and not just a limited panel of lenders. The best way of choosing such a broker is by personal recommendation (if possible), or searching on the Internet and checking in your local paper.

Check how the broker is paid – by a fee from you or commission from the lender he ends up recommending – to avoid getting a nasty shock at the end of the consultation when the broker asks you for several hundred pounds for the advice you've just received. Whether the broker is paid by fee or commission shouldn't affect his independence as long as you use a good, reputable broker. (See Chapter 4 for more on choosing a broker and fees.)

Solicitor or Licensed Conveyancer

Unless you do your own conveyancing (and I advise against this unless you know what you're doing) you must use a solicitor to oversee the legal transfer of the property from the seller to you. (See Chapter 10 for details of the legal process in England, Wales, and Northern Ireland, or Chapter 11 for what happens in Scotland.) Fees vary between solicitors so shop around, but remember that the solicitor offering the cheapest quote may not provide the best service.

Any old solicitor won't do: You must use one who is experienced at conveyancing. If your friend, relative, or neighbour knows a good solicitor, try using him. Or contact the Law Society in England and Wales (www.lawsociety.org.uk) or call 020 7242 1222 for a database of solicitors. If you're buying in Scotland, try the Law Society in Scotland at www.lawscot.org.uk or call 0131 226 7411; or in Northern Ireland, try the Law Society of Northern Ireland (www.lawsoc-ni.org) or call 028 90 231614.

You don't have to use a solicitor: Another option is a licensed conveyancer. Try the Council for Licensed Conveyancers (CLC) on 01245 349599 or www.conveyancer.gov.uk, for a list of specialist conveyancers.

Surveyor

Skimping on a survey isn't a good idea in the long run – the survey is there to pick up faults and problems with the property that you may otherwise miss until they cause difficulties once you've moved in (see the Cheat Sheet or Chapter 9 for details on the type of survey available). A survey buys you peace of mind if nothing else: If there are no structural problems you need worry about, you know you won't face a hefty repair bill at a later date. And if problems are discovered you at least have a choice – give the property a wide berth if the necessary repairs blow your budget, or see whether you can persuade the seller to reduce the asking price accordingly.

Your estate agent, mortgage broker, or lender may be able to recommend a surveyor. Otherwise, contact the Royal Institution of Chartered Surveyors (RICS) for your nearest member if you're buying in England, Wales, or Northern Ireland. You can reach RICS on the phone (0870 333 1600) or visit their Web site at www.rics.org. For RICS Scotland, call 0131 225 7078 or visit the Web site at www.rics-scotland.org.uk.

A Rich Relative

The more you can get your hands on, the better. Try looking closer to home than your mortgage lender: What about your relatives? Is there a rich aunt you can call upon? If someone in the family has cash to spare, appeal to their better nature and convince them of the benefit of helping you out – the feeling of satisfaction it can give them, for example.

Aunt Betty doesn't even have to hand over thousands of pounds to you; she can put it in a savings account that's offset against your mortgage debt (see Chapter 13 for more on family offset mortgages). Or your parents can act as guarantors (see Chapter 5 for more on this), which means they promise to pay your mortgage if you default on the repayments. If your relatives do make an effort to help you out, however, make sure they know what they're getting themselves into before they commit any cash.

Mates in a Similar Position

No matter how tough things get while you're trying to buy your first home, it won't seem nearly as bad if you know someone who is also struggling. Someone you can compare notes with, complain about your respective solicitors, or just have a large vodka tonic with at the end of a stressful day of flat hunting, is a welcome relief.

If you know someone who is struggling to buy, why not club together? Buying a property with a friend doesn't suit everyone but may be the solution for you. Think carefully about the pros and cons beforehand and get a solicitor to draw up a legal document stating who contributed what to the deposit, the share of the mortgage, and how long you're both committed to living in the property. If you get all this right, sharing a property can work very well, enabling you to get a bigger mortgage – and help paying it every month. See Chapter 2 for more details.

Therapists – Masseurs, Counsellors, and so on

Buying a property is not only one of the most expensive purchases you'll ever make, the process is also one of the most stressful – it's up there with getting divorced. I don't personally know about that (thankfully) but I do know that as you fret over the details, it can all get very stressful.

Try not to worry in the first place. I realise this can be difficult, so at least make sure you only worry about the things you can change: Forget about those you can't. Do everything you can your end to make sure things go smoothly – returning forms to the solicitor as soon as possible and organising your finances so everything is ready when the money is needed. But don't fret about what the surveyor is going to discover until he's completed the survey, or whether the seller's own purchase is going to fall through until – worst luck – it actually does.

If all else fails, pamper yourself: A massage, reflexology treatment, or going for a swim or a run will relax you and put it all into perspective. If you want to pour your heart out, a counsellor may be the answer. Don't be afraid to ask for help.

Insurance Broker

The topic of insurance may be one that is guaranteed to send you to sleep but it's very important. Insurance is another area where you may be tempted to cut corners to save money – but it protects you against the unknown so you never know when you may need it. Skimping on cover is extremely short-sighted.

Only buildings insurance is compulsory (see Chapter 4 for more on this) but several other types of insurance are worth buying: home contents, life assurance, and some form of income protection to cover your mortgage if you can't work. Because there are so many companies offering insurance, the easiest way of finding the best deal for you is to use an independent broker. He can access all the deals on the market and find you the cover you need at a price you can afford.

To find an insurance broker, try the Internet. Log onto www. insuresupermarket.com or www.moneyextra.co.uk – two independent sites that can help you find the best deals.

Removal Company

You can move your own stuff but it's far easier to employ a man with a van to do it for you. If you have a lot of belongings and can afford to do so, hire a removals firm that does all your packing, transporting, and unpacking. But you can also employ a firm just to shift your belongings to your new home (with you doing the packing and unpacking). Use a removal firm that comes recommended, if possible: If not, contact the National Guild of Removers and Storers on 01494 792279 or www.ngrs. org.uk, for details of removal companies in your area.

If you've run out of cash by this stage, bribe your mates to help (choose the strapping six-footers over those with slighter builds), bend the arm of someone with a van, and prepare to flex your muscles.

Appendix

Resources

• •

*T*his appendix lists some of the main organisations I refer
to throughout this book. You may want to contact one
or more of them for more information on specific aspects of
buying a home on a budget.

Professional and Trade Organisations

Association of British Insurers (ABI): The trade association
for the UK insurance industry, the ABI represents around 400
companies. Contact: 020 7600 3333 or visit www.abi.org.uk.

Association of Relocation Agents (ARA): The professional
body for the relocation industry in the UK and Ireland, ARA
can provide you with details of local members. Call 08700
737475 or visit its Web site at www.relocationagents.com.

Citizens Advice Bureau (CAB): The CAB offers free, confiden-
tial and independent advice on a range of financial issues to
those living in England and Wales. Locate your nearest CAB
at www.citizensadvice.org.uk. For **Citizens Advice
Northern Ireland**, go to www.citizensadvice.co.uk. For
Citizens Advice Scotland, visit www.cas.org.uk.

Council for Licensed Conveyancers (CLC): The CLC publishes
a list of licensed conveyancers. Contact: 01245 349599 or visit
its Web site at www.conveyancers.gov.uk.

Council for Registered Gas Installers (CORGI): The National
Watchdog for gas safety in the UK can suggest a CORGI-
registered installer local to you. Call 0870 401 2300 or visit
its Web site at www.corgi-gas.com.

Council of Mortgage Lenders (CML): The CML is the trade association for UK mortgage lenders and promotes good lending practice. Call 020 7437 0075 or visit www.cml.org.uk.

English Heritage: This organisation aims to help people understand and appreciate why historic buildings matter. Visit www.english-heritage.org. In Northern Ireland, try the **Environment and Heritage Service in Northern Ireland** www.ehsni.gov.uk; in Scotland, try **Historic Scotland's** Web site wwwhistoric-scotland.gov.uk; in Wales, go to www.cadw.co.uk.

Federation of Master Builders (FMB): The largest trade organisation in the UK for the construction industry is a good place to start if you need a builder. Call 020 7242 7583 for details of FMB members in your area or visit its Web site at www.fmb.org.uk.

Financial Ombudsman Service: If you have a complaint about your mortgage, first take it up with your lender or broker who should have its own complaints procedure. If you aren't satisfied, cotnact the Financial Ombudsman Service. Call 0845 080 1800 or visit www.financial-ombudsman.org.uk.

Guild of Master Craftsmen: Membership of the Guild is recognition of a company's skill and integrity. Call 01273 477374 or visit www.thegmcgroup.com for more information.

Institute of Plumbing: The UK's professional body for plumbers can help you find a local registered plumber. Telephone 01708 472791 or visit its Web site at www.plumbers.org.

Law Society of England and Wales: The Law Society provides advice on choosing and using a solicitor. For information, contact the Society by phone (020 7242 1222) or visit its Web Site at www.lawsociety.org.uk.

Law Society of Northern Ireland: For more information on choosing and using a solicitor in Northern Ireland, contact the Society on 028 90 231 614 or visit www.lawsoc-ni.org.

Law Society of Scotland: For more information on choosing and using a solicitor in Scotland, contact the Society on 0131 226 7411 or visit www.lawscot.org.uk.

National Association of Estate Agents (NAEA): The NAEA is the leading professional body for estate agents in the UK and aims to improve their professionalism and accountability. Members are bound by a Code of Practice and adhere to professional Rules of Conduct. For more information, call 01926 496800 or visit NAEA online at www.naea.org.uk.

National Inspection Council for Electrical Installation Contracting (NICEIC): The NICEIC is a voluntary regulatory body and charitable organisation, which aims to protect the public from unsafe or unsound electrical work. Call 020 7564 2323 or visit its Web site at www.niceic.org.uk.

National House Building Council (NHBC): The NHBC is the regulatory body for the building industry. The advantage of using an NHBC-registered builder is that inspectors carry out checks during the building process to satisfy themselves that the property conforms to NHBC standards. You can contact NHBC on 01494 735363 or visit its Web site at www.nhbc.co.uk.

Office of the Ombudsman for Estate Agents (OEA): The OEA Scheme is devised to address disputes between estate agents who are members and the public. Consumers can register complaints if they feel that their legal rights have been infringed or an agent has not complied with the OEA Code of Practice. Telephone 01722 333306 or visit the OEA's Web Site at www.oea.co.uk.

Royal Institute of British Architects (RIBA): RIBA has a database of architects in the UK and can put you in contact with a member near you. Members follow the Code of Professional Conduct and RIBA can offer practical assistance if they fall foul of this. Contact RIBA on 020 7580 5533 or visit its Web site at www.riba.org.

Royal Institution of Chartered Surveyors (RICS): RICS is a global professional body representing, regulating, and promoting chartered surveyors. If you are looking for a surveyor, contact RICS for your nearest member. You can reach RICS by phone (0870 333 1600) or online at www.rics.org. For RICS Scotland, call 0131 225 7078 or visit the Web site www.rics-scotland.org.uk.

Society for the Protection of Ancient Buildings (SPAB): This national pressure group fights to save old buildings from decay, demolition, and damage. It offers advice, educates, and campaigns. For more details on conservation, call 020 7377 1644 or go to www.spab.org.uk.

Further Information

This section includes some of the Web sites I have found most useful. I recommend that you check them out as well.

Buildstore: Provides a useful and comprehensive Web site for the self-builder or renovator, enabling you to search for land that's already received planning permission, specialist mortgages, and plenty of advice and tips. Check out the Web site at www.buildstore.co.uk.

Bricks and Brass: Offers information on buying, maintaining, and renovating a period house. Be guided through the renovation process with plenty of invaluable tips and advice at www.bricksandbrass.co.uk.

Moneysupermarket: Offers a comprehensive service allowing users to compare the cost of a range of financial products from mortgages, credit cards, and personal loans to home insurance and life cover. Visit the Web site at www.moneysupermarket.com.

Self Build ABC: Offers lots of advice and practical tips on self-build and what you need to consider before taking the plunge. Visit www.selfbuildabc.co.uk.

Up My Street: Provides comprehensive details of shops and services near a property. Visit www.upmystreet.com if you're considering buying in an area you're not familiar with.

Credit Reference Agencies

Equifax and Experian are the two main credit agencies, which hold a copy of your credit file. Lenders contact these agencies to check your credit file before they decide whether to let you have a mortgage or not. If you've missed payments on a personal loan or previous mortgage, for example, this information is recorded on your file. With so much riding on what's contained on your file, it's worth checking that it's correct, *before* you apply for a mortgage. Write to Equifax or Experian, enclosing a cheque for £2 for a copy of your file.

Equifax PLC

Credit File Advice Centre
PO Box 1140
Bradford, BD1 5US
Phone 0870 0100 583
Web site: www.equifax.com

Experian Ltd

Consumer Help Service
PO Box 8000
Nottingham, NG1 5GX
Phone 0870 241 6212
Web site: www.experian.co.uk

Index

Notes

_____
_____
_____
_____
_____
_____
_____
_____
_____
_____
_____
_____
_____
_____
_____
_____
_____
_____
_____
_____
_____
_____
_____
_____

Notes

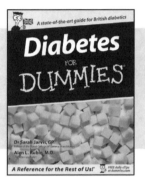
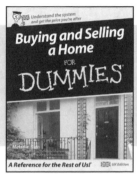
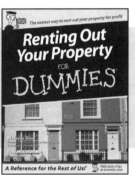
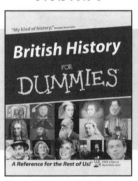
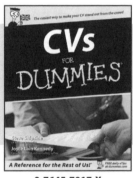
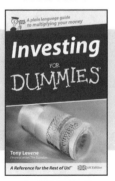
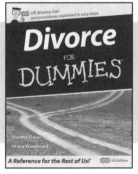

FOR DUMMIES

The easy way to get more done and have more fun

GENERAL INTEREST & HOBBIES

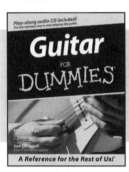

Guitar
FOR DUMMIES

Play-along audio CD included!
The fun and easy way to start playing the guitar

Mark Phillips
Jon Chappell

A Reference for the Rest of Us!

0-7645-5106-X

Spanish
FOR DUMMIES

Speak Spanish — the fun and easy way!

Dialogues from the book on audio CD

A Reference for the Rest of Us!

Berlitz
Susana Wald

0-7645-5194-9

French
FOR DUMMIES

Speak French — the fun and easy way!

Dialogues from the book on audio CD

A Reference for the Rest of Us!

Berlitz
Dodi-Katrin Schmidt
Michelle M. Williams
Dominique Wenzel

0-7645-5193-0

Italian
FOR DUMMIES

Start speaking Italian in no time with this fun and easy guide

Dialogues from the book on audio CD

A Reference for the Rest of Us!

Berlitz
Francesca Romana Onofri
Karen Antje Möller

0-7645-5196-5

Psychology
FOR DUMMIES

Your fun and easy guide to the basics of human behavior

Adam Cash, PsyD

A Reference for the Rest of Us!

0-7645-5434-4

Managing
FOR DUMMIES

2nd Edition

Covers managing people, projects, and teams

A Reference for the Rest of Us!

Bob Nelson, PhD
Peter Economy

0-7645-1771-6

Also available:

Japanese For Dummies®
0-7645-5429-8

Architecture For Dummies®
0-7645-5396-8

Rock Guitar For Dummies®
0-7645-5356-9

Anatomy and Physiology For Dummies®
0-7645-5422-0

German For Dummies®
0-7645-5195-7

Weight Training For Dummies®, 2nd Edition
0-7645-5168-X

Project Management For Dummies®
0-7645-5283-X

Piano For Dummies®
0-7645-5105-1

Latin For Dummies®
0-7645-5431-X

Songwriting For Dummies®
0-7645-5404-2

Marketing For Dummies®
2nd Edition
0-7645-5600-2

Parenting For Dummies®
2nd Edition
0-7645-5418-2

Fitness For Dummies®
2nd Edition
0-7645-5167-1

Religion For Dummies®
0-7645-5264-3

Selling For Dummies®
2nd Edition
0-7645-5363-1

Improving Your Memory For Dummies®
0-7645-5435-2

Islam For Dummies®
0-7645-5503-0

Golf For Dummies®
2nd Edition
0-7645-5146-9

The Complete MBA For Dummies®
0-7645-5204-X

Astronomy For Dummies®
0-7645-5155-8

Customer Service For Dummies®, 2nd Edition
0-7645-5209-0

Mythology For Dummies®
0-7645-5432-8

Pilates For Dummies®
0-7645-5397-6

Managing Teams For Dummies®
0-7645-5408-5

Screenwriting For Dummies®
0-7645-5486-7

Drawing For Dummies
0-7645-5476-X

Controlling Cholesterol For Dummies®
0-7645-5440-9

Martial Arts For Dummies®
0-7645-5358-5

Meditation For Dummies®
0-7645-5166-7

Wine For Dummies®
3rd Edition
0-7645-2544-1

Yoga For Dummies®
0-7645-5117-5

Drums For Dummies®
0-7645-5357-7

Singing For Dummies®
0-7645-2475-5

**Available in the UK at bookstores nationwide and online at
www.wileyeurope.com or call 0800 243407 to order direct**

Also available in the United States at www.dummies.com

WILEY

FOR DUMMIES

...and have more fun

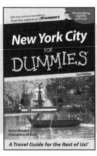
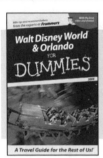